FAST,
FRESH AND
UNBELIEVABLY
DELICIOUS

plum   Pan Macmillan Australia

MATT PRESTON

FAST, FRESH AND UNBELIEVABLY DELICIOUS

204 RECIPES YOU'LL WANT TO COOK AGAIN AND AGAIN

plum. Pan Macmillan Australia

CONTENTS

INTRODUCTION

This is my second cookbook. It is full of recipes for stuff that I like to cook for my family and friends. That hasn't changed.

For me deliciousness should always be paramount and I still feel it should be achieved as simply as possible, using ingredients that are easily found in your local supermarket and with equipment that is found in most Aussie homes. There are no waterbaths, $2000 mixers and blast chillers needed here!

Sometimes, however, you might find yourself reaching for a can or going to the freezer because so many of the recipes take very commonplace ingredients and then twist them up into something rather exciting. The very elegant tinned peach soufflé on page 242 is a great example of that!

This second cookbook is a wee bit different from my first. It has a much longer title than 'Matt Preston's 100 Best Recipes', for starters. Oh, and the work shirt I'm wearing on the cover is green, not blue.

The food is a wee bit different too – fresher, lighter, healthier and with many more Asian flavours. You'll find heaps of vibrant summer salads loaded with pep, punch and crispiness; crunchy dishes that eat light but are so jam-packed with flavour they taste like they should be bad for you (but aren't); and other simple and more responsible alternatives to my bad ways of the past.

Oh and many more vegetarian dishes – not that you'll notice. These recipes are meat-free because they don't need it to make them delicious. You won't miss it. This is vegetarianism by stealth. Rest assured there is also some seriously carnivorous stuff too. That's why this book is so much bigger than the last one!

Fresher, healthier and more delicious recipes; well, that was the idea – and then it all went wrong...

I suggested a section full of those really naughty over-the-top dishes that I love to cook for friends as a treat. These went into the sealed section because, like a Bangkok nightclub act, they are just a little too full-on for the delicate stomachs of some people and, like a night out with a top netball team, they should be limited to a once-a-year indulgence for the good of your health. That section is sealed for your own safety. Please resist opening it if you are a helpless slave to your passions.

The trouble is that once the sealed section got filled up, this salaciously finger-licking decadence overflowed, threatening to overwhelm my best intentions to "eat light, eat fresh".

Sure, there's still a lovely vibrant dish of pineapple with black pepper, no-churn ice creams made with very little added sugar and no added cream, and just about the lightest, most low-fat chocolate mousse you'll find. The rot sets in with probably the world's two biggest panna cottas, a rather blousy trifle, the sexiest little pavlovas, a couple of really rather debauched cheesecakes, alcoholic slushies and milkshakes and enough chocolate recipes to satisfy Willy Wonka. Page after page of addictively tasty stuff that will keep you smiling from teatime to the merriest Christmas. Yes, I know, I'm a terrible backslider.

In short, this book is like me. It starts out with REALLY GOOD intentions and its willpower holds for quite a while until suddenly it is overwhelmed by temptation. Once that self-control is gone, it slips into a bit of an orgiastic free-for-all. Good times! Welcome to the Pleasure Dome, my friend, please grab a fork!

The most satisfying thing about writing a cookbook is discovering that people have cooked from it. I know from my own experience too many of the cookbooks on my shelves are never used and have never had the privilege of being stained by the cook. For me, the book you are holding is only relevant if you cook from it.

The recipes in your copy of this book only achieve validity when you share them with your friends and family – the highest accolade for any recipe being when it becomes a regular family favourite. At that point I feel the recipe should become yours. Please take it as a gift and when you pass it on to your loved ones plaster your name on it accordingly!

Love,
Matt

PS. Oh, and don't forget to send me your pictures of what you cook and who you enjoy it with to facebook.com/mattscravat

SOME THOUGHTS ABOUT COOKING FOR KIDS

Looking at life from the misty mountain top of old age, which is where I find myself these days, there seem to be four phases or ages that we go through.

The first is when we are trying to work out what adults want.

Then from about thirteen you are trying to work out what the opposite sex really want. For some of us this phase can linger, while others decide that what the same sex wants is more important.

The next age is trying to work out what kids want and then, the final stage is not caring what anyone wants.

I am firmly in phase three (and probably still on my 'Ps' when it comes to phase two). Both are perplexing but nothing – not even Chinese flat-pack furniture instructions – can be more perplexing than trying to work out what your kids will eat if you aren't cooking for them on a daily basis.

There are some rules, however, that I have been discovering now that I am spending a whole heap more time in the marital home with MasterChef filming in Melbourne. Here are the ones that I could note down in the time it took to drink half a cup of tea – half a cup because any parent will tell you that you never get the time to drink a full cup.

✴ Kids' tastes are always changing; always maturing.

✴ Shapes matter to an earth-shattering degree; whether it's a zucchini cut into dice or batons, a carrot cut into discs or grated.

✴ No one is more stubborn than a small child who doesn't want to eat something. But adults can be tougher and that's our only chance!

✴ Kids will try what they want; sometimes what they want corresponds to what you want.

* If you crumb it, they will eat it

* If there is nothing else, they will eat some of it

* If you tell them everything is 'chicken' they will eat it until they are six. Then they will see through your subterfuge and resent you accordingly. It may be worth it.

* The threat of 'no dessert' still has power – even with a grown man.

* Some kids can throw up at will when you insist they eat something they really don't want to – my wife is still reeling from that revelation.

* If you pluck three kids at random they will all have different likes and dislikes especially if these make it impossible for you to cook just one dish.

* All kids know what they like – until they try something they hate and realise that actually they like it.

* A wise nanny of 20-years experience also pointed out to me that too often kids are too full from drinks to eat dinner and so therefore they should go 'nil by mouth' for the half hour before dinner, which is another rule to enforce.

* Outside influences are best for engendering change.

* If your kids sit in front of the computer or TV all day they won't be as hungry as if they have been outside swimming, swinging, surfing, skating, skipping, skiving or playing soccer. So limit screen time and they'll eat more.

* Many kids are more likely to eat what you cook if you get them to help you choose what's for dinner, help with the shopping and prep the meal. 'Cook with them not for them' is what one wise mum once told me (Thanks, Alex!).

* With this in mind why not give them this book to flick through and get them to pick what they'd like to eat – and then get them to help you shop for it and to make it.

* Always try to give kids a choice – but just make sure that choice is between two 'good' choices! Otherwise they will just choose 'lollies' no matter what the question!

* They don't like 'bits'; especially suspicious 'green bits'.

* Remember you are the parent. You are the one who should be in charge!

I don't know when it happened but these days a parent is expected to have about fifty different recipes at their fingertips to satisfy the culinary demands of junior. Back when I was a boy my mother had just a revolving list of eight things she fed us and we didn't complain! (Of course, I should note, compulsory complaining about young people and how cushy they have it today is a mandatory part of the entrance exam to becoming a card-carrying oldie.)

Currently, however, my brood and I have reached a sort of uneasy peace about a group of foods that are 'approved' by all three members of the kiddie kitchen cabal. I should note that the youngest is also the unusual child who refuses to eat both lasagne and pizza, marking her down as someone who will go hungry at uni or alternatively, end up a potential supermodel.

Here is what might be described as 'safe territory' when it comes to meal times in our house:

WRAPS

Won't eat pizza, will eat flatbread made with exactly the same dough?!????? Go figure! but I have to say that there is something rather good about folding bread, warm and fluffy from the pan, oven or toaster around everything from a jumble of blushing pan-fried prawns tossed with lime juice and cubes of avocado to cubes of Sunday's leg of lamb re-cooked on the BBQ till it's all sizzly and crusty. The presence of tzatziki and some cucumber ribbons or the usual taco combo of shredded iceberg and diced tomato provide a way of getting some veg into them too. You can also try the same approach with avocado, shredded chook and some mayo. I still suspect that the mere act of them rolling the wraps for themselves makes them more acceptable. I think the sociologists would call it 'ownership'.

PASTA

The flexibility of pasta makes it such a staple in our house. If one of the kids is being fussy and is 'off' zucchini or tomato sauce then a dollop of pesto, whether it is a classic basil and pine nut or something more exotic like coriander and cashew, is an easy alternative. As is serving the pasta nude with just a little grated cheese, melted butter and black pepper. This sounds simple but the Romans worship it as one of their three favourite pasta sauces alongside *carbonara* and *all'Amatriciana*, perhaps that is because it sounds far sexier in Italian – *cacio e pepe*. There's a rather sexy adults-only version of this on page 134.
Currently the fave pasta at home – other than the ubiquitous Bolognese – is one that is featured on page 129, where you cook florets of cauliflower in the same water with the pasta, then when it is cooked you toss it in a hot pan with the bacon or pancetta that has just been cooked! The other pasta that they are all loving at the moment is the chicken Bolognese on page 148.

RICE

Rice is like the unassuming bloke in the corner of the room that no one objects to and is pretty hard to hate – even for kids. Rice dishes like pilafs and risottos are always popular, as is partnering rice with something saucy like a simple braise of chicken legs in a tomato sauce – my kids do love a braise, though – or that old nursery staple, tuna mornay. You'll find rice ideas on pages 142.
Tuna mornay might well be my favourite comfort food. Especially if the white sauce is loaded with peas and corn kernels as well as shards of canned tuna and served with boiled white rice. I reckon the secret is a little lemon to cut the richness and accentuate the sweetness of the corn and peas.

SKEWERS

There also seems to be a strange fascination about skewers. In fact, pretty much anything that won't be eaten as a lump on a plate will be treated with far more interest if it has to be pushed off a bamboo stick, whether it's cubes of lamb, chicken breast, prawns, fish or beef. Interestingly, this doesn't seem to be related to my children's desire to use the skewers as jabbing implements on each other!

One of my several failed attempts at plating the dessert on page 251!

The two secrets here seem to be to keep any flavourings to a minimum and ideally get their nimble little fingers to help with the threading. Tossing chook skewers in teriyaki sauce or something Chinese-y always seems to go down well and while rice and a steamed veggie might be traditional, the wrap approach can also be employed here to encourage more veg eating. Ribbons of cucumber or blanched carrot cut with a potato peeler which would be ignored on other dishes always get the seal of approval from my kids in this arena. There is a skewer recipe on page 67.

BALLS

I am assuming that this falls into the same area as skewers but for some reason anything that's ball-shaped seems to go down well with most kids, whether it is meatballs, dumplings, chicken balls, risotto balls (aka arancini) or kofte. And yes, they can go on skewers, and be served in wraps too making them super kid friendly! I'd put this down to our love of ball sports from tennis and footy to golf and netball. See the recipes for dumplings on page 107, the Vietnamese bun cha on page 69 or the lamb burger on page 64, which is sort of like a large, flat meatball!

FRITTATA

Kids might turn their noses up at quiche but for some reason this simple block of baked egg hiding all manner of usually unmentionable vegetables is always a sure-fire winner with most kids, whether loaded with zucchini and parmesan, peas, mint and feta on page 116 or all manner of Med veg like capsicums and corn kernels with cubes of ham. Maybe it's because those eggs are shaped like a footy? On the following pages you find a very kid-friendly Spanish omelette and both corn fritters or pea fritters too: See pages 108, 104 and 33 respectively. All have some kiddie dinner miles on them – just dial back the herbs and the chilli. Remember – kids' palates are for more keen and sensitive than ours.

IN THE OVEN

I've tried to cut out frying food for the kids, replacing this approach with chops, steak or sausages cooked on the BBQ or crumbed chicken breast or fillets of fish baked in the oven with a simple potatoey mash. So far no complaint about the absence of frying. If either of the older two read this that might change! Try the crumbed fish with oven 'fries' on page 82 as a start.

About the only thing that does get fried in my house is stir-fry which might be a good way to get the kids to eat veggies but for me is about as enjoyable as being forced to build that Chinese flat-pack computer desk with three drawers while small children jab at your eyes and bare feet with the sharper pieces of Lego.

Now, good luck and do share your success and failures with everyone else reading this book and facing the same kid challenges by heading to facebook.com/mattscravat and sharing your experience. Remember the pickiest food critic is a seven-year-old child. And as they get older they just get better and better at expressing it.

SALADS

SUMMER SALADS

I know it's a stereotype but even in these days of liberation and equality it's often the blokes who gather round the grill to marvel at its shiny grandeur, grunt at each other in short sentences punctuated by words like 'Holden … Slater … Duckworth-Lewis … Fastcut-32 Standard', and argue over who gets to hold the tongs and prod the meat to make sure that it is really, truly, dead.

Now I like having a chat about the upcoming Test series as much as the next girl but really, given the choice, I'd rather surrender the tongs in favour of the far more creative work of coming up with the salads. While there are probably only about 15 proteins you are likely to grill on the BBQ, when it comes to salads there are thousands. For me salads make a BBQ as much as the proteins or the game of backyard cricket. And on their own they can be far more interesting than meat and two veg for lunch or dinner but with so many possibilities, deciding which salad to make can be perplexing.

First, I like to think about what salads go best with the meat or seafood being served. For example, ingredients like avocado, spinach and bacon go really well with chicken, while roast beetroot, walnuts and soft goat's cheese are perfect with lamb. Fish such as salmon loves flavours like lemon, dill and cucumber. So why not combine each of these trios into a salad to match the meat?

The next thing to think about is how your dressings can build bridges between your salad and protein. For example, how about using a fresh mint vinaigrette if you are serving that beetroot salad with lamb? Or a simple creamy horseradish dressing, made from sour cream with a good dollop of horseradish, if you want to serve the same salad with beef? (With that latter dressing, feel free to make it looser by mixing in some lemon juice or warm water.)

Also think about how the dressings will react with the proteins. Salads are a great partner to grilled meats and fish because they provide freshness and acidity against the richness of the meat or fish. So don't forget the acidity, whether it comes from citrus, vinegar, sour cream, mustard or any other source. While a creamy potato salad is ace with rich fish like salmon, and there are few things better than prawns with mayo, generally I prefer the tartness of an oil and acid vinaigrette for salads served with fish or seafood, which already have creaminess in their flesh.

Another important factor is contrast – both in flavour and texture. This might be a smooth sour cream dressing used over a crunchy slaw of finely sliced red cabbage, a fine dice of blanched red onion and a big handful of chewy currants. If you add chunks of red apple as well, for a different sort of wet crunch, then your dressing could morph into something saltier using blue cheese to give some bite against the sweetness of the apple. You could also add walnuts and celery for even more crunch as this plays on the classic Waldorf salad and it's always fun to twist a classic.

Those are the basics but there are many more rules for perfect salads – as I shall now reveal.

18 RULES FOR PERFECT SALADS

1. DON'T DRESS TOO EARLY

The main pitfall with salads is dressing them too early so they go soggy – remember that acid in the salad is going to 'cook' your leaves. So dress them just before you or your guests will eat them. A creamy salad like a potato one, where you want the dressing to soak into the potatoes a little before eating, is the only exception.

2. BUSY SALAD IS BAD SALAD

Another pitfall to avoid is the busy salad. The very thought of one of those US salads that combines cucumber, corn, lettuce, tomato, grated carrot, pea shoots, alfalfa sprouts, celery, onion, marshmallows and so on fills me with horror. The only exception is when this is an array of myriad complementary flavours working against a robust carb like couscous or brown rice.

3. GRATED CARROT IS EVIL

Flannelly, flaccid and adding nothing to any salad other than bulk, grated carrot should be banned from salads the way toddlers are banned from driving fast cars – for the good of everyone involved.

4. SIMPLE SALADS RULE

Rather than throwing everything in the crisper drawer into a salad bowl, it is far better to concentrate on serving a big bowl of simply dressed leaves. Then make a couple of those other ingredients into stars of their own little salads. This might be something as perfect as crescents of de-seeded cucumber tossed with wine vinegar and sugar to pickle; then 30 minutes later tumbled with loads of chopped parsley and diced celery. Then there are few things better than slices of perfectly ripe tomatoes sprinkled with good olive oil, salt flakes and leaves of marjoram or oregano just before serving.

5. START SIMPLE AND THEN STEP IT UP

Too simple for you? Then step up this tomato salad by adding a little very, very finely sliced red onion and sticky balsamic dressing made by reducing balsamic with a little caster sugar. Only dress the tomatoes at the very last moment before serving. Feta or canned tuna can be added to turn this into a summer dish all of its own. Just remember, in my salad world the tomato must be the star or not there at all. While those peeled and thinly sliced cucumbers could be layered with sliced strawberries, lots of black pepper and a simple vinaigrette to make an unusual summer salad.

6. LETTUCE SALADS SHOULD ALWAYS BE SIMPLE

As I mentioned earlier, usually I'll serve salad leaves on their own – just well chosen iceberg, butter lettuce or cos lettuce leaves tossed with a classic vinaigrette. Three parts oil to one part acid is the basic rule for a vinaigrette which is also great used to dress steaks or fish. The only rule is be prepared to deviate from this ratio depending on the acidity level of the oil and what other sweet ingredients might be added, like honey, or tart ingredients, like Dijon mustard.

7. AVOID LOOSE MIXED LEAVES

I'm not a fan of mixed or mesclun salad that you buy loose at the supermarket as you risk getting bits of dodgy salad leaves like coral or red oak; far better to get a whole head of one lettuce for your summer greens. Oh, and when buying leaves loose do keep an eye out for brown ends to the stalks of the leaves or damaged leaves. Leave them in the supermarket. This is called 'picking' the salad.

8. MORE ROBUST THE LEAF; TOUGHER THE PARTNER

While simple lettuce leaves work well in the simplest of states I am partial to mixing more flavourful leaves with ingredients that can match their intensity. Rocket leaves go wonderfully with shaved parmesan salads, especially if some sliced ripe pear and balsamic dressing is added. That combination of parmesan and balsamic also goes wonderfully with the succulent but bitter leaves of witlof; in fact, with pretty much any of those bitter leaves Italians love. Although when it comes to those beautiful purple, red and white-veined radicchio leaves, I struggle to go past teaming them with anything more than fennel, blood orange, a little oil and salt flakes. You'll find a nice little recipe for that at the end of the chapter. This brings a touch of summer warmth to the table from August to October (when the blood orange is in season in Australia).

9. USE FLAVOURS THAT COMPLEMENT YOUR PROTEINS

Think also about how you can flavour what you are cooking with spices or herbs that will echo or complement the salad. A rub of salt, cumin and coriander seeds on that lamb, and give your beetroot, walnut and feta salad a little lift with orange or lemon zest that will pick up the citrus notes of the coriander seeds.

10. ADD CRUNCH

Think about crunchy bread croutons in your Caesar salad or the walnuts in the Waldorf. They are there as much for texture as taste. So, does your salad need more crunch? Nuts and seeds not only add crunch and flavour but also set the culinary accent of the dish. Change those walnuts in the beetroot salad to pistachios and it starts to look Middle Eastern rather than French. Use crumbled feta instead of goat's cheese; throw in some coriander and cumin seeds and now you could be eating this salad in a souk, with your friend Amir dressed in a 'thawb', discussing the relative merits of medjool and baam dates.

11. SOME THOUGHTS ON CARB-DRIVEN SALADS

Some salads are there like a condiment, salsa or sauce, to provide strong flavours to set off or complement your protein or to refresh your palate, while others are there to provide bulk like couscous, potato or rice salads. Pasta salads too often are claggy or dried out; a good rice, couscous, or potato salad, however, is a thing of beauty. Everyone has their favourite potato salad whether dressed in something creamy like a 50/50 yoghurt and mayo dressing or just with a simple vinaigrette lifted with loads of chopped chives or dill. Serve it warm or cold but always use waxy potatoes.

12. PEPPING UP THOSE CARBS

With other bulking salads like couscous, rice, quinoa or barley, I think the main aim is to keep things as peppy and exciting as you can with your choice of ingredients. I always use something crunchy like a nut or two, some acidity and finally something salty whether it's cheese, bacon, capers, olives or just salt.

13. SWEET BURSTS

That reminds me. Adding sweet little highlights with dried fruit such as sultanas, chopped dates, currants, mango or even honey-roasted carrots is another way to add more texture and flavour contrast.

14. THINK OF WHAT GOES WITH WHAT

When composing a salad think of the classic accompaniments to the meat or fish you'll be serving. For example, lamb chops are very comfortable with minted peas so make a salad of a cup of fresh peas, fresh mint leaves, a little lemon zest and some creaminess from fresh ricotta or feta. Make boiled new potatoes your carb of choice. The great thing about this pea and mint salad is you can add almost pretty much anything else to it like peeled broad beans, blanched sugar snap peas, chopped asparagus, diced zucchini (both raw and blanched) or any of the above. A little lemon juice or white wine vinegar will add some acidity.

15. PICK A THEME

Generally the choice of flavours to use in salads is driven by the overall picture of the type of meal you are aiming for and what else you are serving. For example, if the menu is grilled beef and a Vietnamese rice noodle salad then go for an Asian slaw with shredded wombok, beanshoots and carrots with tangy Thai-style dressing made from fish sauce, lime juice and a little sugar.

16. THERE IS NOTHING WRONG WITH A CLASSIC

How about just dressing a large plate of steamed green beans with a vinaigrette and then making them look pretty by grating over first the white and then the yolk of a couple of hard-boiled eggs. It's called a mimosa salad and it's a classic! To take this up a notch, add some blanched spears of asparagus and something to give your vinaigrette a little pep, whether it is some baby capers or the cheeks of green olives.

17. MAKE A BLUE CHEESE DRESSING

To make a blue cheese dressing that pretty much goes with anything – try it on a plain iceberg lettuce salad, sliced celery with walnuts, or just spinach and bacon, wow! – just whisk 50 ml of yoghurt or sour cream with 40 ml of milk and then add 100 g of crumbled or cut soft blue cheese with a teaspoon of white wine vinegar. Now taste and adjust the flavour and texture by adding salt and more vinegar or milk.

18. WHEN IN DOUBT, ADD PIG

Porky goodness, in terms of bacon or crispy prosciutto, is also a sure fire winner in terms of adding both texture to salad, as well as a good savoury hit that will bring the other ingredients alive. It is especially good used with sweeter salad ingredients such as roast pumpkin, mango, grilled peach or roast corn.

ROASTED BEETROOT, GOAT'S CHEESE AND ORANGE SALAD

1 large beetroot (about 400 g)

1 orange

1 pickled beetroot (optional)

100 g goat's cheese rolled in ash

30 g toasted hazelnuts, roughly chopped

2 tablespoons of your favourite dukkah

salt flakes and freshly ground black pepper

TIP: No dukkah? Make it!!! Crunch a handful of almonds or hazelnuts with 1 teaspoon of coriander seeds, ½ a teaspoon of cumin seeds, a pinch of salt flakes and some sesame seeds (if you have them). Doneski.

Simple, classic and extremely virtuous – this salad has absolutely nothing in common with me ... other than good taste.

Preheat the oven to 200°C.

Wash the beetroot and pat dry. Wrap the beetroot loosely in foil and roast in the oven for 50–60 minutes, or until your knife slides easily into the middle.

Remove from the oven and peel: the skin should come off easily while still warm. Use rubber gloves. Allow to cool to room temperature before cutting into thin wedges.

Zest the orange. Segment the orange over a bowl, catching the juices as you cut. Reserve the juice.

Plate the roast beetroot and pickled beetroot (if using) with the orange segments, crumble over the goat's cheese, pour over the reserved orange juice and top with hazelnuts and dukkah. Finish with a sprinkle of salt and pepper and a little of the orange zest.

SERVES 4 AS AN ACCOMPANYING SALAD OR 2 AS A MAIN

PEA AND MINT FRITTERS WITH ICEBERG LETTUCE

300 g (½ cup) frozen peas, thawed,
    blanched in boiling water and
    drained
2 whole eggs lightly beaten, and
    1 egg white
35 g (¼ cup) plain flour
¼ level teaspoon baking powder
¼ bunch mint leaves, chopped,
    plus extra to serve
½ bunch chives, finely cut, finely
    chopped, plus extra to serve
½ teaspoon salt flakes, plus extra
lots of freshly ground black pepper
vegetable oil, for frying
½ small iceberg lettuce or salad
    greens of choice
100 g feta or ricotta, crumbled
½ lemon, to serve

Once chefs stacked; then they smeared, then the smear evolved into the skid. Then food was strewed seemingly randomly, first of all across the plate but then on either side of an off-centre linear axis of the chef's imagining. I've always been more of a fan of the tumble and the tear myself. I'll tell chefs it's because I am searching for the order that comes from natural chaos and, as such, it's so very 'now' but it's really because it's easy and looks natural. Just like this salad.

Mash about half the peas with the back of a fork and leave the rest of them whole, glad and relieved to have avoided the evil tines of the giant fork that so cruelly crushed their brothers.

Whisk your single egg white.

In a separate mixing bowl, sift the flour and baking powder, then add two whole eggs and gently combine. Add the herbs and peas and season with salt and pepper. Gently fold in the whisked egg white.

Heat a drizzle of oil in a non-stick frying pan over medium heat. When hot, drop small tablespoons of the mixture into the pan and flatten just a wee bit with the back of a spoon. Cook for 2–3 minutes on each side, or until golden brown. Continue cooking in batches, adding a splash more oil if needed.

Allow the fritters to cool to slightly warm or room temperature before adding to the salad.

Lay the lettuce leaves on a serving plate and with your hands break each fritter into a few pieces and pile on top of the lettuce. Crumble over the feta or ricotta, scatter on the extra chives and mint leaves and squeeze over the lemon juice. Season with salt and pepper and serve.

SERVES 4–6

SLOW-COOKED TURKISH LAMB SHOULDER WITH CUCUMBER, GREEN OLIVE AND DATE SALAD

ROAST LAMB

1.5 kg boned lamb shoulder
   (2 kg with bone in)
olive oil
2 tablespoons cumin seeds
3 teaspoons salt flakes
packet of flatbread, cut into
   triangles and warmed, to serve

THE SALAD

1 pomegranate (optional but pretty)
1 bunch coriander
2 long green English cucumbers,
   peeled and seeded, cut into
   5 mm dice
2 pale green celery stalks, tough
   strings removed, cut into
   5 mm dice
12 dates, pitted and cut into
   rough dice
24 Sicilian green olives, pitted and
   chopped into quarters
200 g (1⅓ cups) shelled pistachios

SALAD DRESSING

80 ml (⅓ cup) extra-virgin olive oil
½ tablespoon pomegranate
   molasses*
½ teaspoon salt flakes
reserved juice of 1 pomegranate

YOGHURT DRESSING FOR LAMB

300 ml (1¼ cups) Greek yoghurt
a good handful of flat-leaf parsley
coriander stalks from the salad
seeds and skin from cucumbers
juice of 2 lemons, to taste
salt flakes

* Available from Middle Eastern
   food stores.

Scary doesn't come any bigger than having to cook for one of the world's great chefs but that's the rash offer I made to Marco Pierre White just after he landed in Australia to film *MasterChef: The Professionals* with me. The only way I survived was to cook a meal that touched on everything I'd learnt about him in a couple of days. To wit, he liked dates, cumin seeds and meat cooked on the bone. This recipe just came to me. It also, phew!, received his seal of approval.

ROAST LAMB Preheat the oven to 200°C.

Make sure that the lamb's tough top layer of skin, or 'bark' has been peeled off to reveal the fat beneath. Score the fat in a 2 cm diamond pattern and rub in a mix of the olive oil, cumin seeds and salt flakes on all surfaces of the lamb shoulder.

Place the lamb in the oven and blast it for 30 minutes. Then turn down to 130°C and leave for a couple of hours. Check to see how it's going. It should be lovely and brown on the outside and still pink at its thickest point. Rest for 15 minutes.

THE SALAD If in season, cut the pomegranate in half and hold a half cut-side down over a bowl. Bang on its back with a wooden spoon to knock out the seeds. Pick out any white pith and save any juice to add to the dressing. The pomegranate adds a prettiness, but you won't miss it if you don't have it.

Shred the coriander leaves, keeping the stems and any cleaned roots for the lamb dressing. While prepping also remember to keep your seeds and skin from the cucumber for the lamb dressing too.

Now mix everything together: coriander, cucumber, celery, dates and olives. Dress the salad just before you eat. Then sprinkle on the pistachios and pomegranate seeds.

SALAD DRESSING The exact ratio for this dressing depends on the power of the olive oil and the elegance of the pomegranate molasses but a ratio of 3 to 1 olive oil to molasses should work. Add any pomegranate juice you might have to freshen the dressing.

YOGHURT DRESSING FOR LAMB Blitz the yoghurt with the herbs and the cucumber skin to make a smooth pale green dressing. Add some of the cucumber seeds gradually until the dressing has the thickness of cream. Add the lemon juice to taste. Add salt to help balance the dressing's acidity and the bitterness of the cucumber skins.

TO SERVE Roughly pull the lamb apart into large shreds. Place the lamb shoulder, salad and warmed flatbread on the table in large bowls. Let everyone help themselves. Squirt the lamb with yoghurt dressing.

SERVES 6–8

SWEET POTATO AND COUSCOUS SALAD WITH ONE DIRTY BIG SECRET

500 g sweet potato, peeled and
    cut into 2 cm chunks
1½ tablespoons maple syrup
3 tablespoons extra-virgin olive oil
salt flakes and freshly ground
    black pepper
250 g (1 cup) couscous
250 ml (1 cup) boiling water or
    chicken stock
zest and juice of ½ orange
zest and juice of 1 lemon
1 orange, segmented and each
    segment cut into 2 or 3 pieces
60 g (a scant ½ cup) dried apricots,
    finely sliced
80 g (a scant ½ cup) dried figs,
    finely sliced
70 g (a scant ½ cup) smoked
    almonds, roughly chopped
1 teaspoon ras el hanout (see Tip)
coriander leaves, to serve

TIP: Ras el hanout is a Moroccan spice mix available from posh food shops or online. You can substitute a grind of 1 cardamom pod, a ¼ teaspoon of ground cumin, ½ teaspoon of coriander seeds, ¼ teaspoon of cinnamon and ½ blade of mace or a grate of nutmeg.

Bet you stopped just to find out what the Dirty Big Secret was, didn't you? Well, for once a cynical attention-grabbing headline is actually followed by a secret that is also a goodie – the secret to fluffy no-stick couscous. Oh, and you'll also discover a salad that's a riot of sweet, sour and smoky flavours. Double win. P.S. The dried figs coud be substituted with dates. P.P.S. The smoked almonds are vital.

Preheat the oven to 200°C.

Toss the sweet potato in the maple syrup and oil and place on a low-sided baking tray. Scatter a couple of pinches of salt and lots of black pepper on top. Bake for 25–30 minutes, or until cooked. Remove from the oven and set aside.

To ensure the couscous doesn't stick together, use your hands and gently rub 1 tablespoon of olive oil into the couscous to coat. Taa-daa! THIS IS THE SECRET! Add ½ teaspoon salt to the couscous and pour over boiling water or stock. Cover with a lid immediately and allow to sit for 5–10 minutes before raking gently with a fork.

Add the zest and juice of the orange and lemon to the couscous. Add most of the segmented orange, dried fruit, almonds and sweet potato (keeping some of each for the top). Sprinkle over the ras el hanout and season with salt and pepper.

Gently toss the couscous to combine and pile on a serving plate or in a large bowl. Pile the remaining ingredients on top and scatter over coriander leaves.

SERVES 4

BLUEBERRIES, WATERCRESS AND GOAT'S CHEESE SALAD WITH LAMB

1 bunch watercress
400 g (2 cups) couscous
400 g lamb backstraps
salt flakes and freshly ground
 black pepper
about 3 tablespoons extra-virgin
 olive oil
150 ml (⅔ cup) red wine
1 teaspoon sugar
250 g (2 packs) fresh blueberries
tub or roll of fresh goat's cheese
 (If you can find ash rolled goat's
 cheese that would be perfect. You
 may find goat's cheese labelled by
 its French name chèvre)
100 g (¾ cup) slivered almonds

Sometimes you stumble across unlikely bedfellows, especially when it comes to ingredients. Not only do tumbled watercress, dusky blueberries and virginal fresh goat's cheese look so very good together, they also taste great in this *ménage à trois*. Strangely, most other unlikely bedfellows don't look so good tumbled together.

Wash and dry the watercress. Clip the slimmer stems from the top third of the bunch and pick off any other leaves that look perky from the rest of the bunch.

Make the couscous according to the packet instructions so it is light and fluffy.

Season the lamb with salt and pepper, then pan fry the lamb backstraps in a heavy pan in a tablespoon of oil for 3 minutes on each side. Remove the meat from the pan. Wrap it in foil and keep warm.

Return the pan to the heat. Pour the wine into the pan, add sugar and using a wooden spoon scrub off any of the yummy tasty bits. The wine will bubble and reduce as the alcohol burns off. This will take a couple of minutes.

Now pour in 50 g blueberries and mash them into the wine. Cook for about 3 minutes and season to taste with black pepper and salt. Mix any of the lamb juices in the foil into the sauce.

Arrange the watercress on a big plate. Sprinkle with the remaining blueberries. Dollop with little lumps of goat's cheese. Serve with your best olive oil, a little salt and twist of black pepper on the side to be applied to the salad at the table. This way you can maintain the dusty bloom on the blueberries for as long as possible; and I'm also not sure this salad actually needs any dressing anyway.

Mix the couscous with the almonds, season and plate with the lamb sliced into finger-width slices. Dress with some of the wine and blueberry sauce.

Eat!

SERVES 4

YIM YAM'S YUM YUM CRUNCHY RICE SALAD

I'm not sure how posterity will remember me but if it is just that my name is on the menu at Yim Yam Thai Laos restaurants next to this dish 10 years after I raved about it in a review, that is good enough for me. And it's lovely that chef-owner Lylah Hatfield has agreed to share the recipe for one of Australia's best but least-known dishes. Interestingly, this salad was an early forerunner of my favourite plating approach, that of the all-natural tear and strew, that you'll see throughout this book.

Place the rice in a sieve and rinse under running water until the water runs clear. Place in a saucepan with 400 ml (1¾ cups) water and the salt and bring to the boil over medium heat. Cover with a tight-fitting lid, reduce the heat to low and cook for 10 minutes, or until the liquid is absorbed. Remove from the heat, set aside, covered for 10 minutes (residual heat will finish cooking the rice).

Meanwhile, bring a saucepan of water to boil, turn off the heat, add the chicken breasts. Cover for approximately 20 minutes or until cooked (the water's residual heat will be sufficient to cook the chicken). Drain and set aside. (Don't leave chicken in water.)

To make the rice balls, place the warm rice, coconut, turmeric, onion, kaffir lime leaves and eggs in a large bowl. Using damp hands, combine well, then press the mixture into 10 balls.

Fill a wok one-third full with the oil and heat over medium heat to 160°C, or until a cube of bread turns slightly golden in 20 seconds. Gently lower the chillies into the oil and fry for 2 minutes, or until lightly cooked and dark red. Remove with a slotted spoon and drain on a baking tray lined with paper towel.

Lower the rice balls into the oil and fry, in two batches, turning, for approximately 8 minutes until golden brown. Remove with a slotted spoon and drain on baking tray lined with paper towel. Cool for 5 minutes.

Meanwhile, using a mortar and pestle, pound 35 g (¼ cup) peanuts to small pieces, leaving the rest for garnish. Transfer to a large bowl, add the chilli flakes, sugar, lemon juice and fish sauce and stir well to combine.

Tear the cooked chicken into small shreds or pieces, then add to the dressing bowl with the spring onions, red onion, coriander and mint. Toss. Using a wooden spoon or your hands, break the rice balls into large chunks, add to the chicken mixture and gently toss until just combined.

Scoop onto a plate with roughly sliced lettuce leaves and scatter over the remaining peanuts, fried chillies and coriander sprigs.

SERVES 4

265 g (1⅓ cups) jasmine rice
½ teaspoon salt
2 × 280 g chicken breasts (skin off)
35 g (½ cup) shredded coconut, toasted (place it in a small frying pan and heat on medium–high heat until it browns – watch it carefully as the coconut changes colour quickly)
1 tablespoon ground turmeric
½ small onion, thinly sliced
8 kaffir lime leaves, centre vein removed, finely shredded
3 eggs, lightly beaten
vegetable oil, to deep-fry
4 red bird's eye chillies, split (depending on taste)
50 g (⅓ cup) unsalted roasted peanuts
2 tablespoons dried chilli flakes (depending on taste)
4 tablespoons white sugar
5 tablespoons lemon juice
3 tablespoons fish sauce
4 spring onions, chopped
½ small red onion, thinly sliced
¾ cup roughly chopped coriander, plus extra sprig to garnish
½ cup torn mint leaves
4 iceberg lettuce leaves, to serve

SOME WAYS WITH QUINOA

My worst kitchen disaster of 2011 was my first attempt at making quinoa. It was so disastrous that even my children took pity on me and asked me 'what happened?' with the sort of concerned tone usually used by their mother surveying a particularly badly grazed chin. Very unlike them …

Like a bad midday movie, however, I heart-warmingly managed to triumph over my ancient-grain tragedy. Now in this, the UN's international year of quinoa no less, I am here to help you too. For no more is this protein-packed Aztec grain the sole domain of little vegan, hippy cafes where the floor staff are called Heaven, Rainbow or Zonk and the cook wears a hat made out of technicolour alpaca wool to stop his dreadlocks dunking in the chai lattes. Quinoa is the grain of the moment.

Think of it as a gluten-free couscous or a brown rice. It is perfect in a salad (as you'll see) or use it warm as a carb to soak up a meaty braise such as slow-braised beef cheeks, to give some juicy bulk to your tuna patties or corn fritters, or even as a twist on rice pudding – perhaps double-twisted by being made with coconut milk, lime zest and served with lychees as well.

It also works well as a substitute for cracked wheat in one of those Arab tabouli salads heavy with garlic, a little tomato and loads of parsley. And here it can be fried as well as cooked with water. It's also really good with chicken – as the heft in the stuffing or served warm with avocado, a little preserved lemon and pistachios under a succulent roast chook breast. Or why not try a warm tumble of quinoa with roasted cauliflower florets, pinenuts and sultanas? Ideal with the lamb skewers that follow.

Now listen carefully because here is the secret of cooking good quinoa. It's as simple as simmering 1 cup of it with 2 cups of water for 12 minutes, then just leave the quinoa off the heat and covered for 10 minutes. The result? Perfect fluffy, nutty and slightly juicy quinoa each time; never water-logged nor like eating flecks of cardboard.

The two quinoa recipes here are very different. One takes the cookery of London's great quinoa pioneer Yotam Ottolenghi as a starting point; he who loves mixing wild rice, sweet potato and dried Persian lime with the grain. The other is just the simplest of salads, made glorious summer by this little grain.

The latter is as neat and easy a way to make use of quinoa as there is; while the former is a massive pfaff and a hassle and is about the only recipe in this book that requires you to shop anywhere other than the local market or supermarket. However, the adventure of sourcing dried limes perhaps from a nut shop, pomegranate molasses from a trendy provedore and 'amchoor' from an Indian deli will make you feel like a true culinary adventurer from those dim, dark days before food was all about maximum flavour and minimum fuss.

It is also the sort of salad only to make if you have a deal with the one you love that if you cook then they wash up … and you want to punish them. It is possible to dirty every saucepan in the house if you are careful!

This is why it's a good winter salad – not just because the warm, earthy flavours of the marmalade, hummus, wild rice and roast sweet potato make it the best salad you taste this year but because all that washing-up activity will keep them nice and warm.

1. REVENGE WINTER QUINOA SALAD

(A DISH BEST SERVED COLD . . . OR EVEN LUKEWARM)

2 large sweet potatoes, peeled and cut into
  3 cm cubes
100 g (1 cup) wild rice
2 red onions
olive oil
200 g (1 cup) quinoa, rinsed
1 Persian dried lime or dried lemon* (use a fresh
  lime, or dried green mango powder (amchoor)
  if you can't find dried lemon or limes)
½ cup hummus
½ cup yoghurt
1 bunch radishes
1 tablespoon marmalade
200 g (1½ cups) shelled pistachios
1 lime
salt flakes
20 mint leaves (a small bunch)
30 coriander leaves (a small bunch)
40 g (2 cups) puffed quinoa (optional,
  but it adds more crunch to the salad)
1 lemon, to serve
1 pair washing-up gloves and a new dish brush

Preheat the oven to 180°C.

Put the sweet potato cubes on an oiled baking tray and pop in the oven. Do this about 60 minutes before you want to eat the salad.

Cook the wild rice as per packet instructions. This will take about 45 minutes, so start this early too. Both the sweet potatoes and wild rice can be done in advance, if you want. Slice the onions and fry them in a little oil so they caramelise – about 25 minutes. We want them soft, sweet and a little burnt at the edges. When this is done remove from the heat.

While the rice, sweet potato and onions are cooking, it's time to make the quinoa. Place the quinoa and 2 cups of water into a saucepan, cover and bring to the boil. Then cook very gently for 12 minutes with the lid on. Take the pan from the heat and leave for a further 10 minutes with the lid on to help the quinoa fluff up. After this, lift and turn gently with a fork and spread on a large chopping board to cool.

So far that's four pans and two chopping boards dirtied already plus various spoons, knives and spatulas.

Make the dressing. Take the dried lime or lemon, cut into quarters and remove the seeds. Grind the lime in a spice mill or decent blitzer. Add the hummus and process together. Add a drizzle of olive oil to smooth out the dressing and add the yoghurt to moderate the intensity of the dried lime flavour to your liking. Remember that as it is a dressing it should be stronger than you think as it will be flavouring loads of other flavours. If not using the dried lime, just mix the lime juice and lime zest of 1 lime with the hummus instead. Or use dried green mango powder (amchoor), which will give a suitably exotic sour flavour. It is readily available in Indian stores and trendy providores.

While the quinoa is cooking, check the onions to make sure they aren't burning and check the sweet potatoes to see if they are softening. Also top, tail and wash the radishes. Then cut into chunks a little smaller than the sweet potato.

In a small pot, warm the marmalade so it goes liquid. Add a little water if it needs help.

Toast the pistachios in a dry frying pan over high heat for about 5 minutes. Keep the nuts moving in the pan regularly so they don't burn. Remove from the pan and reserve.

Drain the wild rice well and leave to cool. So that's two more pots, a blender, colander and frying pan for them also to wash up.

Peel the fresh lime and using a small sharp knife carefully cut out the lime flesh from between the segment walls. Cut these roughly into little 1 cm pieces.

Check the sweet potato. When it starts to soften and taste sweet, toss it in the warmed marmalade and return to the oven for a few minutes. Turn the heat up to 200°C and cook until the edges of the sweet potato start to blacken. Remove them from the oven.

Now you are ready to assemble the salad. Place the wild rice and the radishes in a large salad bowl. Toss in the onions and the sweet potato. Just before serving sprinkle with some salt and layer on, in this order, the lime pieces, the shredded mint and coriander leaves, the pistachios, and the puffed quinoa (if you are using it). Tossing this at the table will keep the crispy things crisp!

Serve with the lamb skewers opposite or on its own drizzled with the hummus dressing and with a squeeze of lemon to taste.

SERVES 4-6

TIP: Persian dried limes (*limu-omani* or *loomi*) are lemons or limes that have been salted and then dried. The darker-coloured or black dried fruit are usually limes, while the paler or browner ones are usually dried lemons. Pierce the skin with a skewer and they work brilliantly dropped into stews or soups using lamb, chicken or even fish. They add an earthy tang. Partner them with other aromatics like nutmeg, cumin, cardamom or saffron. You can also use them to make a tea by steeping them in boiled water.

*Dried limes and pomegranate molasses are available from Arab or Persian specialty stores and some Indian stores. The limes are very light so they are also good to order online or over the phone if you can't get to a suitable shop.

WASHING UP REQUIRED:
1 LARGE CHOPPING BOARD
1 KNIFE
1 BAKING TRAY, 1 SAUCEPAN, 1 FRYING PAN, ANOTHER SAUCEPAN, 2 SPOONS, 1 SPATULA, ANOTHER KNIFE, A FOOD PROCESSOR OR BLENDER, ANOTHER 2 SPOONS, A SMALL POT, ANOTHER FRYING PAN, A COLANDER, A SALAD BOWL, 2 SALAD SERVERS, SERVES YOU RIGHT

2. LAMB WITH POMEGRANATE MOLASSES

1 cup pomegranate molasses*
600 g lamb fillet, cut into 4 cm cubes, free of any sinew
wooden BBQ skewers, soaked in water

In a bowl or zip-lock plastic bag, pour the intensely sweet–sour molasses over the lamb. Massage it in. Leave for at least 40 minutes – but longer is better.

Heat a ridged grill pan over high heat.

Thread the lamb onto the skewers. Grill until cooked on the outside but still nicely pink in the middle. Leave them to rest for 15 minutes under foil before serving. Serve with the quinoa salad.

SERVES 4

3. SUMMERY CONCILIATION QUINOA SALAD
(WITH MINIMAL WASHING UP)

200 g (1 cup) quinoa, rinsed
3 Lebanese cucumbers, peeled, halved and seeded
2 punnets cherry tomatoes
2 tablespoons extra-virgin olive oil
2 tablespoons red wine vinegar
salt flakes

Place the quinoa and 2 cups of water into a saucepan, cover and bring to the boil. Then cook very gently for 12 minutes with the lid on. Take the pan from the heat and leave for a further 10 minutes with the lid on to help the quinoa fluff up. After this, lift and turn gently with a fork and spread on a large chopping board to cool.

When cool, toss the quinoa – and here's that word again – gently with the cucumber and tomatoes. Sprinkle on the oil, vinegar and salt (in that order). Toss gently again. Serve with skewers of chicken or sliced steak.

SERVES 4 AS AN ACCOMPANYING SALAD

WASHING UP REQUIRED:
1 SAUCEPAN
1 CHOPPING BOARD
1 KNIFE
1 FORK

SEARED PRAWNS WITH VIETNAMESE NOODLE SALAD

1 × 250 g packet of rice noodles;
   medium (5 mm) thickness
2 carrots
1 telegraph cucumber
1 bunch coriander, with roots
   if possible
1 bunch mint
60 g grated palm sugar
zest and juice of 1 lime, juice of
   3 more
2 garlic cloves, peeled
2 tablespoons fish sauce
1 long green chilli, stem removed
2 small red chillies, seeded and
   diced, plus extra for serving
2 teaspoons soy sauce
a little warm water
24 green prawns, peeled with tails
   left on and cleaned of poo shoots
3 tablespoons peanut oil
salt and freshly ground black
   pepper
3 tablespoons unsalted peanuts,
   roughly chopped for garnish

This is a great little quick salad for a hot evening – especially when friends stay over. The slippery white Vietnamese rice noodles seem to cool the ambient temperature automatically by about 8°C. The wet crunch of the cucumber, raw carrot and the mint all help you feel like you are sticking your head in the icebox. Obviously the salad works equally well with some chook thighs baked in the oven with soy sauce or just with some rags of seared beef tossed through it.

Soak or cook the rice noodles in boiling water as instructed by the packet.

Peel the carrots and cut into matchsticks.

Take the cucumber, wash it and then peel it with a potato peeler. Save the peel. Now cut the peeled cucumber in half lengthways. Using a teaspoon, remove the seeds. Do this by dragging the teaspoon down the centre of the cucumber. Keep the seeds with the peel. Cut the cucumber into long matchsticks a little bigger than the carrots.

Take the coriander and mint and discard any discoloured stalks and leaves. Cut the leaves off the head of the coriander bunch. Slice into pieces about half the size of a 5 cent coin. Do the same with the mint. Save the coriander stalks and roots.

To make the dressing, scrape the coriander roots clean of any dirt and stringy bits. Wash well. Slice up the roots and stalks. Throw these into the blender with the palm sugar, juice of 1 lime, the garlic, fish sauce, 1 chilli, soy sauce and water. Blitz. Throw in the cucumber seeds and half the cucumber peel and blitz again. Taste. Now balance. It will probably taste sweet and will therefore need the juice of at least another lime plus a couple more drops of fish sauce. If you want more heat, gradually add the other chilli, tasting as you go.

To cook the prawns, sear them in a hot oiled pan for 2 minutes. Toss regularly.

To assemble the salad, toss the noodles, carrot, herbs and cucumber batons together. Toss in half the prawns. Dress with about three-quarters of the dressing, stir and top with the remaining prawns. Serve the rest of the dressing on the side with a little bowl of the red chilli. Serve immediately, sprinkled with peanuts.

SERVES 6

HOW TO PERFECTLY POACH CHICKEN

Dive into recipe books and you'll find myriad suggestions for how to perfectly poach chicken. Jamie might tell you to cover the chook with liquid, bring it to the boil and then simmer for 1 hour and 20 minutes. Other chefs – and this is Gary's preferred way – will tell you the only way to poach chook is to slip it into boiling stock, bring the stock back to the boil for between 5 to 15 minutes and then lift the covered pot off the heat to let the chook cool.

Instructions for Chinese poached – or white cut – chicken, which tends to result in flesh that is softer and silkier, can be even more tortuous. How would you feel about bringing the chook to the boil in the stock and cooking for 5 minutes then removing the pan from the heat for 20 minutes, then returning it to the boil for another 3 minutes, then cooling it in iced water! Phew people, isn't poached chicken supposed to be simple?

I have over the last couple of months been conducting a number of experiments for poaching both whole chook and chicken breasts and my findings have been fascinating. I've found that the two most cogent factors when poaching chicken are how quickly do you need the chook, and secondly what texture do you want in the flesh of your poached chicken? Think about the end use of your poached chicken when deciding. Firm is good for shredding for robust salads, like the Thai salad that follows, or for chicken mayo sandwiches. Springy and moist is perfect for taking lighter dressings like the curried mayo and whipped cream combo of coronation chicken. While satiny, slippery and only just set is how I like my chicken for softer salads, for pie fillings or for dishes such as Hainanese chicken rice. Ironically, it seems that the softer-set the flesh of the chook the longer it will take to achieve, as you have to cook the bird gently by using the residual heat of the stock.

So, here's how to simply poach your chook for that delicate softer-set flesh using a simpler version of the steps taught to me by Peter Gilmore of Quay in Sydney. It's also the way George likes to poach his chook.

First take a 1.5 kg bird. Buy the best you can afford as the quality of the flesh will shine through with this form of poaching. First check the bird's cavity and remove the giblets if included. Now rinse the bird inside and out and dry using paper towel or a spotlessly clean tea towel.

Pick a pot with a lid that will comfortably hold the bird without swamping it. Now bring 3 litres of stock or a 2:1 ratio mixture of stock and water with your choice aromatics to the boil. Have a kettle of freshly boiled water handy. Slip the bird in breast-side down into the pot so the stock covers it. Add more boiling water from the kettle, if needed, to cover the chook.

Now just remove the pot from the heat, bang the lid on and leave for an hour. Do not let the chook sit in the pot until the stock goes cold but remove it from the stock after an hour and place in the fridge to cool. After an hour or so the barely poached pink chook flesh will be ready to pull apart perfectly for salads or popping in a pie. Or you can just rub the chook all over with a little sesame oil, cut into segments and serve with boiled rice and steamed bok choi for a healthy meal. Served this way, the chook is perfect with my spring onion relish or red chilli relish that you'll find on page 74.

It's not an exact science but for a larger bird, I use more stock and leave it in the stock for 15 minutes longer.

The same approach works well for poaching chicken breasts. I pour enough stock to cover the breast into a pan with a lid and bring it to the boil. This is about 500 ml of stock per skinless breast. Then I slip the breasts in, remove from the heat and leave covered for 45 minutes. I'll then check them to see if they have firmed up which shows they are cooked. If I'm in a hurry I'll bring the stock back to the boil after adding the breasts and then remove from the heat. Check them 10 minutes after being covered and off the heat. I'm looking for a firm-set flesh, which when cut is smooth and not fibrous at all. This meat is perfect for mixing with a 50/50 combo of mayo and whipped cream for coronation chicken. Flavour the mayo to taste with about ½ teaspoon of curry powder or a teaspoon of tandoori paste and add some sweetness and tang with ½ cup of 1 cm pieces of dried apricots, softened by soaking in a little of the hot stock. Don't overload the chook with the dressing. Toasted slivered almonds can make a nice addition. This is delicious served with a green salad of iceberg lettuce, celery and cucumber or in sandwiches.

THE LEFTOVER STOCK
Poaching chicken results in an excellent stock that can then be used as the basis of a cracking pumpkin soup or minestrone. Just make sure you strain the stock and then cook it at a rolling boil for a few minutes before adding the softer veg.

MAKING A MASTERSTOCK
If you do want to add flavour to your poaching stock – and thus to your poached chicken – do think about where the chicken is destined. If it's for a lovely fresh French-inspired salad or a chicken pie, then how about throwing in fresh bay leaves, the greens of spring onion, black pepper, a few sprigs of thyme and a handful of crushed garlic cloves? If I'm serving it with steamed bok choi and rice, or tossed through freshly stir-fried Chinese veg, I'll make a basic masterstock by boiling up a stick of cinnamon, a star anise, ½ cup of soy sauce, a handful of brown sugar and some slices of fresh ginger. Chinese cooking wine or sherry, cloves, some long peels of orange zest and garlic are all other fine additions. For that coronation chicken think of Indian spices like crushed cardamom and coriander seeds. Simmer the stock for 10 minutes with these aromatics to kick-start the infusion before adding the chook.

THAI SHREDDED CHICKEN SALAD

1 bunch coriander (leaves picked and stalks reserved for the dressing)

4 chicken breasts, skin off

1 litre (4 cups) chicken stock, plus water to cover

1 wombok lettuce (iceberg can be used at a pinch)

4 fat spring onions

2 fat green chillies, like jalapenos (but long green or red chillies will do)

1 bunch mint

200 g unsalted peanuts (salted will suffice if you can't find unsalted or a stupid premium is being charged for them)

THE DRESSING

coriander root

2 garlic cloves

salt

2 tablespoons good fish sauce

juice of 3–4 limes

60–75 g palm sugar (or caster sugar if you really can't get palm sugar), to taste

NOTE: you may not need all of each of these as making this dressing is a balancing act.

TIP: You don't need to use the garlic and coriander if you want a more neutral salad. If you can't get palm sugar follow Thai cooking guru David Thompson's advice and use caster sugar but never brown sugar. He'd also probably suggest pounding the chillies into the dressing and using ember-hot scuds rather than sunshine-warm jalapenos, because he's like that.

Admission time. This recipe started out as Stephanie Alexander's but it has, over the years, evolved into a salad all of its own. It's the most perfect of Aussie summer dishes – fresh, light but packed with waves of flavour and texture. It uses a more intense poaching method than I would usually use, which results in chook that is easier to shred using two forks. That means it's perfect as a holiday dish because you can easily poach extra chicken breasts at the same time, which can used for sandwiches the next day.

Wash or scrape clean the coriander roots; cut them off and reserve. Bruise the remaining stalks by thumping along their length with the blunt edge of the knife.

Next, poach the chicken breasts in a wide pot so that they can be placed side by side along with the coriander stalks. Pour in the chicken stock and top up with water if the breasts aren't covered. Bring to the boil and then immediately turn down to the barest shimmering simmer for 5 minutes. Then turn off, cover with the lid, and leave the breasts to cool in the stock until needed.

DRESSING While the chook is steeping, make the dressing. Mince or mash the coriander root and the garlic cloves with a little salt into a smooth paste. A mortar and pestle is ideal. You can do it on a wooden chopping board with the flat side of a chef's knife but chop the root and garlic first. Mix in 6 teaspoons of fish sauce, the juice of 3 limes and 60 g of shaved or grated palm sugar until the sugar dissolves.

Now balance the dressing. You want there to be a little salty stinkiness from the fish sauce and some fresh acidity from the lime juice but both held in check and made slurpable by the sweetness of the palm sugar. To achieve this balance, add more fish sauce, lime juice or sugar little by little, tasting all the time. Spend some time doing this as the dressing is what makes this salad so addictive.

When you are ready to prepare the salad, drain the chook and shred it, scraping it apart with a fork. You'll end up with a bowl of shredded chook.

Cut the wombok in half and slice thinly from the nose to about 2 cm from the root end. This way you'll get both frilly wombok shreds and juicier, stemmy slithers. Pile on top of the chicken.

Peel the tough outer leaves off the spring onions and trim off the frilly root end. Slice thinly into coins – both white and green. Slice the chillies lengthways and scrape out the seeds and veins with a teaspoon. Chop into small dice. Throw both onto the wombok.

Pick the leaves off the mint and chop. Toss into the salad so everything is evenly distributed.

At the table pour on the dressing and toss in the peanuts. Eat immediately.

SERVES 4

SUPERMARKET BBQ ROAST CHICKEN, MANGO AND CASHEW SALAD

There is something forlorn about those BBQ roast chooks that supermarkets line up to sell at a knock-down price at the end of the day. Like the last kids to be picked for the footy team, the sight tugs at my heartstrings. The thing is that they might be forlorn but they are also very tasty, especially when paired with some of chicken's best friends – fragrant herbs, toasty cashew crunches, slippery sweet mango, creamy avocado and more flavour fireworks from the chilli. It's really like throwing one of the poor little buggers a big, bright, brilliant party – and there's even fancy dressing too.

To make the dressing, grind the garlic, ginger and palm sugar in a mortar and pestle. Add all the other dressing ingredients and stir well to combine.

On a big share plate or individual plates, layer all the salad ingredients and top with the cashews and the chillies. Pour over the dressing.

SERVES 4–6

1 store-bought chicken, cut or torn into pieces
2 mangoes, peeled and sliced
3 avocados, peeled and sliced
salad leaves or watercress
½ bunch Thai basil leaves, torn
½ bunch mint leaves, torn
140 g (just under 1 cup) unsalted roasted cashews
2–3 red chillies, bullet or long, finely sliced

DRESSING
2 garlic cloves, peeled and smashed
2 teaspoons peeled and finely chopped fresh ginger
20 g palm sugar
juice of 2 limes
½ teaspoon salt flakes
2 teaspoons fish sauce
1½ tablespoons mint jelly
2 tablespoons grapeseed oil

SEARED BEEF WITH FISH-SAUCE CARAMEL AND A LIME SLAW

salt
1 kg prime grass-fed beef fillet
6 long red chillies, seeded and
  thinly sliced

LIME SLAW
½ head iceberg lettuce
¼ head white drumhead cabbage
juice of 3 plump limes

FISH-SAUCE CARAMEL
250 g palm sugar, roughly chopped
220 ml (almost 1 cup) water
40 ml or so of the best/most
  expensive fish sauce you
  can afford

There is a theory on a certain TV show that some dishes defy the usual rules of good taste. This is one of those yum–yuck dishes. There is nothing wrong with seared beef sitting on slaw zinging with fresh lime but the very idea of making a caramel out of stinky old fish sauce is the logic of the mad house – and yet somehow it works and works very well. The lime on the slaw, the salty crust on the meat, the fresh crunch of the lettuce and cabbage, and the sweet salty funkiness of the sauce all marry beautifully to create a harmonious whole.

Rub the salt into the fillet.

Heat your BBQ or ridged grill pan to as hot as you can. Sear the meat on all sides, taking care always to apply the meat to a spot on the grill that has not had its heat dissipated by cooking. Get all the edges good and crusty brown with 2–3 minutes on each side.

Slice thinly. It will still be rare in the middle.

Lay the beef on the lime slaw and drizzle with the caramel. Top with the sliced red chillies.

LIME SLAW
Using a mandoline, or your maddest knife skills, slice the lettuce and cabbage thinly. Dress generously with the lime juice.

FISH-SAUCE CARAMEL
(inspired by the Vinh Ky Garden restaurant in Hue – and Teage Ezard)
In a heavy pan, heat the palm sugar with 180 ml of water. Bring to the boil and simmer until it becomes a golden caramel. This will take about 8 minutes. Remove from the heat before it gets too dark (or burnt) and splash in the last 40 ml of water to stop it cooking further. Stir in the fish sauce little by little until the salty stinkiness of the fish sauce starts to peek through and reduce the aggressive sweetness of the caramel.

SERVES 4–6

GRILLED PEACH, PECAN AND PROSCIUTTO SALAD

60 ml (¼ cup) balsamic vinegar

55 g (¼ cup) caster sugar

100 g baby rocket, aged or yellowing leaves and any stalky bits removed

10 mint leaves, torn roughly

70 g mild, soft goat's curd

8 slices prosciutto, torn into little strips

4 firm but ripe yellow peaches, cut into thin wedges

70 g (½ cup) toasted pecans

Our culinary souls are set by moments such as these. I'm standing on a street corner in a northern Spanish town with my friend Catherine; we're giggling like idiots, or children. We've both bitten into our first *paraguayos*. This donut peach is so loaded with honeyed juice that every bite is like taking a drink – the soft pastel flesh sends springs of sweetness flashing around our mouths, overwhelming our lips so it escapes, running down our chins. It's a deliciousness that is so timeless that it should be rose-tinted and shot in flickering, over-exposed, colour-saturated Super 8 film, as only the best memories are.

The humble peach owns far more than its fair share of my finest, and most vivid, culinary memories. There's the time sitting in the shade of a dusty stone barn, with an old man as wrinkled as a walnut, when his sons returned from the midday heat with a crate of peaches, each the size of a baby's head. They cried as much, and made my fingers sticky enough to catch passing flies.

Then there was the white peach pulled from an old, twisted tree of a stone-fruit farmer by the banks of the Murray. It was like sinking your teeth into sunshine but finding it cool and slippery instead of warm and golden like hay. 'We don't grow peaches like this any more,' he said with sadness.

Sadly, ranged on the side of darkness, are those peaches that crack or crunch in a way that is frankly unnatural. Here's the thing: those soft, juice-bombs of peaches don't like to travel and sit on shelves for days on end. They aren't the peaches giant supermarket chains want because they don't pack and ship as well as those pretty but bullet-hard peaches. Peaches that might look as fine as a firm-fleshed prom queen but, as everyone with a little life experience knows, you can't judge the sweetness of supermarket fruit by its appearance. Often if it's pretty, it's hard. Then you need to heat up the hard-hearted little buggers for this salad.

Make a balsamic syrup by simmering the balsamic and sugar in a small saucepan over low heat, stirring regularly so it reduces down to half its volume, to make ¼ cup of liquid. Do this gently – don't let it boil. Let it cool before using. The syrup will thicken as it cools.

Put the rocket in a wide, flat salad bowl with the mint leaves. Top with small dollops of goat's curd about the size of a fingernail and the torn prosciutto.

Using a ridged grill pan (or a flat-bottomed pan if you don't have a grill pan), cook the peach segments so they soften and get nice char bars on them or a lovely golden brown colour.

Arrange the peaches on the salad and drizzle with the cooled balsamic syrup. Scatter the toasted pecans on top. Eat.

SERVES 4

INNOCENT PEA SALAD WITH EVIL PORKY PEPITA CRUNCH

Recently I have had the pleasure of discussing the vagaries of television, advertising and the shortcomings of the Melbourne Football Club with ad guru and charming star of television's Gruen series, Russell Howcroft. One of the great insights the man we call 'boss' shared with me was that to be successful names have to combine contrasting soft and hard words like 'Iron Butterfly' or 'Steele Sidebottom'. So henceforth this salad shall be known as 'Sweet Pea; Salty Crunch'. It combines an innocent salad of fresh uncorrupted flavours ravished by the sort of garnish that is the equivalent of a heavy metal groupie in laddered fishnets and too much eyeliner seducing the geek from IT.

Lay the shredded lettuce down the middle of a platter. Layer the peas and the celery on top. Toss the apple in the lemon juice and sprinkle over the platter.

Make the bacon and pepita crunch. Fry the bacon in the butter until it's tanned in places. Throw in the pepitas and let them start to toast. When some of the pepitas are starting to go golden at the edges, stir in the sugar and let it melt. Keep stirring and a caramel will form from the brown sugar and the rendered pork fat which will coat the pepitas and bacon. Sprinkle with some salt flakes and spread out on baking paper.

Now finish the salad. Crumble over the cheeses – large lumps of ricotta; smaller lumps of feta – and scatter on the herbs. Dress the salad with olive oil and a splash of sherry vinegar. Smash up the pepitas of evil and strew over the top. Done! Serve!

SERVES 4–6

1 cos lettuce, dark leaves discarded and the paler inner leaves finely shredded
360 g (3 cups) frozen peas, cooked
140 g (1 cup) celery, cut into pea-size dice
100 g (½ cup) green apple, peeled and cut into pea-sized dice
juice of 1 lemon
6 rashers streaky bacon, diced
40 g butter
160 g (1 cup) pepitas
100 g (½ cup) brown sugar
salt flakes
200g fresh ricotta, cut from a wheel at the deli counter, not in a tub
100 g feta
1 bunch mint, chopped
1 bunch flat-leaf parsley, chopped
4 spring onions, cut into rings
3 tablespoons olive oil
1 tablespoon sherry vinegar

TIP: This pepita crunch is great with the pumpkin soup on page 98

GERMAN FOOD AIN'T ALL BAD

My Bavarian–Barossan friend Caroline taught me these recipes. She is quite strict, so no extemporising.

1. GERMAN POTATO SALAD

This simple salad dumps the traditional sour cream and mayo in favour of a more austere dressing that is actually far more tasty.

To make the salad, cut **6 medium-sized Dutch cream potatoes** into large bite-sized pieces and place in a pan of cold water over high heat. While the potatoes are cooking, take **150 ml veggie stock** (or 2 teaspoons of good stock powder diluted with 50 ml of boiling water and 100 ml of iced water) and place over low heat to reduce by half. Cook the potatoes until just cooked. Drain the potatoes and toss with ½ **finely diced brown onion**. Pour over the reduced stock and let the potatoes soak it up for a minute or two. Throw over a simple dressing made from shaking **4 tablespoons olive oil** and **3 tablespoons vinegar** in a jar along with ½ **bunch curly parsley**, finely chopped. Great with anything off the BBQ.

2. GERMAN CUCUMBER SALAD

The idea of something as understated and fresh as cucumber even contemplating mixing with a sour cream and milk dressing seems wrong, and rather corrupting, but given a little time the change wrought in the cucumber by the dressing has to be tried to be believed.

According to Caroline, the Germans don't like chunky cucumber so take a peeler and shave **1 whole cucumber** into ribbons. Stop when you reach the seeds. Finely chop ½ **medium-sized onion** and add to the cucumber. In a separate bowl **mix 2 tablespoons white vinegar** with **2 tablespoons oil** then stir through **4 tablespoons sour cream**, **2 tablespoons milk** and **lots of salt and pepper**. Pour this dressing onto the cucumber and onion and gently toss to coat. Let them sit for 15 minutes. It will taste sour and the onion hot but the cucumber will mellow all that as it gives up its juice. Serve with pretty much anything!

BBQ SALADS

Every BBQ needs salads, and here are two easy classics. They are ace with the German ones too.

3. LEEK AND MINT SALAD

Don't get freaked out, like chefs do, about this recipe. Trust me.

Take **6 leeks** and trim them, removing the coarse green tops and the frilly bits at the bottom, *but* don't remove the bulb bit that keeps the leek together. The length should be about 12 cm. Working at the non-bulb end, take a sharp knife and make 2 × 5 cm deep incisions in a cross pattern. Wash the leek well under cold water to remove any grit.

Place 2 leeks on a plate with a splash of water and cook in the microwave for 90 seconds. Do the same with the remaining leeks. If you put them all in together they don't cook evenly. Cut the leeks into 1 cm slices and arrange on a serving plate. While still warm, splash **red wine vinegar** and **extra-virgin olive oil** over the top. Finish with **salt flakes**, **freshly ground black pepper** and lots of **julienned**, **fresh mint leaves**.

4. TOMATO AND MARJORAM SALAD

For the dressing, mix **1 tablespoon good-quality red wine vinegar** and 1½ **teaspoons caster sugar** together. Once the sugar is dissolved slowly incorporate **3 tablespoons extra-virgin olive oil**.

Cut **4 tomatoes** into thickish slices and lay the tomato slices on a serving plate or in a bowl, drizzle over the dressing and scatter over **fresh marjoram leaves** (you'll need the leaves of about ¼ bunch).

Serving suggestion: add dollops of soft goat's curd, if you like.

WARM SPINACH, PRUNE, BACON AND BLUE CHEESE SALAD

100 g (⅔ cup) dried pitted prunes
125 ml (½ cup) balsamic vinegar
1 tablespoon soft brown sugar
2 tablespoons grapeseed oil
½ teaspoon English mustard
½ teaspoon salt
freshly ground black pepper
8 rashers back bacon, cut into strips
200 g baby spinach leaves
60 g (½ cup) walnuts, lightly toasted
1 plum, cut into thin wedges
50 g creamy blue cheese (yes,
   daggy Danish blue will do)

TIP: For extra crunch you could candy the walnuts or add croutons of dark rye bread that are crispy on the outside but still moist inside.

Warm salads, or *salades tièdes*, were all the rage back in the eighties and that warmth does some marvellous things to this combination of flavours, very similar to those in a salad I ate last summer at a little café called Piknik. Serving the salad warm means the blue cheese softens slightly and the flavour of the taut young plum really comes alive against the soft, gnarly prunes. It's like watching young kids cheeking the sweet-and-sour old folk. Note that this salad is in the 'salad as four Mars bars' category and is so rich you'll want to eat it in moderation … maybe.

Put the prunes, balsamic and sugar in enough water to cover and bring to a gentle simmer. Let the prunes soften without breaking down too much (about 7–8 minutes).

Mix the oil, mustard, salt and pepper together to form a dressing and set aside.

Remove the prunes from the vinegar and set aside. Discard the vinegar.

In a large frying pan, cook the bacon until crispy, drain on paper towel and wipe out the pan.

Now get ready to work quickly. Five, four, three, two, one, GO!

Reheat the large frying pan, return the bacon to the pan and let it heat up again, tossing constantly for a minute or two. Add all the spinach leaves and then pour over the dressing. Keep the spinach moving, turning with tongs just long enough to toss the spinach together with the bacon and for the spinach to start wilting but don't let it go soggy. This final tossing needs to be accomplished in no more than 1 minute.

To serve, layer the salad with some spinach and bacon, scatter over some prunes, a few walnuts, some plum pieces and crumble over a bit of blue cheese, then keep layering till all the ingredients are used up. Serve straight away.

SERVES 4 AS AN ACCOMPANYING SALAD

WINTER SALADS

As the weather gets colder, my pelt gets thicker and my thoughts turn to finding a cosy cave to hibernate in. They also turn to eating lots as if some primal self-defence mechanism against failing food sources has kicked in. My first reaction is to demand huge steaming bowls of carbs sozzled with butter and mounds of juicy meat and treacle tart or sticky toffee pudding to finish, of course.

Winter also opens itself up to some of the world's most classic salads; without having to the break the rules of seasonality or break the bank. Of course, some of these winter salads do revolve around slathering everything with mayonnaise such as the classic crunchy Waldorf salad combination of celery, walnut and apple. A modern take on Waldorf can be made by keeping the use of (low-fat even) mayo to a very bare minimum or replace the apple with hunks of very ripe pear, which will give the salad the impression of juiciness without all those mayo calories and fat.

Or instead how about Skye Gyngell's wonderful take on a pear and gorgonzola salad. The talented Sydney-born cook marries the creamy saltiness of the Italian blue cheese with pear quarters poached in sweetened red wine with juniper berries, thyme and a bay leaf. These provide a wonderful foil for the bitterness of the endive and the crunch of walnut halves.

There is also the prospect of salads made with bitter winter leaves like spiky endive, chicory or dandelion which are much loved by the Italians and some parts of France. Endive, in the form of spiky frisée lettuce, perhaps reaches its pinnacle in a classic Lyonnaise salad with chunks of bacon (lardons) and crunchy croutons topped with a poached egg and acidic French mustard dressing.

I am also a fan of chicory, which seems to be known by as many pseudonyms around Australia as a character from *Underbelly*. Chicory aka Belgian endive, witlof, and Sammy Knuckles – OK, I admit it, I made that last one up – is a pretty, pointed dart of a salad bulb. The fat succulent white leaves peel away into little boat shapes that are wonderful paired with a salty flavour like freshly peeled shards of parmesan, perhaps balanced by the sweetness of a balsamic vinegar dressing or maybe with soft poached eggs, chunks of pan-fried pancetta and some crunchy croutons as a take on *salade Lyonaisse*.

Then there is the whole universe of shredded cabbage salads that you'll find in my last book (you do have my last book, don't you? It's pretty good – if not quite as vibrant as this one). Or those salads that work around grains or seeds and other dried goodies whether that be couscous or quinoa.

While winter is traditionally about roasted root veggies there is nothing to say that these can't also be used in a winter salad. I always like to do double the amount of veg with the Sunday roast as this can then be saved for a delicious Monday night dinner of leftover meat and a salad of those veggies tossed in a light vinegar dressing (I use sherry vinegar). Add a handful of toasted pine nuts and a few fresh thyme leaves to perk things up. Roasting naturally sweet veg like this intensifies their sweetness making them a great foil for acid-driven dressings and the tang of fresh cheeses.

Pairing beets with goat's cheese, hazelnuts or walnuts and dill is a classic combination that you'll find elsewhere here. While roasted carrots go perfectly with a crumbling of fresh or dried ricotta, toasted almond shards and a dusting of dukkah. Dress with a little orange juice that's been reduced in a pan to a drizzling consistency. Add shredded flat-leaf parsley for greenery.

When it comes to winter salads, however, two take centre stage on my table. Both pair wonderfully well with a lamb shoulder roasted in the oven, or boned leg, grilled slowly on the BBQ. One is inspired by the mythology of the ancient underworld and how winter came about; the other by a trip to an altogether more tangible netherworld, that of eighties New York.

The ancient world believed that winter was due to Persephone, daughter of earth goddess Demeter, being abducted by Hades and tricked into staying in the underworld after eating pomegranate seeds. The sweet, juicy, garnet-red seeds of this fruit can also be somewhat astringent, which makes them perfect for this pomegranate salad given the obvious sweetness of the redcurrant jelly. Cucumber adds crunch, feta adds salt and the redcurrant jelly nods to the classic English partnership for roast lamb.

On my first visit to New York in the days long before I was a food writer, a meal in the arty district of SoHo, at a trendy Italian restaurant called Vucciria, was made memorable by a brilliantly simple combination of blood orange, radicchio and fennel dressed with no more than the leaching juice from the citrus and a scattering of salt. Just peel **3 blood oranges**, removing all pith and skin. Slice into rounds 8 mm thick. Reserve any juice that is released during cutting. Remove seeds. Remove the flannelly outer leaves and break up **1 head red radicchio** into individual leaves; wash and dry. Remove the tough outer petals from **2 bulbs of fennel** (basically you need the same amount of fennel as oranges). Cut off the 'fingers' at the top of the bulb. (Remove and reserve the feathery leaves for the pomegranate salad on page 40.) Cut off the hard nub at the base of the fennel. Slice the fennel as finely as you can. On a plate, arrange the bitter red leaves, then the blood orange and fennel slices. Dress with a splash of good **olive oil**, if desired, then any reserved blood orange juice and a good pinch of **salt flakes**.

NOTE:
If blood oranges aren't in season, you can use ordinary oranges.

POMEGRANATE SALAD

2 fat ripe pomegranates
1 Lebanese cucumber, peeled and
  cut into small dice (i.e. smaller
  than the pomegranate seeds)
80 g good-quality crumbly feta
2 tablespoons toasted almonds
2 tablespoons Greek yoghurt
1 small jar redcurrant jelly
fennel fronds (from the fennel
  salad on page 39)

NOTE: If pomegranates aren't in
season you can use oranges instead.

TIP: If you can't
get redcurrant jelly,
buy mint jelly instead
and also add a
few mint leaves
to the salad.

Cut the pomegranate in half around its middle and knock the seeds onto a plate, saving both seeds and juice. Pick through the seeds removing any of the pith that might have come away from the pomegranate's husk along with the seeds.

On a long thin plate, lay out an even line of the seeds in the middle, leaving loads of white space on either side; this 'negative space' will make the dish extra appealing and elegant, thus fooling people about its simplicity.

Sprinkle the cucumber dice along the middle of the seeds. Crumble the feta over the top of this long mound. Sprinkle along the length with the toasted almond shards.

Then line the mound with seven scant teaspoon-sized dollops of yoghurt. Top each yoghurt mound with a little (½ teaspoon) dollop of redcurrant jelly. Sprinkle the fennel fronds over the length of the barrow-shaped salad.

SERVES 4

22 NOT SO SECRET HERBS AND SPICES EVERYONE SHOULD HAVE ...
AND HOW TO USE THEM

For me, having the right herbs and spices on hand is like having a full set of colouring pencils – everything on hand to draw flavours that range from the piquant and the fragrant to the warm and the earthy.

MY FAVOURITE HERBS

HOW TO USE FRESH HERBS

This may ruffle feathers: I don't like dried herbs. Their pungent flavour is inextricably linked in my mind to bad seventies tomato sauces. Over the years I've managed to disinter those little glass bottles of desiccated dead dust from my spice drawer in favour of planting little fresh pots of my favourites to use in my cooking. Along with salt flakes, access to fresh herbs has been one of the things that has taken my cooking to – as they say on the TV – another level. Fresh herbs have a delicacy and fragrance that lifts dishes; you just need to use three times as much as you would do with dried. So if a recipe calls for 1 teaspoon of dried basil use 3 teaspoons of fresh instead.

Fresh herbs are the backbone of so many of the classic sauces of the world, whether it's the tarragon in your Béarnaise, the parsley and oregano paired with chilli and vinegar in Argentina's classic chimichurri for steak, or a whole world of 'green' sauces. The French *sauce verte* flavours mayonnaise with chopped tarragon, parsley or sage, while Italian *salsa verde* is a classic multipurpose sauce that goes with just about anything from lamb, roast chook or fish to beef – roasted, boiled or BBQ'd. You can even toss your boiled potatoes in it. It's made from combining chopped parsley and basil with garlic, capers, oil and lemon. I like adding anchovies, mustard and a little mint to mine, which is very Jamie Oliver.

In Mexico you'll find *salsa verde* slathered on tacos or grilled pork but theirs is built around coriander with tomatillos, chillies and a little lime juice. Neither should be mistaken for France's *sauce vierge*, which is a great simple dressing for fish, made from olive oil, lemon juice, chopped tomato and shredded basil. I like to add a few coriander seeds. The name doesn't refer to the colour of the basil but the clean-tasting, virginal nature of this peppy combination.

A fresh pesto is probably the best-known herb sauce there is in Australia but it's also one of those things you tend to have to make in bulk – if you aren't using the old fashioned muscle of a mortar and pestle – as you need lots of basil leaves, pine nuts, parmesan, garlic and oil for the food processor to blend them effectively. The trouble then is that you are eating pesto from now till eternity. What I've started doing each time that I make a batch of pesto is to take half of it and pep it up with a handful of capers, a couple of anchovies, a good squeeze of lemon and a little water to make a wonderful pungent herb dressing that is like a cheat's salsa verde. This is great slathered over roast meats, dolloped on tomato pizzas or spread on sandwiches or wraps instead of mayonnaise. Throw in some extra-virgin olive oil and it's a lovely dressing for fish or roast chook as well. It's delicious with cured meat like pancetta and prosciutto, fresh tomatoes or slices of boiled egg with iceberg lettuce. Add some chopped green olives and suddenly it's working wonderfully with beef and lamb as well.

The thing that sets all these sauces apart is that they are uncooked and partner the fragrance and flavour of the herbs with a touch of acidic bite and often some oil for texture. Another cracking cold sauce for everything from fish like whiting to cured and cold meats is *sauce gribiche* where chervil, tarragon and parsley are chopped together with hard-boiled egg, capers, gherkin and mayo, or vinegar, and a little oil.

Obviously fresh herbs are delicious just as they are, sprinkled on raw or cooked foods or in dressings but they are just as flexible thrown in with stuff that's cooking. Adding a branch of rosemary to your roasting potatoes or a sprig of mint, stalks and all, to your boiling new season's potatoes will add an edge. If using herbs in a sauce I like to add half at the start of the process and then freshen up the sauce by stirring through the rest just before serving – this will bring some freshness to the sauce as well as the complexity of the herb's flavour, both cooked and raw.

So now, how about some different ideas for how to use some of Australia's most popular herbs:

MINT

This breath of fresh air isn't just for lamb and peas. Try adding it to your tabouli, pair it with Asian herbs, like holy basil and Vietnamese mint (which isn't a mint at all, but I digress), in a zippy Thai salad; or let it give a lift to fruit salads or berries. It is wonderful rolled up and very finely sliced on melon or pineapple (see page 227). I also make a tomato sauce for pasta that pairs fresh mint and lemon with loads of feta for a very different impact from the usual Italian flavours. As it grows like billy-o round my place I also douse it with almost boiling water to make a refreshing herb tea.

FLAT-LEAF PARSLEY
(also called Italian or Continental parsley)

This is my every time herb. I use it as much for colour and freshness as flavour to finish servings of everything from soup to casseroles but I also chop it up to stir through mashed potato or the mince for hamburgers or meatballs. It can bulk up a pesto and has a wonderful friendship with fish, seafood like mussels, garlic and lemon zest. While a slab of gammon with parsley sauce will have me humming 'Danny Boy', curly parsley is the devil and should never be used unless you are arranging raw meat in a butcher's window. It is tickly and flat-leaf parsley has a better, stronger flavour. Knödel are the only exception to this rule!

BASIL

We all know that basil is BFF with tomatoes, at the core (with pine nuts, parmesan and garlic) of a Mediterranean pistou and a good pesto but why not try this pungent herb with pink salmon for an interesting change – or if you are feeling really radical, very finely sliced on your strawberries. That is a match made in heaven. Basil also goes wonderfully with zucchini as you see on page 116. There are numerous different basils out there, so think about plain purple basil for colour, holy basil for the breath of aniseedy freshness it brings to Thai stir fries, or lemon basil as its pronounced citrusy flavour is a real surprise.

SAGE

These fuzzy, spear-shaped leaves are the traditional herb for pork but sage also marries well with onion for a stuffing for any poultry. Why not try it to flavour your next porky Bolognese, or crisp up the leaves in a little foaming butter and then toss your gnocchi or pasta in this sage-scented pan with a grate of parmesan and a squeeze of lemon. Even a few nuggets of anchovy will thrive in this environment. Also try sage with pumpkin. Mixing very finely sliced or fried sage leaves through mashed pumpkin is wonderful with either pork chops or roast chicken. Be careful, though, as sage is pretty potent and can overpower a dish.

CORIANDER

This frilly-edged herb is a fixture in Indian, Mexican, Middle Eastern and Thai dishes and you'll find it popping up all through this book. Try some stirred through your next batch of mushrooms on toast for a bit of a departure from the norm. Or try making a coriander pesto with cashews instead of pine nuts. It also seems to have a natural affinity with white meat so try it in stuffing for a turkey or tossed through carrots with some orange zest to serve with roast chicken. It's also at the core (along with parsley) of my take on a Moroccan chermoula that's great slathered on fish or chook.

THYME

This might well be my favourite herb. Those delicate little leaves look so beautiful picked from their woody stalks and add a very French twist to eggs, potatoes, chicken, mushrooms and anything with leeks and onions. Try using it to flavour bean casseroles or toss some thyme leaves through your crumb for schnitzels. It's also great – as are so many of the herbs here – added to a simple vinaigrette. Think about adding a branch of thyme to soups like French onion and to stews, especially when there is wine, rabbit, beef or Dijon mustard involved. I also love thyme tossed through braised mushrooms, either with goat's cheese, or a little Dijon mustard blended into the pan juices.

MARJORAM

This herb was the Greek and Roman symbol of happiness and it seems happiest with tomatoes. So try it anywhere you might use basil, such as sprinkled on a pizza fresh out of the oven or in the mince for Bolognese, homemade snags or meatballs. It is also great adding a herby waft to your scones, focaccia or breads – something that most herbs are great for. 'Wild marjoram', aka oregano, is a softer-tasting version that's perfect for all these uses as well as pepping up a Greek salad.

DILL

This delicate, frondy herb has a powerful hold over the kitchen of the north and east of Europe from Istanbul and Greece to Scandinavia. Its pretty, fine pluches go classically with fish, chicken and eggs. Try it in a mayo or vinaigrette-based dressing for any seafood like mussels, prawns or fish. It also goes well with oranges and in pickles and is great in a potato salad or with pretty much anything that contains cucumber, sour cream or yoghurt, whether it's a tzatziki or vinegar-dressed cucumber salad. Try it in an omelette with smoked salmon and a generous dollop of sour cream.

BAY LEAVES

Bay leaves have fallen out of fashion but, fresh, they still play a big part in my kitchen: on skewers woven between hunks of beef for the BBQ; tossed in a Bolognese; in a bouquet garni – the classic French herb bundle of bay, parsley and thyme – to flavour soups, stews and stocks; or just to scent milk for everything from white sauce to even your rice pudding. Try a handful thrown into the water next time you are cooking crabs. Interesting!

CHIVES

Chives can happily tread anywhere that spring onions go – snipped and sprinkled on boiled potatoes or potato salad, omelettes, a melted cheese toasty, garnishing soup, casseroles or your baked potatoes. It's great adding a gently oniony bite to vinaigrettes instead of garlic or just mix finely chopped chives with Greek yoghurt and salt to make a simple but different salad dressing. My favourite use is to toss snipped chives into the butter in which I've cooked thin strips of steak. I'll then serve the steak on mash with the chive butter poured over the top. This works equally well for gently cooked fillets of delicate white fish. Always use chives at the end of cooking rather than at the start.

ROSEMARY

Rosemary has been dating lamb for as long as anyone can remember but that's not to say that it can't stray and add its powerful aroma to your roast blue eye or your baked quinces or apple tart. The flowers are perfect for this. Just sprinkle them on the quinces or apple tart before serving as a pretty, flavour-packed garnish. It's the key to the stuffing of perfect Northern Italian *porchetta* but it's also pretty funky in your syrup to candy oranges. Just go easy as it's such a powerful herb and always keep it away from beef.

TARRAGON

The delicate aniseed flavour of tarragon makes it perfect with beef in a Béarnaise or with chicken. Why not work tarragon butter under the skin of your next roast chook. It goes really well in a tartare sauce for fish instead of parsley, or sprinkled over steamed potatoes with a little butter. It's also great as part of a mayonnaise or just sprinkled over any egg dish. As with pretty much any of these herbs, if you have a glut of them, use them to stuff the cavity of a chook or whole fish. Or better yet, make a *petite salade* with fresh tarragon leaves and fresh grapes. Toss grilled pieces of BBQ'd chicken or goat's cheese through it. Resist the temptation to load this with mayonnaise as our American cousins do but instead just dress it with a little simple vinaigrette.

MY FAVOURITE SPICES

Spices are by definition any 'dried seeds, fruit, root, bark, or vegetative substance primarily used for flavouring, colouring or preserving food'. Their recorded use by humans dates back over 4000 years but undoubtedly it's much, much longer than that. The Arab world dominated the world of spice, at least until seafaring nations like England and Spain (and their early dependents) sought to cut out the middlemen by opening up their own direct links to the spice islands of the East Indies.

Spices are very much the domain of those cuisines that were built on trade and of the places from whence they came, such as India, Mexico and South East Asia. The Middle East and North Africa bestrode the spice routes and built their wealth on the spice trade. Even today a visit to the spice markets of Istanbul, Cairo and Damascus (hopefully one day again) should be on the bucket list of anyone serious about food. They are an education in both range and quality; just to smell the heady fragrance of truly good saffron is to have your perception of that spice realigned.

Drag open the drawers where I keep my spices and it's like discovering a store of flavour postcards from my travels. Packs of 'crab boil' spices from the American south, vacuum packs of dark fruity janissary spice blend from Istanbul and a *masala dabba* from Mumbai's Crawford Market. This container of stainless steel spice pots contains everything from sour mango powder and oniony 'hing' to more familiar cardamoms and mustard seeds, which the Indian kitchen cannot do without.

Certain spices get more of a workout than others in my kitchen. Here are my 10 most used picks:

PAPRIKA

The dried and ground fruit of the capsicum or chilli plant makes up the base of this ruddy powder that is another supercharger of flavour. I use a couple of teaspoons to add flavour and a rich red colour to everything from a simple casserole of sliced capsicum and chicken thighs to braises made with tomato and chorizo. It also works well in a rub for roast pork or adding a little complexity to everything from lamb mince fillings for stuffed capsicums or filo parcels to fish stews. Obviously it is also essential in my goulash and when I'm making a decadent creamy chicken *paprikash*, but here I note that with numerous different grades I want a paprika that is at the sweet end of the range rather than pungent and slightly bitter. Paprika is also one of the spices that deteriorates most markedly and quickly, so buy it in small quantities. Also keep any eye out for smoked paprika, which is delicious spiking a mayonnaise for prawns or sprinkled across braised octopus and boiled potatoes in a take on the classic Galician dish. Use it sparingly though, as it easily overshadows other flavours.

CORIANDER SEEDS

These seeds are another 'warm' spice but with a slightly lemony or citrus fragrance under their earthiness. They are an essential partner to the honey in any of my carrot dishes, whether roast, braised, mashed or puréed. They also go beautifully with pork and are the essential spice when I am cooking cubes of pork on the BBQ to make a Cypriot-style souvlaki. Their fragrance is much lighter than their best mate the cumin seed. I find that a little toasted and ground coriander seed is great with white fish and in pilafs – usually because I'll also partner it with a little fresh coriander, which is like pairing a cello with a violin in an orchestra. They both make a similar sound but they fill a different space in the taste spectrum. I've also had much success partnering coriander seed with anything that loves the citrusy zip of orange or lemon such as roast beetroot, braised mushrooms or the chicken or prawn filling for tacos. Feel free to add a little fresh lemon or orange zest to further cement this partnership. Chicken seems to have a particular affinity with coriander seed, so next time you are making a gravy for your Sunday roast chook, add some ground coriander to the pan juices and see the lift it will give them.

FIVE-SPICE POWDER

Spice blends are a world all their own, from the simplest curry powder to the most complex 28-ingredient Moroccan *ras el hanout*. Few blends, however, capture the flavour of a cuisine as completely as the mix of fennel seed, cloves, cinnamon, star anise and Sichuan pepper known as Chinese five-spice powder. I'll rub it in to the skin of duck breast before pan-frying and then serve with a sauce of orange or mandarin juice and the pan juices reduced to a syrup. I'll mix five-spice powder with honey, soy, ginger and garlic to make a simple marinade for baked chicken wings, or use it to add some fragrance to stir fries and braises – especially Chinese red braises – where soy is present. I'll also mix a little into the flour for coating chook before frying to give fried chook an exotic Mandarin twist.

STAR ANISE

Star anise is perhaps the most marginal of the 10 spices here as in my kitchen its role is largely limited to flavouring masterstocks for poaching meat and birds, for mulled wine or to add a lift to sugar syrups in which I'll poach fruit such as peaches, oranges or pears (where its strong, sweet, aniseed flavour marries well with vanilla). It also works wonderfully with cinnamon and black peppercorns. My favourite use of star anise is, however, to put a couple of blades in with onions that I am browning to make the base to any stew, soup or braise. This alchemy of mixing onion with star anise gives the onion an unexpected meatiness. It sounds a little weird but once you've tried it, you'll be a convert. Heston Blumenthal discovered this. Thanks Heston.

CINNAMON

These quills of fragrant bark are the king of spices for me. No other spice is quite as warm, quite as fragrant, quite as reassuring. I'll heat milk with a stick of cinnamon if I can't sleep and it will soothe me back to a deep and restful snooze. I'll use it as a funky flavour in braises of beef or lamb alongside the zest of orange, which is something you'll find in ancient recipes from back when battles were fought in armour and dragons were almost real.

Cinnamon is essential in my apple pie or apple crumble, or even the butter-roast apples I serve with roast pork. I also love using it to add an exotic note to chicken and almonds cooked with rice in the Lebanese manner. Pears, carrots (and carrot cake), pumpkin, sweet potato, chocolate, apricots and banana all also love the cosy warmth cinnamon brings.

Cinnamon is also great stirred through ricotta and then spread on toasted Turkish bread for breakfast. Add a little drizzle of honey for sweetness!

ALLSPICE

These dried berries that originated in the Caribbean are like a spice mix all on their own. Taste the spice and it contains notes of everything from cloves and mace to cinnamon in each berry. I love a little ground allspice sprinkled over my roast pumpkin, flavouring fruit cake or underpinning the flavour of my spicy Jamaican-style 'jerked' chicken. Partnered with onion powder and garlic powder allspice is at the very heart of most great US BBQ sauces and spice rubs that I've ever made for anything, from pork ribs to beef brisket. Like bay leaf in the herb world, I reckon allspice is the most undervalued of all spices.

CUMIN SEEDS

Earthy, warm, a little pungent – the presence of cumin seeds adds a very distinct and prominent flavour to so many of the things that I love to cook. I'll pan-toast them to toss through braised red cabbage, or over cauliflower I've par-boiled and then fried until the florets are patched golden. I'll toss a teaspoon through buttered, boiled potatoes to give them a wake-up call or sprinkle a little ground cumin over the top of cucumber, yoghurt, or the two mixed together.

Cumin is also the perfect partner for eggplant, whether it is a little mixed with the creamy, smoky flesh of BBQ'd eggplant perhaps used as a babaghanoush or ground with a pinch of salt flakes to sprinkle over homemade eggplant chips. In fact, cumin goes rather well with any smoky flavours, which is why I use it as the main spice in my roast corn and green capsicum salsa that you'll find online at taste.com.au.

If I am feeling exotic, I'll toast the seeds and grind them up with a little zingy and almost metallic Sichuan pepper to make a simple dry rub for lamb skewers.

NUTMEG

This rather large seed is magnificently versatile. It goes wonderfully well in cakes or with any milk-based desserts. I love it grated over the top of rice pudding, your Christmas eggnog or creamy Brandy Alexander cocktail. The Dutch grate a little over cauliflower and the Scots use it to hide the flavour of lung in their haggis but in my house I tend to use it most to add a nutty perfume to everything from pan-wilted spinach, braised leek or roast pumpkin to flavouring the apple filling in an apple pie or apple crumble. The main thing with nutmeg is to go easy on it as too much will give your dish a rather nasty metallic or medicinal zing. Nutmeg is also reportedly hallucinogenic, which perhaps helps explain the spell it casts over everything that it is paired with. In the Middle Ages Arab authors suggested that a cup of warm milk with honey and nutmeg was a fine way to get a night of passion started. Apparently.

FENNEL SEEDS

Certain ingredients inspire an almost Pavlovian response in the kitchen. If I use feta, I almost immediately reach for a lemon. If I use cucumber, the yoghurt usually isn't far behind. So it is with pork and fennel seeds. These pretty little ribbed flavour-bombs impart a wonderful aniseed fragrance to my slow-roasted pork shoulder or rough Italian-style sausages. Fennel seeds are also important in both Indian and Chinese cuisine where their flavour is one of the elements of five-spice powder. I've also been eating a lot of fennel seed biscuits recently; crisp, buttery biscuits where the seeds add lightness, perhaps because they are credited with helping digestion. In fact, they are an essential part of most Indian *mukhwas,* which are those colourful sugar-and-spice rubbles that are served as an after-meal digestive and breath freshener.

BLACK PEPPER

It's an old kitchen saying that you season with salt but you spice with black pepper. It's quietly omnipresent in so much of what I cook but there are a few times when I'll let the pepper shine for itself and here the secret is to grind the pepper into a fine sieve to get rid of the hot dust so the fruity flavour of the pepper can star. This way, black pepper is wonderful coating a fillet of beef or used as the lead flavour in a beef braise, whether Western or Chinese. Mushrooms sit very well here. I love using black pepper with the zippy precociousness of lime juice on whole, buttered sweet corn, BBQ chook or prawns as well. Use a little of the lime zest as well as the lime juice. More unusual, but actually a delicacy that dates back to Roman times when pepper was a luxury that cost more than gold, is to pepper your strawberries. Try it, you'll love it!

Each country tends to build up a particular reputation – the English for roasting, the Americans for deep-frying, the French for sauciness. Around the globe the culinary technique that Australia owns is that large hunk of metal that we call the BBQ.

Sure the Argentines, Jamaicans and Malaysians might share our love of cooking outdoors over an open flame with their *asadors*, oil-drum grills loaded with jerked chicken or slowly turned skewers of satay but we are happy to share because Australians are just that sort of people.

The BBQ is a perfect way to cook as it can cook fast or slow, imparts flavour (sometimes unwelcome if you haven't cleaned it!) and provides the perfect modern fire-pit or campfire around which to hold important conversations on such vital subjects as designing the perfect Esky or the best tackle ever made in a Grand Final.

The first secret of a true Aussie BBQ is in the preparation. For example, cut and make the elements for your salads in the morning but don't assemble and dress them until your guests arrive. Actually, the real number one rule is to check that you have enough gas in the cylinder and if not, buy more. More BBQs have been ruined by the gas running out than by burnt snags.

Next, make sure that the BBQ is clean after you've scraped off any old congealed fat. And yes, it is easier to clean the BBQ immediately after cooking, when it has cooled down but is still warm.

Then pick a menu that can come off the BBQ in waves. Start with sausages and chops. Perfect for the kids, who are likely to be less patient, and ideal because both can be eaten in the fingers. For adults that might be enough, but if you want to step up your BBQ, think of slow-cooking a boned leg of lamb on your grill perhaps rubbed with a mix of North African flavouring made from combining 2 tablespoons of roughly ground coriander seeds with a tablespoon of cumin, some olive oil and salt. The lamb can be cooked just before your guests arrive and then rested in a warm place. Partner it with garlic and mint-spiked Greek yoghurt and a mound of onions or cucumber pickled lightly in a mix of vinegar and sugar. Don't forget to season any meat from the BBQ with a good pinch of salt flakes.

I tend not to cook whole fish on the BBQ but, if I do, I have found that using the flat plate and laying down silicon paper first will help those problems of the skin and flesh sticking to the metal.

There is much debate about marinades and spice rubs at BBQs. I use more dry rubs these days as they are quicker and tend to give meat a good crust but really if you buy the best meat you can afford it doesn't need as much help to taste delicious. I'd rather a small piece of good steak than a slab of cheaper stuff. If you are cooking unrubbed or unmarinated meat, then coat the meat lightly with a little oil rather than the grill. This helps limit the amount used – and the unwelcome flare-ups that too much oil can cause.

The one thing to watch out for with marinades is sweetness from brown sugar or honey as sugars can burn easily and end up adding bitterness instead. Cook meats with this type of marinade, like chicken with a sweet soy honey marinade, on indirect or low heat to avoid this risk. Overall, however, I'd rather add the flavour after cooking with sauces, salsas, smoking and herb butters rather than marinades.

FOUR WAYS <u>WITH</u> SAUSAGES

There are certain things we tend to take for granted. The seasons, electricity, our mothers, fresh sausages … Yes, few things are as accommodating as the humble snag and yet earn so little appreciation in this country where they are disparaged with the tag 'mystery bags'. Oh, shame on you Australia!

The snag will wordlessly help you raise money for the local kinder at the sausage sizzle or fill up little kids cheaply and with barely more fuss than squidging a little sauce on a sheet of soft white bread. It will happily spill its guts so you can splodge it on a pizza or toss its meaty filling in a tomato sauce for pasta like lazy man's meatballs.

Yet behind this humble exterior lurks a nobility, a nobility that is inherent in the prime flesh from whence it came and that is enhanced by trappings that steak or fillet could never have, for the sausage comes ready-barded and already adorned in spices like a debutante princess dressed in the family's best jewels. But then the sausage should have pride for it is, in itself, a matter of pride for many countries around the world whether it is the spicy merguez of Morocco, the Boerewors of South Africa seasoned with vinegar and coriander or the curried *pork sai ua* or fermented *sai krok Isan* of Thailand.

The hot dogs of Copenhagen can rightly stake a claim to being the national dish of Denmark as the skinless *cevapcici* do in Bosnia and Herzegovina, Bulgaria and Serbia. Greece has its *loukaniko*, Italy has its *salsicce* and in China, Thailand and the Philippines the local sausages are a thing of no-little importance. And we haven't even touched on the 470 separately identified and catalogued sausages of England, Ireland and Scotland … or the eye-popping wonder world of wurst that is Germany. No wonder the humble sausage sings such a fine song as it dances in the pan.

The thing that I find slightly weird however in a 'Hello, Mr Freud is that a gun in your pocket' sort of way is that whenever you look at pictures of butchers or check out books on making fresh sausages, there's always a bloke at the helm. Perhaps that's why each year the Australia Meat Industry Council searches for the national Sausage King but no sausage queen.

So, with this in mind, I set the charming and rather demure Kate from my food team the task of researching the perfect cooking of sausages. 'There's a sort of secret society of sausage sizzlers talking online about how they fry, grill, bake, poach (really), BBQ and casserole snags, with varying degrees of OCD. We're talking bath temperatures, fat to meat ratios, and core temperature,' she told me later.

'I'm pretty sure there wasn't a single female voice among the discussions on the subject. It felt a bit like intruding on "secret men's business" but then this must be men's business because I'm pretty sure there is not a woman on earth that would spend 45 minutes watching a sausage fry slowly on low heat!'

So let's assess those four different ways of cooking your humble snag perfectly.

POACHING

Poaching your sausage is more common than you might think; there are two schools of thought here. One way is to gently poach them in a small amount of water to cook them through before browning them in a pan or on the BBQ. To do this, place your sausages in a pan with about half a centimeter of water and bring it to the boil. Before the water boils away completely, turn the sausages to even up the cooking, then allow them to continue cooking in the pan to brown the skin. This does make for a nicely cooked sausage but there are no fat reducing benefits to this method of poaching.

The second way is to submerge the sausage in a cold water bath over a medium heat. Hold it there for as long as it takes to bring the internal temperature of the sausage to 150°C or 70°F. Then sear your snags in a hot pan to brown the outside. The danger here, however, is that to get a good colour on the snags, you risk overcooking the snags in the pan as you do it.

FRYING

The main thing here is to avoid rapid cooking or a too-hot pan which can lead to a burnt sausage with a raw centre or, worse still, the exploding sausage where the moisture in the snag turns to steam bursting the skin.

The secret of frying is to cook the sausages very slowly over a low–medium heat until just cooked through, while getting a nice brown on the outside. For a fat snag this might take up to 45 minutes. The sausages will not split and, yes, you can use your probe thermometer to measure the internal temperature.

BAKING

Baking your sausages is often seen as the easiest way to cook sausages, especially a large number, and the most effective use of energy to do so. The danger is that baking can dry them out, so the best way to cook sausages in the oven is to pop them in a baking dish with some vegetables and tinned tomatoes to make a one-pot meal.

Then there is that other sausage oven favourite, Toad in the Hole. Here the secret, like a Yorkshire pudding, is ensuring that the fat in the baking dish is sizzling hot when the 'hole' batter is added. Making Toad in the Hole is as easy as setting the oven to a blistering 240°C and pouring **2 tablespoons** of **sunflower oil** into a standard 35 cm × 25 cm cheap roasting pan. Add a **sprig of fresh rosemary**. As everything is going to be very hot, grab your oven mitt and use tongs.

When the oil is sizzly-hot around the rosemary, remove the herb stick and slip in **8 fat beef sausages**. Brown for about 3 minutes or so a side. While the snags are frying to a lovely golden brown, make the batter. Sift **115 g** of **plain flour**, a **teaspoon** of **mustard powder** and ½ **teaspoon salt** together. Whisk in **2 eggs** and **300 ml milk** until you have a smooth batter. Now this is where things get interesting – and potentially dangerous! Carefully remove the roasting pan from the oven and pour the batter around the sausages. Note that the batter will bubble and the fat in the pan may spit. Return to the oven and bake for 25 minutes, or until puffed up and golden. An onion gravy is the traditional accompaniment to Toad in the Hole.

BBQ

For me the BBQ has the greatest affinity with the snag. The BBQ has a number of different heat zones perfect for evenly cooking snags both big and small. Also any fat rendered out of the snag drips away rather than hunting out your waistline. Note, however, that this fat can cause flare-ups., which can burn your snags.

So here's the skinny on cooking snags on the barbecue. First, take the sausages out of the fridge about 30 minutes prior to cooking. This allows the internal temperature to rise for more even cooking through of the snags and reduces their cooking time. Next, turn the outside burner on the BBQ up to high and the one inside it on to low to create a hot side and a cool side of the BBQ.

Now separate the sausages from their links and lightly oil them. Start cooking over the hot burner to seal the sausages. Leave them there until they are a nice medium brown but make sure they are kept away from random flames and flare ups. At this point, move the thick snags between the low burner (and a switched off burner next to it) so they can continue cooking longer without burning. Thin sausages can be moved directly over to the low burner to finish cooking.

To reduce cooking time when BBQing thicker sausages, you can always try poaching them for 4–5 minutes first in a pan and then searing them on the grill. Don't limit yourself to water, however, why not try red wine, beer, stock or even miso soup as the poaching liquid and to add extra flavour.

After extensive research, one glaring question still remains when it comes to snag cookery. All the sites talk with a white lab-coated fervour about using a calibrated meat thermometer or thermo-probe to tell when the snag has reached the desired internal temperature of 150°F or 65.6°C but they also all agree that UNDER NO CIRCUMSTANCES SHOULD YOU PIERCE THE SKIN of a cooking sausage. Tricky to probe 'em then, blokes, and that's a real snag!

BBQ BEEF FILLET WITH HORSERADISH VINAIGRETTE AND ROAST SPRING ONIONS

8 potatoes

1 × 2 kg beef fillet

160 ml (½ cup) good olive oil, plus extra

salt flakes

16 long fat spring onions, tough outer layers peeled off

zest and juice of 1 lemon

1 heaped tablespoon horseradish cream

2 garlic cloves, finely chopped and mashed with salt, using the flat side of your cook's knife

freshly ground black pepper

1 head cos lettuce, rough darker leaves removed, cut lengthways into eights

200 ml sour cream

chives or parsley, finely chopped

TIP: This dish would work wonderfully with a salsa verde rather than this horseradish dressing. To make this, mix olive oil, smooth Dijon mustard, capers, a couple of finely chopped anchovies and garlic cloves, lots of chopped parsley and some wine vinegar to add bite. Or just sprinkle the beef with a couple of tablespoons of crispy fried capers. Or dispense with the dressing altogether and splash the meat with a 2:1 ratio of good olive oil and good balsamic vinegar. Sprinkle on salt. Use rocket instead of the cos lettuce.

My holiday luggage always contains a box of salt flakes and a cryovaced frozen beef fillet. Maybe it's because I'm born under the sign of Cancer – we do like to travel with ALL the comforts of home. The beef fillet is thawed perfectly for a celebratory 'we're here!' meal.

Preheat the oven to 200°C (180°C fan-forced).

Wash and dry the potatoes and wrap in foil. Pop in the oven at least an hour before you want to eat.

Heat the BBQ hotplate (or roasting pan if you want to cook indoors).

Wipe the fillet dry and cut off any thin, shimmery silver skin or sinew. Rub lightly with the olive oil and a little salt.

When the hotplate is really hot, and about 40 minutes before you want to eat, sear the beef on all sides. When you do a new side, shift the fillet to find a new dry, hot point on the hotplate. This searing will take about 12 minutes. We want to get a nice crustiness on the outside of the fillet.

Oil the spring onions and pop on the BBQ. It's OK if these catch a little as that charry sweetness adds another level of flavour complexity.

When the beef is good and brown in places, drop the heat of the BBQ. If the BBQ has a lid, remove the meat and veggies from the direct heat (or turn off a set of burners). Let the meat cook through. This will take about 20 minutes, depending on how well cooked you want it and how thick the fillet is. (If you don't have a lid, just leave the fillet on the heat but turn all the burners down.)

To make the dressing, mix half the remaining olive oil with the lemon juice, horseradish, garlic and loads of pepper. Season and add more horseradish if the lemon is too prominent. Now pour in the remaining oil. The dressing should look split, not emulsified.

When the meat is almost done to your liking, take off the heat to rest for 10 minutes. Cover loosely with foil and an open copy of the local paper to keep the heat. This heat will finish off the cooking of the meat. Slice the beef finger-thick.

I like to serve this on a large chopping board. Place the lettuce along the bottom edge of the board. Place the roasted spring onions that will be sweet, limp and charry along the top edge. Place the beef slices along the middle of the board. Sprinkle on the lemon zest. Dress the meat heartily with the horseradish vinaigrette. This is delicious on the spring onions and the lettuce too.

Serve with the potatoes, split and flesh gently mashed. Add a good dollop of the sour cream and sprinkle with the chives or parsley.

SERVES 8

PORK CHOPS WITH ROAST FIGS AND A BYZANTINE SWEET-SOUR BALSAMIC AND ORANGE GLAZE

FIGS
4 fresh figs
1 heaped teaspoon brown sugar
2 tablespoons Marsala

BALSAMIC AND ORANGE GLAZE
250 ml (1 cup) balsamic vinegar
220 g (1 cup) brown sugar
peel of 1 orange
juice of ½–1 orange
salt flakes and freshly ground
   black pepper

PORK CHOPS
2 teaspoons fennel seeds
2 teaspoons salt flakes
20 black peppercorns
4 × 200 g pork cutlets
olive oil, for cooking

TIP: Any leftover balsamic glaze keeps well in an airtight jar.

So, it's as simple as this: I come from a cultural background that prizes the partnering of red meats with sweetness as a throwback to the days of the crusades. Duck and berries or blackcurrant; venison with oranges or redcurrants; lamb with mint or quince jelly; turkey with cranberry sauce. So see this dish as a thousand-year genetic throwback and think on the wonder that my crude and dusty ancestors must have felt on encountering the studied perfumed elegance of the ancient Arab world with its exotic fruits and spices. And if you don't, you risk me thundering through your house on a destrier, dressed in chainmail, waving a mace. That's the heavy metal spiky thing not the spice known as mace usually found near nutmeg.

Preheat the oven to 200°C (180°C fan-forced).

FIGS Cut the figs from stem to base in quarters, place in an ovenproof dish, sprinkle with the brown sugar and drizzle over the Marsala. Bake in the oven for 15–20 minutes.

BALSAMIC AND ORANGE GLAZE Bring all the ingredients to the boil in a small saucepan, reduce the heat and simmer for 10–12 minutes until the liquid reduces to a syrup. Don't be tempted to keep cooking or it will thicken to a molasses. If it does get too thick, add more orange juice. Discard the orange peel. Check for seasoning.

PORK CHOPS Grind the fennel seeds, salt and peppercorns in a mortar and pestle, spice grinder or bash them in a bag. Rub the pork chops with the dry spice and be sure the meat is at room temperature before cooking.

Heat a large frying pan over high heat, add a dash of oil and the pork and fry for 3–4 minutes on each side, or until cooked.

Drizzle the balsamic glaze on a plate, follow with the pork chops and top with the baked figs.

Serve with baked sweet potatoes and something green of your liking. I like beans or Brussels sprouts.

SERVES 4

PRAWNS À LA PLANCHA

Two little words have given us more pleasure on the set of *MasterChef* than any other. This has been thanks to the ground-breaking decision, especially rare in the prurient, euphemism-laden world of TV, to call a spade a spade, or in this case to call the dark grit-filled intestinal track of a prawn its 'poo shoot'. Top chefs have not been immune to the power of saying these two little words. Rick Stein seemed to revel in this freedom when he was on and, the producers used to instruct Marco Pierre White to say 'poo shoot' just for the fun of it. Marco says 'poo shoot' better than most of us. The words have a wonderful staccato impact and the presence of two double 'o's allows you to wallow in either word or both. Try it!

Toss the prawns in a bowl with the olive oil, garlic and paprika. Set aside.

Preheat the BBQ flat plate to medium. Tell your friends that you are heating 'la plancha'. Cook the chorizo on the hotplate until it gets some colour. Take if off and add the capsicum to the chorizo oil left behind and let it cook long enough to blister and soften a little before adding the cherry tomatoes. Let these blister too. You may need to add a splash more oil to the BBQ at this stage.

Add the prawns to a dry part of the grill plate and toss for a few minutes until cooked. Add the chorizo to the capsicum and tomatoes. Once the prawns are nearly done, toss everything together.

Remove from the heat using a spatula and taking as much of the cooking juices as possible. Pour over the sherry vinegar, season with pepper and possibly a pinch of salt to taste (the chorizo is salty so it may not be needed) and toss to coat. Leave for a couple of minutes. Pile on a serving plate and scatter over the parsley leaves.

Serve with crusty bread to mop up the fats and juices.

SERVES 4

12 large green prawns
3 tablespoons olive oil, plus extra
5 garlic cloves, peeled and
   sliced thickly
1 heaped teaspoon sweet paprika
1 (about 100 g) hot or mild chorizo
   sausage, cut into slices on the
   angle
4 smallish red capsicums, cut into
   cheeks, seeds and veins removed
1 punnet cherry tomatoes,
   left whole
2 tablespoons sherry vinegar
freshly ground black pepper
salt flakes
¼ bunch flat-leaf parsley

TIP: To remove the poo shoot on a prawn that you plan to grill with the shell on, gently bend the tail joint so that the flesh is exposed a little. Insert a metal skewer or fork tine about 4 mm from the ridge and gently tug the vein. It should remove the shoot in one smooth movement.

TIP: Remember that crunchy prawn noses and prawn legs are tasty too. Poo shoots aren't.

WHOLE BBQ SNAPPER WITH LEMONGRASS-CHILLI SAMBAL

While you find lemongrass and chilli sambals in Indonesia, they don't have quite the sweet funkiness of this Vietnamese one. Frankly, this is one of the most delicious chilli sauces I have ever tried. The lemongrass makes it ideal served with rice and chicken or grilled or steamed fish (as a fillet or a whole fish).

THE SAMBAL Slice the chillies in half lengthways. Use a teaspoon to scrape out the seeds and veins. Oh, and do wear plastic gloves and don't rub your eyes. Most of the heat of the chilli is in the veins not the seeds.

Blitz the lemongrass with a little of the oil using a stick blender (or mince it). Fry the resulting purée in a large wok. While it is frying very gently, purée the garlic and spring onions with the same blender – there is no need to clean it. Again use a splash of the oil to lubricate this process. Stir this into the lemongrass and simmer gently together.

Now blitz the chillies with that same blender and throw them into the sauce too. Add the rest of the oil. You want to see oil on top of the cooking red mass.

After a couple of minutes, throw in the sugar, 1 tablespoon of the lime juice, salt and 1 tablespoon of the fish sauce. Stir. Add more fish sauce to taste. Don't use more than 2 tablespoons for fear of overpowering the lemongrass. Taste and fine tune the seasoning with a splash of extra lime juice or a pinch more sugar to achieve a balance you are happy with. Now cook out the sauce for 8 minutes.

THE FISH Preheat the BBQ to high.

While the sauce is simmering, prepare the fish by patting it dry with paper towel inside and out. Using a sharp knife, make 2 or 3 horizontal slashes in the thickest part of the fish flesh, this will help ensure even cooking. Season and oil the fish in and out and stuff the cavity with a few herbs to complement the flavour profile you are after. I use slices of lime and ginger but you could also use coriander roots and stems, lemongrass, ginger, kaffir lime leaves, garlic and slices of lemon.

Take 2 large sheets of foil and lay in opposite directions. Line the foil with baking paper and place the fish on top. Bring the edges together to form a sealed tent like parcel over your fish. Cook for around 15–50 minutes, depending on the size of your fish and the BBQ temperature.

With 5 minutes to go, open the parcel and fold back the edges to expose the fish so the skin becomes crispy. Check if the fish is cooked by looking into the slashed part of the fish – it should be opaque, not pink or translucent-looking. The foolproof way is to use a thermometer. You want the internal temperature to reach 55°C–70°C. Over 70°C and it will dry out. Under 55°C and it will be just cooked but there will still be blood on the bone.

Serve with rice, shredded wombok and the lemongrass–chilli sambal.

SERVES 4

THE SAMBAL

300 g small red chillies, stems removed (about 24 chillies or 370 g unprepped weight)
3 lemongrass stems, white parts finely chopped
250 ml (1 cup) grapeseed oil
6 garlic cloves, peeled and smashed
4 spring onions, finely sliced
1 tablespoon white sugar (purists can use palm sugar if they want, but it isn't essential)
1 lime (we'll use 1 tablespoon or so of the juice)
2 teaspoons salt flakes
2 tablespoons fish sauce

THE FISH

1 × 1 kg whole snapper, cleaned and scaled
250 ml (1 cup) grapeseed oil
1 lime, finely sliced (optional)
4-cm knob of ginger, finely sliced (optional)
coriander roots and stems (optional)
lemongrass stem, bruised (optional)
kaffir lime leaves, torn (optional)
garlic cloves, bruised (optional)
lemon, finely sliced (optional)
rice and wok-fried wombok cabbage, to serve

TIP: This sambal can be eaten immediately with just about anything. Or let it cool and store the sauce in a clean jar under a layer of oil and use within a few days. Use when needed. Note that it will get better after a day, so feel free to make it a day in advance. Warning – I suspect that this sauce is addictive and equally as good with BBQ chicken.

CHICKEN FILLETS WITH OREGANO, LEMON AND GARLIC

1 large bunch oregano leaves
4 garlic cloves
120 ml olive oil
zest and juice of 2 lemons
2 heaped teaspoons salt flakes
loads of freshly ground black
　　pepper
4 chicken fillets, skin left on

I have a small plot outside the back door of the kitchen that is perhaps the most perplexing part of my life. Brussels sprouts and beans get bullied by bugs and usually heavy-fruiting tomatoes baulk at setting fruit but some things grow here as if I was blessed with fingers so green, people could mistake me for the Incredible Hulk. Nasturtium, mint, parsley, basil, silverbeet, bay leaves, society garlic, borage, thyme, sage and oregano grow like billy-o. A surfeit of oregano meant the creation of this dish, which celebrates one of the garden's forgotten herbs, a herb that has dropped out of favour in the face of the omnipresent parsley, coriander, mint and basil in Australian cooking.

Blitz the oregano leaves with the garlic or finely chop both.

Combine the oregano and garlic with the oil, zest and juice of the lemons, salt and freshly ground pepper and stir.

Add the chicken to the marinade and allow to sit for 15 minutes or so before cooking on the BBQ for 3–5 minutes each side depending on the thickness of the fillets.

The trick to cooking these fillets perfectly is to start them on a high heat on one side and then pull the heat right back to cook through. Flip each breast and then whack the heat up to sear off the other side. You want the meat succulent and juicy so the breast should have some give when you give it a little squeeze.

Serve with a potato salad and a crisp green salad.

SERVES 4

LAMB BURGERS WITH FETA, MINT AND YOGHURT DRESSING

1 tablespoon olive oil

DRESSING
200 g Greek feta
250 g (1 cup) Greek yoghurt
½ bunch mint leaves

PATTIES
500 g lamb mince
1 large garlic clove
½ red onion, finely chopped
¼ bunch flat-leaf parsley,
   finely chopped
1 heaped teaspoon dried
   Greek oregano
1 egg, lightly beaten
30 g (½ cup) fresh breadcrumbs
salt flakes and freshly ground
   black pepper

EXTRAS
1 punnet cherry tomatoes,
   cut in quarters
1 tablespoon red wine vinegar
1 teaspoon sugar
4 crusty buns (sourdough if you
   can get them), cut in half
olive oil
2 Lebanese cucumbers, sliced
   into long ribbons with a peeler
¼ bunch basil leaves

Here's the dilemma. Every time I read this recipe I think it deserves to have some olives there somewhere but I'm worried that if I add them it will wreck the simple freshness of this burger. And then what sort of olives – green, black or Kalamata? Maybe the flesh of those last mentioned fruitily-juicy and bruise-purple olives should be ground with a little of the olive oil that dresses the sourdough to add some pep – even if only to the inside of the top piece of bread. But then maybe throwing the cheeks of a dozen black olives into the lamb burger mix would add texture and a salty bitter hit that would contrast beautifully with the lamb. Or should chunks of green olive be added to the sweetly dressed tomatoes to add a salty counterpoint. Or perhaps the green olives would make a better rudimentary tapenade than the black? And here suddenly we see the heart of the malaise of the Greek economy. Look at the debilitating amount of time spent making – or actually 'not making' – a decision as simple as whether olives should be in a lamb burger and if so where. How much worse would it be if we were discussing something more pressing like international bail-outs or loan repayments!

DRESSING Blitz the feta, yoghurt and mint in a food processor until smooth and place in the fridge to thicken up a bit. This can be done ahead of time.

PATTIES Combine all the patty ingredients in a large bowl. Mix together. Now shape into four, equal-sized patties.

Heat a frying pan on medium heat with the oil. When hot, cook the patties for 4–5 minutes on each side. Alternatively, quickly brown the patties and then cook them in a preheated 190°C oven for 10 minutes.

Toss the tomatoes in a bowl with the red wine vinegar and sugar and set aside for 10 minutes. Drain the vinegar before you use them.

Brush each bun half with oil and lightly toast in the oven or on, or under, the grill.

To assemble, lay the cucumber and some basil leaves on the bottom slice of toasted sourdough bun. Then layer with the lamb patty, feta dressing and a spoonful of the tomatoes. Top with bun and compress so the burger's juices, the dressing and the tomato pulp intermingle with the basil.

MAKES 4 ENORMOUS BURGERS

CHICKEN SKEWERS AND SATAY SAUCE

Satay sauce was the first bit of culinary exotica I ever encountered. If seemed so wonderful that anyone would think of making a sauce for meat out of the stuff that I spread on my bread (with raspberry jam) for tea. This confusion came about because my Dad's mate Jan from Holland would visit each year and would, without fail, produce a couple of jars of both a rather superior Dutch peanut butter and of a sort of ready-made dehydrated satay sauce that didn't taste nearly as good on toast. This recipe has become a firm favourite with my kids now too and to keep things a whole lot less confusing, crunchy peanut butter is rather cheatingly at its core.

Preheat the BBQ on medium heat.

In a frying pan over gentle heat, toast the coriander seeds. Grind them to a powder. Set 1 teaspoon aside and combine with the turmeric. Dust the chicken in this spice mix, thread the chicken cubes onto the skewers.

Cook the chicken skewers on the BBQ, or under the grill, for a couple of minutes on each side.

SAUCE To make the sauce, use a blender or food processor to combine the peanut butter, sugar, soy sauce, lime zest and juice, fish sauce, chilli, garlic and sesame oil. Blend on high speed until very smooth. Pour into a saucepan and very gently heat for a few minutes. Stir in ¼–½ cup coconut cream, depending on the consistency of sauce you like.

Serve the chicken with the dipping sauce.

SERVES 4

3 teaspoons coriander seeds, toasted and ground, divided
½ teaspoon turmeric
500 g chicken thighs or breasts, without skin, cut into 3 cm cubes

SAUCE
140 g (½ cup) crunchy peanut butter
2 tablespoons packed brown sugar
2 tablespoons soy sauce
1½ tablespoons grated lime zest
2 tablespoons fresh lime juice
1½ teaspoons fish sauce
1 long red chilli, finely diced
2 garlic cloves, peeled
½ teaspoon sesame oil
¼–½ cup coconut cream

wooden skewers soaked in water, or metal skewers

TIP: I like to serve these with chunks of cucumber, chunks of pineapple and cubes of compressed cooked jasmine rice. (To do this, cook the rice. While it is still warm, spread it 5 cm thick in a square dish or baking paper-lined cake tin. Place baking paper on top and press down on the rice to compress it. Pop in the fridge to set. When the rice sets, cut it into cubes.)

BUN CHA WITH NOODLES

In Hanoi, the best food is found in the streets, from meat-filled dumplings and all manner of rolls to more esoteric dishes like a punchy soup full of teeny crabs pulled straight from the rice paddies, or a turmeric fish stew flavoured with beetle essence that's so loved in the city that a whole street is named after it.

Pre-eminent in this glittering galaxy of gastronomic gems is *bun cha*; fragrant rissoles served with thin squiggly rice noodles all wrapped in lettuce.

Warm the oven to 120°C.

Cut off the coriander stalks. Cut off their roots and slice as finely as you can. Mash these up with the garlic and lemongrass. Use a mortar and pestle, otherwise just chop and scrape them together on the chopping board.

Take a large bowl and mix the pork mince with the dark soy. Add the pounded aromatics (coriander stems, garlic and lemongrass). Now stir in the fish sauce and egg. Keep stirring vigorously. By now the mix should be getting almost sticky. Season with a good twist of black pepper. Finally, stir in the spring onions. Add these last as you want them to be crunchy little surprises in the patties. Place a long sheet of baking paper on the bench. Now make walnut-sized balls of the mix and drop on to the paper. Press them down to make a patty about 2 cm thick.

Soak or cook the rice vermicelli as per packet instructions.

Fry the patties in the peanut or vegetable oil in batches of half a dozen or so. Do not crowd the pan so the oil remains hot. They'll take about 3 minutes in total. They will continue to cook with their residual heat, so don't cook them so much that they become sawdusty. When they are tanned on both sides, remove to a heatproof dish in the oven.

To serve, split the noodles across four bowls. Top each bowl with four of the pork patties. Serve extra noodles and patties together in a bowl in the middle of the table, with piles of leaves of iceberg, mint and coriander on a separate plate.

To eat, take a piece of iceberg lettuce, place a mint leaf, some coriander leaves and some noodles in it. Top with a pork patty. Wrap, dunk in nuoc mam pha dipping sauce and eat messily so the juice runs down your chin. Delicious!

NUOC MAM PHA DIPPING SAUCE Mix the fish sauce and rice wine vinegar together. Stir in the sugar until it dissolves. Now gradually add the lime juice until the sauce is balanced and not too limey. Depending on the juiciness of your limes and their acidity, I reckon you'll need about 80 per cent of the juice but let your palate decide and add water if you feel it's needed. Feel free to add a little more sugar if your palate demands it. Not one flavour should dominate and the acidity of the lime juice will even out the funky saltiness of the fish sauce and the sweetness. Stir in the garlic and chilli. You can use this sauce immediately or, if kept in the fridge, within the next couple of days.

SERVES 4

1 bunch coriander
2 garlic cloves, very finely chopped
1 stem lemongrass, soft centre only, finely diced
500 g pork mince
1 tablespoon dark soy sauce
1 tablespoon fish sauce
1 egg
freshly ground black pepper
4 spring onions, cut into coins
200 g rice noodle vermicelli
peanut or vegetable oil, for frying
1 iceberg lettuce, leaves separated
20 mint leaves (Vietnamese mint, if you can get it)

NUOC MAM PHA DIPPING SAUCE
3 tablespoons fish sauce
2 tablespoons rice vinegar
2 tablespoons caster sugar (with more on hand if needed)
juice of 3 limes
125 ml (½ cup) water (optional)
2 garlic cloves, very finely chopped
1 small red chilli, very finely diced

TIP: Go to Thailand or Vietnam and you'll find a vast choice of fish sauces in the local supermarkets. These range from cheap and pretty brutal to fragrant and almost delicate (and expensive). How much sugar and lime juice you'll add to your sauce depends on how potent your fish sauce is – follow the recipe by all means but let your palate lead you. First time you make a Vietnamese dipping sauce it can pay to put the fish sauce in last rather than first. This means you can see how the fish sauce wells up in the sauce as you add it. Stop when it becomes noticeable rather than dominant.

RECIPE TO KEEP THE BOSS QUIET, OR SQUARE HALOUMI SLIDERS WITH AGRODOLCE BEETROOT (SHE'S MORE AGRO THAN DOLCE)

AGRODOLCE BEETROOT

2 tablespoons extra-virgin olive oil
about 400 g (1 large) beetroot,
   peeled, topped and tailed, finely
   grated
1 teaspoon salt flakes
½–1 teaspoon dried chilli flakes
2 tablespoons brown sugar
zest and juice of 1 orange
freshly ground black pepper

HALOUMI SLIDERS

1 × 250 g packet haloumi
1–2 tablespoons extra-virgin olive
   oil, plus extra to serve
sourdough rolls or Turkish bread,
   cut into squares the same size
   as two pieces of haloumi
handful toasted hazelnuts, roughly
   chopped
¼ bunch mint leaves
¼ bunch flat-leaf parsley
1 lemon

There was a vigorous clamouring to include a vegetarian haloumi 'burger' in this volume. I was unsure until I tried this bright and light citrus beetroot that is somewhere between a chutney and a salsa. It goes really well with pretty much anything – meat, goat's cheese, rocket, walnuts and rye bread, Christmas ham, even salmon – and its tangy but earthy sweetness makes the haloumi dance among the fresh herbs in these sliders. And it's not only versatile but also stores well in an airtight jar in the fridge. So why not make double quantities?

AGRODOLCE BEETROOT Heat the oil over a low–medium heat in a large non-stick frying pan. When it's hot, add the grated beetroot, salt, chilli flakes and brown sugar. Cook for about 5–7 minutes to allow the beetroot to cook through and some of the juices to reduce. Now add the orange zest and juice. Cook for a further 4–5 minutes, which will make things a little sticky and syrupy. Now the beetroot chutney is ready and it can be served hot or cold.

HALOUMI SLIDERS Cut the haloumi into 8 slices about 1–1.5 cm thick. Cut the slices on the thinner side if the haloumi block is smaller than 250 g as not all blocks of haloumi are created equal.

BBQ, grill or fry the haloumi on a lightly oiled surface over high heat for about 1 minute each side until each slice is golden. Squeeze over some lemon juice. At the same time, toast the outside of your bread so the middle gets all hot and steamy, and the outside crusty and hot.

To assemble the burger, cut the bread or rolls in half and layer with some beetroot chutney, a sprinkling of the hazelnuts and a slice of haloumi topped with a couple of leaves of each herb. Drizzle with a touch of olive oil and sandwich on the other half of the bread.

SERVES 4

FOUR WAYS WITH CORN

1. SURINAME CORN

I wanted to balance the sweetness of Dutch brown-sugared corn with the Caribbean tang of fresh lime. Hence Suriname corn, a suitable name given the resurgence of lime production in the old Dutch colony of Suriname in South America, since 2000.

First make your Dutch butter for corn. Cream together **125 g room temperature butter** with **2 teaspoons dark brown sugar** and **¾–1 teaspoon salt**. If you love salty caramel, you'll love this on your corn. To Suriname it, add the **zest of ½ lime** and the **juice of ¼ lime**. Easy as that. Pop it in the fridge to chill.

Serve 8 cobs of cooked corn slathered with the Suriname butter. Add a **squeeze of lime**, a dusting of **freshly ground black peppe**r and, if you are in the mood, a green **storm of fresh coriander**.

2. BACON, MAPLE MUSTARD AND GRATED TASTY CORN

OK, so this corn cob looks like a hairy caterpillar but it tastes rather fine and is inspired by my love of how corn, bacon, bitey cheddar cheese and maple syrup all go so really, really well together. It also comes from having a tub of maple mustard inspired by my current bucket-list restaurant, Joe Beef in Montreal, in my fridge. This anchors the cheese and bacony bits to the corn and is as easy to make as thickening **200 ml maple syrup** over medium heat for about 7 minutes, or until really big bubbles start forming. Let it cool, then whisk in **125 ml smooth Dijon mustard** and a very generous **heaped tablespoon of mustard seeds** – and I mean 'very' because their pop is imperative to the yumminess of the mustard. It is ready to use once it's cold. It'll keep in an airtight container for about 2 weeks.

Now cook **4 cobs of corn**. While they cook, microwave **4 slices prosciutto** between two sheets of baking paper for between 60 seconds and 2 minutes until crisp. Smash this into a sort of bacon dust with a couple of pinches of **salt flakes**. Finely grate **150 g tasty or cheddar cheese** and sprinkle with **½ teaspoon black pepper**. To serve, paint the warm corn with the maple mustard, sprinkled with the bacon dust and the peppery cheese. Do this over a sheet of baking paper, so you can use the bits that fall off.

3. FESTIVAL CORN WITH CHILLI AND COCONUT

I fell for this at my second Glastonbury. It's tasty, crispy, spicy, salty and sweet in equal amounts. Oh, it's so simple too.

First turn up the tunes. Now make the spicy goodness that's going to be sprinkled on the corn. Carefully toast **70 g (1 well-packed cup) shredded coconut** in a dry pan until golden brown. Mix this together with **1 tablespoon brown sugar**, **2 teaspoons salt flakes** and **½ teaspoon chilli powder or flakes** and then balance the sweet saltiness for your palate by adding more salt or sugar. This is even better if you replace the chilli powder with **a couple of long red-hot chillies** that have been very finely diced, but do that just before serving! Oh, and **a little ground allspice** can be another sexy addition.

Next boil **2 corn cobs per person** in water spiked with **salt** and **a little brown sugar**. Then toast the cobs to burnished roastiness on the BBQ. Just keep turning the cooked corn until the corn kernels are a little scorched in places. When they are ready brush them generously with **melted butter** and then roll, dunk or sprinkle each in that canny mix of sweet, salty and hot coconut.

4. MISO-BUTTERED CORN

This next recipe is addictively good. Cook and roast **8 cobs of corn**. While you are doing this roast **100 g blanched almonds** until golden and toasty. Allow to cool. Blitz all the almonds with **80 g miso paste** and **80 g softened butter**. This works best with fancier white miso paste. Heat **2 tablespoons rice wine vinegar** with **2 tablespoons caster sugar** until combined. Season your miso almond butter with about 2 tablespoons of this sweet vinegar mix. Use less or more as your palate dictates. This light syrup also serves to brighten and soften the saltiness of the miso. Serve the corn hot and toasty from the BBQ, slathered with the butter and sprinkle over some **finely diced spring onion**.

This almond miso butter is almost so delicious just spooned onto crusty BBQ'd steaks, on steamed broccoli or dotting the fudgy middles of baked sweet potatoes. Leftover butter can be placed on baking paper, rolled into a log and stored in the freezer for future use. Slice off pieces as needed. This is one recipe you must make!

SEVEN THINGS TO DO WITH CHILLI

If vegetables were able to claim frequent flyer miles you'd be hard pressed to know who'd have the most. The humble potato, which has spread around the world from its origins high in the Peruvian Andes? The plump and softly curved tomato, which started out life in Central America before hitching a lift back to Europe in 1493 with Columbus' returning fleet of Spanish explorers? Both would be pushing for multi-platinum status but really no member of the vegetable world has had the international impact of the chilli.

Since the chilli was first cultivated in Ecuador some 6000 years ago its use has spread around the world from Calabria, Turkey and Hungary to the Philippines, India, China, Korea, Japan and all across South East Asia, including Thailand, Vietnam and Indonesia. In fact, the Indonesian island of Lombok is reputedly named after the savagely hot 'cabe taliwang' chilli, which grew there.

1. LOMBOK SAMBAL

Just mash up **6 fresh, long, skinny red chillies** that you have partially roasted to soften, along with **4 similarly toasted cherry tomatoes** and **2 minced shallots**. Add in a **scrunched-up dry red chilli** along with **a knob of galangal** that you've grated, **some grated palm sugar** to add sweetness and to accentuate the chilli heat. Let your palate decide – grate until you almost taste sweetness. Finish with **a little shrimp paste** (or about a tablespoon of fish sauce), added bit by bit to add both salt and savouriness. Throw the sambal in a small pan with **a little oil** and cook out this fishiness so that it just becomes another layer of subtle flavour. Then let it cool before slathering on meat or fish.

2. AYAM BAKAR TALIWANG

Make Lombok's favourite dish – chicken Taliwang using the Lombok Sambal. Take **1 kg chicken** pieces (ideally thigh fillets), scratching up the flesh with a small knife and then rubbing with **salt**. Let the chook stand for a few minutes to come to room temperature. Next grill or BBQ until the chook is half-cooked (about 3–5 minutes a side). Squeeze the juice of ½ **lemon** into the **sambal** and mix. Now reserve two-thirds of the sambal. Place the other third in a separate bowl to brush onto the chook on all sides as you continue to cook it for about 10 more minutes. You want the chook cooked through but golden and even a little caught in places. Serve with the gently warmed reserved sambal and rice.

3. SAMBAL OELEK

Sambal oelek is perhaps the most famous of the dozens and dozens of sambals to come out of Indonesia, Malaysia and the Philippines. It is apparently named after the mortar it was traditionally made in but you don't need to develop a Wimbledon champion's right forearm unless you value the textural interest this pounding tends to provide over the mechanical alternatives. For the simplest sambal, blitz **half a dozen raw chillies** with **a little caster or palm sugar**, **water**, **a little salt and vinegar** to taste! A dollop of this is delicious just tossed through grilled prawns hot from the BBQ.

Most sambal oeleks, however, combine a mixture of chillies, peanuts, maybe a little vinegar and sugar, shallots, lime leaves, garlic, lemongrass, and other aromatics. Have fun with these, creating your perfect sambal oelek at home.

HOW HOT IS YOUR CHILLI?

The heat of chillies is measured in Scoville units. Use this scale as a ready reckoner for amping up the heat of your chilli sauce. Remember dropping in a scalding hot Thai bird's eye or scud chilli is a great way of pepping up tamer recipes.

THE HEAT (Scoville units)	THE CHILLIES
1,750	Poblano
6,000	Jalapeno, Chipotle, Espelette Pepper, Tabasco sauce
17,000	Serrano Pepper, Aleppo Pepper
40,000	Cayenne Pepper, Tabasco Pepper
75,000	Bird's Eye Chilli
200,000	Habanero, Scotch Bonnet
1,000,000+	Naga Viper, Trinidad Scorpion Butch T pepper
1,500,000	Pepper spray – with those numbers you'd certainly want to keep that out of your eyes!
2,009,231	Trinidad Moruga Scorpion (the plant produced the hottest officially recorded pepper in the world.)

4. CHINESE RED CHILLI SAUCE

The king and queen of these sauces have to be Chinese red chilli sauce and its perfect partner of spring onion relish. They are both ridiculously easy to make.

For the fresh red chilli sauce, first blend **a whole head of peeled garlic cloves** with about **250 g (about 20) stemmed and seeded red chillies**, a grated thumb-sized **piece ginger (about 20 g)**, **1 tablespoon white sugar** and **¼ cup white vinegar**. Taste and adjust seasoning by stirring in more of the vinegar, sugar and ginger if required! Add **a pinch of salt** to finish. If you want to be really hard-core Chinese, pour in some **warmed, melted chicken fat** as you process the sauce. This sauce is brilliant with pretty much anything but wonderful with chook – roasted or poached – especially if you make this spring onion relish below.

Trim and thinly slice **a bunch of spring onions** into coins. Add **3 tablespoons grapeseed oil**, **1 teaspoon soy sauce**, **¼ teaspoon white vinegar** and **½ teaspoon salt** to the spring onions. Now mix all this lot together roughly, bruising the spring onions. Then stir in **some grated ginger** bit by bit until the ginger becomes noticeable but not dominant. (A ratio of about 15 g ginger to 90 g sliced spring onions is about right for me, but you might want more.) Adjust the seasoning with **salt to taste**, as this sauce needs to be primarily about the spring onions and the salt.

5. HARISSA

It isn't just our Asian neighbours who have the monopoly on chilli fun; the red chilli has also found a home in North Africa where, paired with roasted capsicums, it forms a go-to, flavour-bomb sauce called harissa.

Roast, peel and deseed **4 capsicums**. Cut the stems off **16 fresh red chillies** and scrape out the seeds and ribs. Cut the chillies into chunks. Place the capsicum flesh, the red chillies and **2 peeled garlic cloves** into a blender and blitz. Add **1 teaspoon ground coriander seeds** and **½ teaspoon ground cumin seeds**. Drizzle in some **olive oil** to make it smooth. Taste. Season with **salt**. This harissa is perfect smeared over lamb or fish before cooking. It's not too hot but it will still spike up dressings or stews.

GREEN CHILLI

While green chilli seems to be much loved back in its birthplace, its uses are far more proscribed and specific in Asia. In Indian cuisine you often find that green chillies are used fresh and red chillies are used dry. These next two recipes from very different parts of the world show how the slight herby bitterness of the green chilli can be a real virtue.

6. AFGHANI CHATNI

I learnt this wonderful, fresh, loose chutney from some Afghani friends who run a restaurant in Dandenong. It is perfect with any grilled or BBQ'd meat such as lamb or chicken. Think of it as a fresher version of an Argentine chimichurri sauce. See www.taste.com.au for a fine recipe for this herby and only mildly hot Buenos Aires BBQ staple. It's mine! He said boasting slightly.

Pulse-blitz **1 deseeded green capsicum**, **2 diced celery stalks**, **2–4 green chillies with stems removed and seeded**, **a bunch coriander**, **a bunch flat-leaf parsley**, **a bunch dill**, **125 ml (½ cup) wine vinegar (or lemon, or cider vinegar if using coriander)**, **3 garlic cloves** and **a pinch of salt** together to make a green sludgy mass. Add a little water to make it the consistency of a pourable paste. Feel free to add a little olive oil (or walnuts added during processing stage) to give a little creaminess to this sauce.

7. JAPANESE GRILLED GREEN CHILLI AND GARLIC PASTE

Place **two dozen whole green chillies** and **a whole head of garlic** on a smouldering BBQ and let them cook away gently until they are soft. Scrape out the seeds of the roasted chillies and the stems. Discard any skins that come away easily. Then blitz the green chilli flesh with the cloves of the garlic to a smooth, brown paste. Add **a little oil** to help combine. Serve with grilled beef. This idea comes from Sydney's Izakaya Fujiyama where they serve it with teriyaki beef ribs. The sweetness of the soy-based sauce on the ribs is perfect with the earthy herbaceousness of the green roast chilli. It's also delicious with chicken or even providing some condiment-pep to a stir-fry.

LIGHT MEALS

4 WAYS WITH SALMON

Four ways with a salmon fillet – it sounds like a chapter in a particularly saucy French cookbook. But then that's part of the attraction of salmon – its ability to swing so many ways with such ease and no guilt. No wonder salmon is Australia's most popular eating fish. Which leads me to wonder what else you might rank fish on: 'most popular pet fish', 'most popular stunt fish', or perhaps 'most popular fish to slap people with'?

The irony, of course, is that fish is also the protein that more Australians are frightened of cooking than any other. This give us a conundrum but one that can only be overcome by me holding your hand and showing you some really easy ways to cook and serve salmon fillets. These recipes will make this fish your new best friend. Really, it's not that hard and all are delicious, family-pleasers. Promise!

Robust fish and whole fish can go on the grill. If cooking whole fish and the fish tail is cooking more quickly than the body, wrap the tail gently in a bit of foil. If the BBQ temperature is too high, the skin will cook too quickly but the flesh won't have a chance to cook, so turn the temperature down to medium once the fish is on the grill.

Always buy salmon fillets the same weight and thickness so they all cook evenly. Remember, too, that salmon is always at its best when the centre is still a soft coral, so take care not to leave it on the heat for too long. Better to take it off and have it at room temperature than overcook it. If in doubt, use a kitchen thermometer to ensure your fish doesn't overcook. It should be around 55°C.

Then if you want to move on from salmon, try these ideas for making friends with ocean trout, which is even more delicious and better textured.

1. PAN-FRIED SALMON

There are a few tried-and-true steps to getting a crispy-skin fish fillet while still having that wonderful soft, coral-coloured flesh that flakes.

First, pat the skin of the **salmon fillet** dry with paper towel. Now rub the skin with **salt flakes** and set it aside for at least 30 minutes. The salt helps draw the moisture from the skin. When it's time to cook, scrape the salt off using the blunt edge of your knife. Then pat dry again.

Always start the fish in a cold heavy-based frying pan with a **touch of oil** and bring it to a medium heat. Cook skin-side down for 4–5 minutes until the skin is golden and crispy. Gently flip the fish over and continue cooking for a further 2–3 minutes, depending on how you like your fish cooked.

Remember the fish will keep cooking with residual heat once off the flame. I love salmon this way served with **mashed potatoes** and the **salsa verde** on page 42 but given a kick by the addition of a **couple of green chillies**, finely chopped.

2. RAW SALMON

The seams of fat in salmon make it a delicious fish to eat raw but always look for the sashimi grade. It is a higher quality product that has followed a number of guidelines and processes to maintain its optimal freshness and flavour. Look for fillets that are bright in colour, and not darkened, dry or dull in appearance.

I love my raw salmon sliced really thin for carpaccio. The best way to do this is to ensure the salmon is cold – near frozen even – and use a super-sharp knife. This firmer fillet allows for finer cutting. To do this, dry the salmon and wrap in plastic wrap. Place in the freezer until the fish starts to firm up – about 1–2 hours, depending on the size of the fillet. Slice finely against the grain. This will make for a more tender slice of salmon when you bite into it.

Allow about **100 g salmon for each person** and make a dressing with roughly equal quantities of **lime juice** and **mirin** with a **pinch or two of salt**. Add some **coriander leaves** and **black sesame seeds** just before serving.

3. CRUMBED SALMON

The richness of salmon loves a little crunch, which crumb-crusting provides.

Dip **salmon fillets** in **milk**, shake off excess, season with a touch of **salt and peppe**r, and then coat with **breadcrumbs**. Heat some **olive oil** in a heavy-based frying pan over medium heat and, when hot and sizzly, place the crumbed salmon in the pan and cook for 2 minutes on each side. If you are using 150 g salmon fillets, this should cook them just enough to flake nicely – if you remove the salmon from the pan and set aside on a warm plate. Pour any fried crumbs that have come off the fish during cooking on to the plate as well.

Salmon this way is delicious served with **125 g linguine pasta for each person**, tossed with **2 fried chopped anchovy fillets**, **2 teaspoons capers** and **30 g pitted black olives** for each serve. Garnish with **lemon zest**, **chopped parsley** and a splash of **sherry vinegar** that you've flavoured by using it to deglaze the pan.

If you are trying to be a little carb-free, ditch the pasta and pan-fry **6 cherry tomatoes** for each person in a little **olive oil** with **capers**, **olives** and **anchovies** instead.

4. BBQ'D SALMON

When cooking salmon on the BBQ, you'll need to follow the usual rules, such as making sure the BBQ is clean and always heating the hotplates before cooking.

Always leave the skin on your salmon when cooking on the BBQ. It will protect the fish from drying out too much during cooking.

Always bring your fish to room temperature before cooking – just as you would if you were BBQing meat. It's best to oil the fish before putting it on the hotplate. Use the solid grill plate for BBQing delicate fish and have a good spatula with a sharp, fine edge to help turn it.

With **200 g salmon fillets**, cook them skin-side down on the flat grill for 3–4 minutes until the skin is crispy, then gently flip over and finish for a few more minutes on the other side – a bit longer if you like your salmon cooked through.

BBQ'd salmon, with its smoky richness, is perfect served with a **tartare sauce** and adding a herb such as tarragon is the ideal way to step this up. It's as simple as mixing **235 g (1 cup) decent mayonnaise** with a **couple of tablespoons of drained capers**, a **finely diced red onion**, **¼ cup chopped gherkins** and about the same volume of both **chopped parsley** and **tarragon**. Season with some **lemon, salt and pepper** to taste.

Serve the BBQ'd salmon fillets with a generous dollop of this tarragon tartare, a lemon wedge and small boiled potatoes, such as chopped chats, tossed with melted butter, chopped mint and parsley.

VIRTUOUS FISH AND CHIPS

8 peeled potatoes, cut into chips
olive oil
4 × 200 g threadfin salmon or other
   thin, white but meaty fish steaks,
   boned and skinned
120 g (2 cups) fresh breadcrumbs
zest of 1 lemon
120 g (1 cup) finely chopped spring
   onions
½ cup finely chopped flat-leaf
   parsley
50 g (½ cup) finely grated
   parmesan cheese … it's important
   the cheese is finely grated as
   otherwise it will be too dominant
salt flakes
green beans or a simple salad of
   iceberg lettuce and cucumber,
   to serve

LEMON-CAPER DRESSING

2 tablespoons good mayonnaise
   (ie Best's)
2 teaspoons Dijon mustard
1 tablespoon capers, drained
   (or washed if they are the dry
   salted ones)
juice of 1 lemon

Magnetic Island, off the coast of Townsville, is one of Australia's special places for me. It's like taking a jaunt back 50 years to when the beaches of the Mediterranean's quieter islands weren't thronged with backpackers and Russian oligarchs in billion-dollar yachts. Besides its natural beauty, there's also the attraction of a fine local fisherman who sells big fat Endeavour prawns by the kilo. It was he who introduced me to threadfin salmon; a FNQ delicacy that has light white flesh, which in my opinion is far superior to both snapper and barramundi. It's also cheap. This recipe makes the most of this: the crumb is savoury and herby, the dressing is sharp and tart. It's like the best modern fish 'n' chips and the flavours are suitably of the Mediterranean that was.

Preheat the oven to 200°C (180°C fan-forced).

Toss the potatoes in a very little olive oil and lay out on a baking tray lined with baking paper. Bang in the oven. These will take about 35 minutes to brown up so you now have 15 minutes to prep the fish.

Lightly oil the fish fillets and place on foil on a baking tray. Leave the fillets to come up to room temperature.

Toss the crumbs, zest, spring onions, parsley and parmesan together. Taste! Season. The bitterness of the lemon zest should be at the back of the palate and the cheese more prominent but the crumbs and the greenery should be the heroes. Moisten the crumbs with olive oil. You'll need a good couple of glugs. Taste again and adjust as required.

Lightly squeeze a handful of crumbs so they hold together and press onto the surface of the fish. Repeat until the fillets are covered quite thickly.

Bang the fish in the oven for 20 minutes. Flip over all the chips.

After 20 minutes, check. Remove when the crumb is golden and the fish is just cooked and starting to flake. Oh, and the potatoes are cooked and dark tanned in places. Sprinkle with a little salt – flakes if you've got them.

While the chips are finishing and the fish is cooking make a simple undressed iceberg salad or pop your green beans on to cook.

Also make the dressing to serve with the fish. Whisk the mayo with the mustard and capers. Add the lemon juice to thin and to taste. The lemon should balance the salt of the capers and loosen the mayo to a thin pourable consistency. You may not need all the juice.

To serve, plate the fish with some chips. Serve with the dressing on the side and your choice of either salad or green beans.

SERVES 4

SCALLOPS WITH SUGAR SNAP PEAS

2 tablespoons olive oil

400 g large scallops, tough
  muscle removed

salt flakes and freshly ground
  black pepper

350 g sugar snap peas,
  strings removed

½ lemon

Mr Marco Pierre White told me there are few things as elegant or as perfect as sugar snap peas partnered with perfectly cooked scallops. See if he's right, make this dish.

Put a large pot of salted water on to boil. In a large heavy-based frying pan, heat 1 tablespoon of olive oil over medium heat until piping hot but not smoking.

Pat the scallops dry and sprinkle liberally with salt. Place the scallops in the hot pan around the rim, noting which scallop went in first. Be careful not to overcrowd them, work in batches if necessary.

Leave the scallops to cook without moving them around until they are ready to flip. The variation in thickness and pan temperatures makes it difficult to pinpoint an exact cooking time. Between 1–2 minutes on each side should give you a golden crust on the outside, and still be lovely and translucent through the centre. Basically it's worth buying a couple of extra scallops to act as 'control scallops' during the cooking.

When the scallops have been turned over, throw the sugar snap peas in the boiling water and cook for about 1 minute. Drain them and toss with a little olive oil and season with salt.

Arrange the scallops on warm plates and divide the sugar snap peas among them, squeeze over a little lemon juice and serve immediately.

SERVES 4 AS A STARTER

FRUGAL MUSSELS
WITH ASIAN FLAVOURS

There is much debate over the de-bearding of mussels. Some argue that it's better to leave the beard – not so the mussel can become a barista in a trendy hole-in-the-wall coffee joint – but because tearing the beard out of a raw mussel is hard and can cause the mussel distress. It is certainly easier de-bearding them after they are cooked and dead – the mussels not the baristas that is.

Clean and de-beard the mussels now, or do it later as you pick out the cooked mussels. Before cooking, purge the mussels in cold water for at least 20 minutes and discard any with broken or open shells.

Blitz the garlic, lemongrass, ginger and coriander roots or chop very finely by hand.

Heat the oil in a high-sided frying pan or pot and sauté the chopped ingredients and the red onion for a couple of minutes, taking care not to burn the garlic. Add the sweet chilli sauce, water and one kaffir lime leaf, finely shredded, and gently simmer for a few minutes.

Add the mussels to the pan, toss in the sauce, turn up the heat and place the lid on. Steam the mussels for 3 minutes.

If they are all open then you're done. If they don't all open, take any that have opened out of the pan and set aside so as not to overcook them. Cover the pan again and check if more open in another minute. If any don't open after this extra cooking, discard them.

Cut the remaining lime leaves into fine shreds and scatter over the top along with the chopped chilli and coriander leaves.

Serve immediately with any bread you like to mop up the juices – roti is great with this dish.

SERVES 6-8

2 kg small black mussels, scrubbed and beards removed
3 garlic cloves, peeled
1 stem lemongrass, white part only, roughly chopped
1 knob ginger (about 20–25 g), roughly chopped, peeled if skin tough
3 coriander roots, scraped of the hairy bits
2–3 tablespoons peanut oil
1 small red onion, halved and finely sliced
125 g (½ cup) sweet chilli sauce
2 tablespoons water
4 kaffir lime leaves
150 ml (just under ⅔ cups) canned coconut milk or light coconut milk
small red chillies, finely sliced
coriander leaves, to serve

COCKLES FOR SIXTUS

olive oil
1 large brown onion, roughly diced
1 kg cockles, cleaned and purged
   of grit
1 glass sweet white wine
1 cup fresh herbs, at the very least
   flat-leaf parsley but dill, chervil,
   thyme as well
salt flakes
thick slices of toast

I have always rather liked the idea of becoming Pope. Papal infallibility would be a plus, silencing that regular argument over whose turn it is to take out the trash or resolving those tedious pub discussions over which footy code is more skilful. After all, I'd always be right and if they didn't like it they could kiss my papal ring.

There are also those grand robes, heavily worked with gold thread, to dress up in, and the prospect of tooling around town in the Popemobile, cruising for dates, using the immortal Papal pick-up line 'Wanna spend the night studying the ceiling of my Sistine Chapel?'

Trouble is I've read Dan Brown and undoubtedly some wowser monsignors would take the Papal car keys off me – or brand them into my chest. So I might be better advised to be a pope from the early years of the church when the clergy wasn't expected to be celibate.

Pope Sixtus is my type of Pope. One of the tougher pontiffs he was famed for his brutal taxation and, suitably for me, was from the home of the cravat, Croatia. He also knew his food as this dish of cockles proves. And could there be a better dish for a Pope to serve? This one has it all – bread and wine (nice transubstantiation reference there Sixty), tears from the slicing of onions, and the fires of hell bubbling under the pot. Delicious, and it is so perfect that I suspect that the recipe could have been written by Dante himself.

Heat the oil until quite hot, then add the onion and fry. When the onion is soft, add the cockles and cover.

When the cockles start to open, usually after about 2 minutes, douse them with the white wine and the picked and chopped herbs. Whack up the heat and toss the pan to burn off the alcohol. This will take under a minute if the pan is hot. Season with some salt to taste.

Serve immediately piled on thick rustic toast to soak up the juices.

SERVES 2-4

MANY WAYS <u>WITH</u> CANNED TUNA

It's a simple as this – canned tuna turns any imaginative home cook into a culinary MacGyver. It's the kitchen equivalent of a ball of fencing wire to a farmer or gaffer tape to a roadie on a big rock tour. It can pretty much do anything other than tell you when the grain is ripe for harvest or pick out Tony Iommi's lead-guitar lick on Black Sabbath's 'Paranoid'. What makes canned tuna even better is that a tuna cannery is the only food factory that I've been where I've still wanted to eat the product after I've seen it being made! You see, it really is just slabs of fish squeezed into a can.

TUNA BURGERS

Mix a cup of cold leftover **mashed potato** with a drained **425 g can tuna**, the finely sliced whites of **6 spring onions**, **2 teaspoons cumin** and a **heaped teaspoon salt flakes** with **½ cup chopped coriander and parsley** leaves. Stir in **2 lightly beaten eggs** and the **juice of ½ lemon** to help bind the mixture. Now use your hands to shape the mix into 8 patties. Toss these in ½ **cup panko crumbs**, mixed with the **zest of a lemon**, to coat. Pop in the fridge on a baking tray to set for at least half an hour. This helps the crumbs adhere to the burgers. Now brown the patties in **a little oil** in a non-stick frying pan over medium heat, frying for a few minutes on each side before transferring to a baking tray in an 180°C oven for a further 15 minutes until hot through. Serve these tuna burgers with **sweet chilli sauce, wedges of lime** and a dressing made of dollop of ½ **cup mayo** mixed with ½ **cup Greek yoghurt** and some **finely chopped coriander leaves**.

TUNA SANDWICHES

Of course, in the United States as I am sure you are only too aware, 52 per cent of canned tuna is used for sandwiches and only 22 per cent for salads. I'm an old bugger and stuck in my ways so in my classic tuna sanger there is always good **whole egg mayo** – just enough to bind the tuna – with a squeeze of **lemon juice**, a good **spoon of drained capers** and a little **finely chopped red onion**. Half a stick of **finely diced celery** adds further crunch. Needless to say, the young generation view things differently hence this Japanese version is 12-year-old Sam's favourite way to make a tuna filling for his school lunchbox baguette. Revolution is always the refuge of the young.

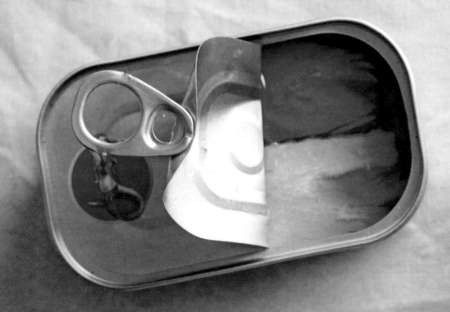

TUNA BAGUETTE WITH A JAPANESE ACCENT

To assemble the **baguette**, first cut it in half lengthways. Spread the bread with a generous amount of **mayonnaise** on one side (½ cup). Then scatter over **3 finely sliced spring onions** followed by **370 g drained, flaked tuna**. Season the tuna with **salt, black pepper** and a squeeze of ½ **lemon**. Top with 2 teaspoons of torn shreds of **pickled ginger**, a layer of **cucumber ribbons** (cut the ribbons from a cucumber using a potato peeler) and half a dozen **coriander sprigs**. Sprinkle over a tablespoon of **black or white sesame seeds**. Cut the baguette into 4 pieces on the angle and devour with your mates as you discuss whatever it is that 12-year-old boys discuss when adults aren't around. Probably how embarrassing their parents are …

OTHER OPPOR-TUNA-TIES – TEE HEE HEE

It's an inoffensive kid's favourite is tuna mornay and as simple to make as tip **a can of drained tuna** into **a white sauce** (**50 g melted butter** whisked with ¼ **cup plain flour** and then **2 cups milk** and heated to thicken) alongside **a drained can of corn**. The tuna brings salt, so the only flavouring this really needs to bring it up to an adult dish is a good **twist of black pepper** and a **handful of sliced spring onion**. This is perfect served on rice, pasta or baked under a grilled, gilded topping of mash potato. Chilli lovers should add **finely diced green chilli** or a good splash of **Tabasco**.

I also like to pair canned tuna with mashed potato to make **tuna patties** that the kids and I like, or make and chill a **thick béchamel** loaded with **tuna, a little smoked bacon and onions**. This can then be shaped when cold, **double-covered in breadcrumbs** and then fried for a couple of minutes on each side to make delicious golden-crunchy but oozy-centred tuna croquettes.

TUNA PASTA

Canned tuna also partners beautifully with that other pantry staple – dry pasta. Some of my favourite combinations are cooked tubular **penne** pasta or linguine tossed with **a can of tuna** and one of the following three combinations: **black olives, chopped oil-fried silverbeet, fried red onion and some crumbled feta**; cooked **peas and loads of lemon juice**; or with **an eggplant** cut into batons and fried with **sliced red onion** and **3 cloves of minced garlic**. A little **lemon juice** and a handful of **chopped parsley** added at the moment of serving helps this last terrific tuna combo too.

Just remember to always add the tuna at the last moment and do no more than just warm it in the pan with the pasta. Remember also to toss the pan with all the ingredients and a splash of the starchy pasta water to help an emulsified sauce form from the oil used in cooking and the sweated juices of the ingredients.

Tuna also goes wonderfully well with the flavours of a classic **puttanesca sauce** for pasta – **capers, rich tomato sauce, anchovies and olives**. You'll find my puttanesca recipe in my last book or online at www.taste.com.au. Less traditional is to make a base Napoli sauce with **canned tomato, fried onions** and **garlic**. Hit this with a **drained can of tuna**, a tablespoon of brown sugar and **a tablespoon of dried tarragon** to make a sweet tarragony sauce. Use lemon to balance the more obvious sweetness. I have no idea why something that reads so disgustingly tastes so good – but it does.

TUNA AND GREEN OLIVE PENNE

Cook **400 g penne** as per the packet instructions in lots of salty water and then drain. Reserve a little pasta water. Meanwhile, heat **60 ml olive oil** in a pan over low heat, toss in a **sliced red onion** and **2 garlic cloves** for a few minutes to soften. Add a **teaspoon of sugar**, **375 g cherry tomatoes** (some halved and some whole) and **30 ml red wine vinegar**. Season with **salt and pepper.** Cook for another 5 minutes to soften everything. Add a generous handful of **pitted and halved green olives**, a **handful of chopped parsley leaves**, and a splash of pasta water. Flake in about **370 g tuna** (give or take a gram) in chunks and warm through. Gently toss the penne through the sauce. Plate the pasta, scatter **another handful of chopped parsley**, a **handful of torn basil** and the **zest and juice of ½ lemon**. Finish with a drizzle of **olive oil**.

TUNA PASTA BAKE

Equally as low-rent but delicious is to make a tuna bake with pasta. The robust juiciness of red and green capsicum tiles are the perfect foil to the tuna here. Cook with **500 g small penne or corkscrew pasta**. Take it out of the cooking water 2 minutes earlier than it says on the packet so the baking doesn't turn your pasta to sludge. While the pasta is cooking, fry **a brown onion** in a little **olive oil** with **a green and a red capsicum**, deseeded and cut into 2 cm tiles. When the onion has softened, throw in **2 finely chopped garlic cloves** and stir. Add **2 × 400 g cans tomatoes** and bubble this sauce away on a high heat for 5 minutes, stirring to reduce. Season with **salt**. Add a **little chilli**, a good squeeze of **lemon juice** or a little sugar if it takes your fancy. Toss a **475 g can tuna** into the tomato sauce along with a **bunch of finely chopped parsley** leaves and the **250 g roughly crumbled ricotta**. Warm an oven dish with boiling water. Don't forget to pour the water away! Dry the dish and butter it generously. Pour in the tuna and capsicum pasta and top with **fresh breadcrumbs** sprayed with **olive oil**. Bang in a 180°C oven until the top goes golden and crunchy. This cheese and seafood combination works well on the pasta even though it is a cardinal sin of the Italian kitchen.

TUNA SALADS

I had four grandmothers. Perhaps that explains why I have always been a greedy boy. The thing is three couldn't cook and one could. One of the ones who couldn't cook did, however, have some mad skills when it came to opening cans and bottles. I have wistful memories of her love of canned tuna – she always referred to it quaintly by the old name of 'tunny fish' and she used to make both tuna mornay in winter and a number of tuna salads including a classic 'salad Niçoise' in summer.

TUNA, LENTIL, LEEK AND FENNEL SALAD

Mix **2 teaspoons sugar** with **2 tablespoons sherry vinegar**, **4 tablespoons extra-virgin olive oil** and some **salt and pepper** to make a vinaigrette and set aside. Heat **2 tablespoons extra-virgin olive oil** in a frying pan over low heat. Add the **white of a leek** cut into 1 cm rounds and caramelise them. As the leeks colour like a 12-year-old boy when his mother wants to kiss him outside the school gates, add **2 thinly sliced garlic cloves**. Remove the pan from the heat and gently toss through a rinsed and drained **400 g can lentils**, a thinly sliced **bulb of baby fennel**, **2 tablespoons torn parsley** and half the dressing. Now, season to taste with **black pepper** and a **little salt**. Plate this lentil mixture and flake over a **185 g can drained tuna**. Sprinkle with **2 tablespoons toasted pinenuts**, the fronds from the top of the fennel and spoon over more dressing. Serve with **lemon wedges**.

SALADE NIÇOISE

This salad is as simple as arranging the meat from a **large can of tuna** in an interwoven pile made up of a **punnet of** halved **cherry tomatoes, 16 pitted and halved black olives, 4 quartered hard-boiled eggs, 20 cooked green beans** and **10 halved waxy potatoes** (like chats or kipflers). Snip a couple of good pinky **anchovies** into small pieces over the salad with scissors. It's great if the potatoes, eggs and beans are still warm from cooking as they'll soak up the dressing. Dress with a simple lemon juice vinaigrette – that's as easy as glugging over some **olive oil**, squeezing over the **juice of a lemon** and giving it a good **twist of black pepper**. Season with **salt flakes**.

MORE SALADS GOOD AND BAD

In fact, canned tuna makes a welcome addition to any juicy tomato-based salad, like a well-dressed Tuscan-style panzanella where the stale bread in the salad soaks up both the flavour of the tuna and the tomato juice. While canned tuna usually works beautifully cold and straight from the can I've seen tuna used unconvincingly in everything from potato salads to Caesar salad. Far better to do what we do on set at *MasterChef* when George, Gary and I need a protein-packed snack; just stir a drained **can of tuna** through a mound of **cooked brown rice, chopped tomato, celery, pickled chillies** and **diced carrot**. Dress with a good squeeze of **lemon juice** and **twist of black pepper** or if we are feeling fancy we'll use a **dollop of hummus** made into a dressing with a little of the oil from the can. We are all class, us three!

BONUS SNEAKY SOUP SECTION . . .

TIPS TO MAKING GREAT SOUP

Great soup is simple soup, and as with any simple dish it's far harder to hide substandard ingredients. This doesn't mean you need expensive ingredients – in fact, some of the best soups are made with less popular cuts of meat or seasonal gluts of vegetables, which are by their very definition cheap.

Chunky, creamy, thick or crystal clear, great soup is made up of four key elements; the stock, the flavourings, the hero ingredient and any garnishes.

TIP 1: IT'S ALL ABOUT THE STOCK

Make sure you use the best stock you can find. Homemade stock is wonderful and frugal but shop-bought stock is fine – just make sure you buy the salt-reduced varieties as stocks will reduce during cooking and you want to be able to control the saltiness. To make great full-flavoured stocks, roast off your stock ingredients before steeping in water, and try to pack in as much flavour at possible. For example, when making chicken stock rather than using the carcass of Sunday's roast chook and the veg trimmings get some chicken wing tips from your butcher, which are dead cheap but once browned-off will give you loads more flavour.

TIP 2: BE ADVENTUROUS, BE SEASONAL

While pumpkin soups and chicken-stock based soups, like chicken noodle, might be Australia's most popular, don't forget about the wonderful choices of other less familiar vegetables, such as broccoli brought to life with the salty tang of blue cheese. Or perhaps celeriac or parsnips, which can both be cooked in milk that can then be skimmed and used to flavour your soup. Purée the veg with some of the milk and stock.

I find there is something particularly reassuring about celeriac soup especially served splashed with butter, poached celery hearts and nice splash of Tabasco. While sweet potato works wonderfully with curry spices and other warm-taste profiles from the Caribbean or US, such as chilli and allspice.

When cabbage is in season ribbons of drumhead or savoy cabbage make every vegetable soup seem heartier and deliver both a luxurious satin texture and a bit of bite. White cabbage is especially good sliced into ribbons, fried in a little butter and then braised until soft in pork broth made from smoked pork hocks. Don't forget to strip off the rosy meat to flash-fry in butter and pour sizzling into the soup when you serve it.

Even something as prosaic as frozen peas can make a great soup. Just defrost them and braise them in chicken stock with some leeks. Crush the peas, season and then warm through with some lettuce leaves until these wilt. Garnish with shredded mint, some crumbled ricotta and a splash of olive oil. It'll feel like spring even in the midst of a Tasmanian winter. Well, almost!

TIP 3: BUILD FLAVOUR

The flavourings of a great soup start with the base whether it's toasted spices, a spice paste or a fine dice of veg like carrots, onions and celery perhaps fried up with a little salty porky goodness (like speck or good old bacon). Even onions slow cooked with star anise will give a meaty-tasting foundation for your soup. The next steps in building the flavour range from the addition of booze, like wine or sherry to deglaze the pan, to adding a dash of flavouring liquors like Worcestershire sauce, tinned tomatoes, soy sauce, mirin or something sour like a splash of vinegar. Even old parmesan crusts will add a lovely savoury complexity to soups with many elements, such as ribolitta or minestrone. When adding herbs in your base flavourings, remember to save some to use in your garnish as well.

Remember, boiling or braising vegetables means some of the flavour and goodness leaches out into any cooking liquid, so instead, think of using other cooking methods like roasting. Or use the cooking liquid from vegetables that grow above ground to drive that flavour back into the soup. Sweet root vegetables, like parsnip, carrot and pumpkin, are particularly well suited for this treatment.

TIP 4: MAKE IT TEXTURAL

Now let's look at textures. Using a stick blender or blender on your soup will give you a purée that can be thinned by the addition of more stock, or maybe milk or cream, for a creamier result. Remember, if puréeing hot soup, do not completely seal the blender as blitzing the soup will release steam and you risk popping off the lid and spraying soup all over the kitchen. Instead seal the blender and remove the little central access stopper in the lid. Cover this resulting hole fully with a well-folded, clean tea towel and carefully apply pressure to stop the soup escaping. The cloth will let the steam escape. If you want your soup even creamier pass it through a fine sieve to remove fibres and any lumps. This will give you a satiny-textured soup.

Many soup recipes suggest adding potatoes. This is as much for how they can add smooth texture to soups as for their cheap bulking properties. I'd rather use more of the soup's core vegetable as I find the potato inevitably dilutes the intensity of the soup. In Spain and Italy, bread can serve the same purpose. Break up stale bread and let it soak and soften in your soup before serving. This works best with looser, clear or brothier style soups.

TIP 5: GARNISH!

The final touch is to garnish the soup. The secret here is to add contrast whether it's in terms of taste, texture or temperature. Think of adding a swirl of something rich, cool and creamy to thick soups – like a thyme herb cream to your leek and potato soup – or something crunchy like toasted nuts, garlicky or parmesan croutons, or even corn chips if the soup has Mexican flavours. When it comes to adding another layer of flavours to your soup, think of the Vietnamese way of adding loads of fragrant herbs to their pho soup or the French way of sprinkling finely snipped chives or carefully chopped soft herbs, such as chervil or dill, to add a fresh herbaceous note to chicken, creamy or fish soups.

You also won't be surprised to discover that, for me, there are few more important garnishes than those that add porky goodness. Sizzly, crispy strips of bacon or shards of toasted prosciutto or cubes of fried speck will meet all three of those garnish aims, providing contrasts in texture, taste and temperature.

There is only one soup that doesn't require any garnish at all and that's a really good pea and ham soup made with loads of smoky ham hocks.

WINTER SOUPS

Sure there are summer soups of great renown, like gazpacho, consommé, pappa al pomodoro and chilled vichyssoise, but winter is when soups really come alive and this is as much to do with the produce in season as the climate.

It doesn't matter whether it's a Scotch broth loaded with beef, barley and carrots, a pea and ham soup so thick and rich it sets like a jelly when it cools, or a Persian ash. The latter is part of an ancient group of soups that pre-date Muslim times and are built around slow-cooked wheat, pulses or barley usually with lamb and veggies.

Pretty much any root vegetable or tuber makes a good soup, whether it is a beetroot borscht, brown onions and beef stock to make a classic Parisian French onion soup, reassuring milky celeriac soup or a sweet and creamy parsnip soup.

It isn't just the stuff growing underground that makes great soup; the soup pot is equally happy with wilting silverbeet or kale wound through a hearty Italian minestrone or ribollita but I draw the line at using spinach in soup – it's just too expensive. Brassicas like cauliflower and broccoli also make good soups as they've got nice strong flavours. This also makes them ideal to partner with strong salty flavours like cheese or cured pork.

The king of all above-ground veg however is the mighty pumpkin. It is the most searched for soup on the internet in Australia and it comes in numerous versions from the simple to the most complex. None are quite as Aussie or have the same lightness and brightness as the one on page 98!

LEEK AND YOGHURT SOUP WITH SLOW-BRAISED ONIONS

520 g (2 cups) natural yoghurt

4 large brown onions

80 g butter

1 star anise

85 g (½ cup) golden sultanas

60 g (½ cup) walnuts

3 spring onions, pale part sliced thinly

2 leeks, pale part sliced into 1 cm rounds

½ teaspoon turmeric

2 garlic cloves, peeled and crushed

½ teaspoon plain flour (used as much to stop the soup splitting as to thicken it)

310 ml (1¼ cups) vegetable stock (you may not use all of this, it's just for thinning the soup to the appropriate consistency)

20 fresh mint leaves, chopped

1 teaspoon dried mint (ideally from Middle Eastern or Turkish food stores)

½ teaspoon curry powder

salt flakes

This dish is inspired by a delicious Afghani yoghurt soup called *kokoutti*, which I tasted at a great little restaurant in Melbourne called Afghan Village. What I love about this thick soup is how the rich tang of the yoghurt plays against the sweetness of the braised onions. I've added some tweaks picked up elsewhere, such as adding leeks, spring onions and fresh mint to give the stew more body and freshness. Definitely go for a long country walk (ideally over the Hindu Kush) before or after eating this one!

Drain yoghurt suspended in a muslin bag over a bowl for an hour to remove some of the whey. Now you have what Afghanis would call *chaka*.

While this is draining, slice your brown onions and cook them gently in a heavy pan with 40 g of melted butter and the star anise. Cook the onion for at least 40 minutes, stirring occasionally, or until it goes a lovely dark brown. Remove the star anise and any blades that have broken off. Reserve the onion and keep warm.

There are a few chores to do while the onion is cooking. First, take the golden sultanas, cover them with boiling water and leave them in a quiet corner so they plump up. Also toast your walnuts in a dry pan. Now you are sorted for the main elements for the garnish.

Melt 20 g of the remaining butter. Fry the spring onion with the leek and the turmeric over medium heat. Don't let them catch. When the leek is almost cooked, add the garlic and soften it. Take the pan off the heat to cool a little.

Mix the flour into a paste with a little of the vegetable stock. Then mix in half of the remaining stock. This will help thicken the soup and also help to stop it splitting. Next, using a hand whisk, mix the yoghurt and the floured vegetable stock together with half the chopped fresh mint and the dried mint. Now, ensuring the heat is low, pour the drained yoghurt and stock mixture onto the leeks.

Warm the soup through. Let it get to a gentle simmer but do not let it boil or else the soup may split. It will thicken slightly but if it starts getting too thick (you want it to coat the back of a spoon well), add a little more of the stock. In a small pan, gently warm the remaining 20 g of butter with the curry powder until it foams and smells of hazelnuts (and curry obviously). Immediately remove it from the heat.

When the soup is creamy and cooked out, it's time to serve it.

Drain the sultanas and pat dry. Crush your walnuts a wee bit.

Pour the soup into four bowls. Dollop a spoon of the warm caramelised onion in the middle of each bowl. Drizzle the brown curry butter around the onion on the surface of the soup. Garnish the onion with walnuts, remaining fresh mint and a few of the golden sultanas. Serve with Afghani (if you can find it) or Turkish bread.

SERVES 4

A LIGHTER, BRIGHTER AND VERY AUSTRALIAN ROAST PUMPKIN SOUP

2 kg Kent pumpkin, cut into wedges
and seeded

2 brown onions, peeled and
chopped into 6 wedges

4 Granny Smith apples, 3 of them
peeled, cored and roughly
chopped, 1 reserved

5 garlic cloves, unpeeled

100 ml extra-virgin olive oil

1 teaspoon ground cinnamon

salt flakes and freshly ground
black pepper

½ nutmeg

2 litres (8 cups) chicken stock

TO GARNISH

250 g crème fraîche, sour cream
or cream

1 Granny Smith apple, sliced into
fine batons, tossed in a little
lemon juice

30 sage leaves, flash fried for
30 seconds in hot oil

50 g (scant ½ cup) roughly
chopped hazelnuts

TIP: Remember not to cut the apple batons until you need them as otherwise they'll oxidise.

In Hong Kong they believe that happiness is defined by a good soup on the stove and an old Chinese proverb claims that contentment is 'having a good wife and rich cabbage soup'. I heartily agree – soup on the stove means a life with a lot less worries – although here in Oz we'd probably plump for a pumpkin not a cabbage soup.

Pumpkin soup is Australia's favourite soup come winter. It's seasonal and therefore very cheap – about 40 cents a portion – and a breeze to make as with this recipe the oven does most of the work. Also in using Kent pumpkin I'm picking a pumpkin that almost peels itself after it is roasted.

The only trouble is that pumpkin soup can be as predicatable as a metronome in a cardigan ... so I have taken an old Aussie country idea, that a journo from Darwin shared with me, of adding Granny Smith apples to give the soup a lightness and luminosity that makes it even more moreish. Any tart apple will do but as Granny Smith is an apple that was first grown in Australia, they are perfect for this soup. It would be un-Australian to use anything else.

Preheat the oven to 180°C.

Put the pumpkin, onions, apple and garlic on a large baking tray. Toss in the olive oil. Sprinkle over the cinnamon, salt and pepper and grate over the nutmeg. Toss again.

Bake your veg and apple in the oven for 30–40 minutes until cooked and nicely softened.

Remove your baking tray from the oven and leave the veg to cool a little. When they are still hot but safe to handle, take the skin off the pumpkin and squeeze the garlic from its papery skin.

Now transfer all the baked ingredients to a large pot – garlic, pumpkin, onions and apples. Add your stock and bring to the boil. Reduce the heat to a mild simmer and allow the soup to reduce for a further 15 minutes.

Turn off the heat and blitz until smooth. Season to taste. If you want a silky smooth soup, pass it through a fine sieve using a wooden spoon but to be honest I usually can't be bothered.

To serve, dollop a generous amount of crème fraîche on the soup, followed by the apple cut into batons, the crispy sage leaves and the chopped hazelnuts, so you have a little pile in the middle of the soup. Oh, and don't forget to season with some salt flakes and a grind of black pepper. Serve!

SERVES 8–10

MY GRANDMOTHER'S JERUSALEM ARTICHOKE SOUP

I love Jerusalem artichokes. Rich and creamy, these winter tubers are easy and prolific to grow, and their flavour is really accented by the butter, hazelnuts and smoky bacon used here. I don't know why the chestnut and the water chestnut work so well, but there is something about their contrasting textures – moist and slippery, powdery and earthy – that is so good against this silky soup. It's worth finding them.

The night before you want to make the soup, peel and slice the artichokes. Place them in a bowl and cover with water mixed with the lemon juice. Leave to soak overnight. This should make them less gassy.

The next day, in a heavy-bottomed saucepan, melt half the butter and sweat the shallots until translucent. Remove the shallots and add the rest of the butter. Drain and pat dry the slices of artichoke. When all the butter is melted and hot in the pan, add the slices of artichoke and cook until they start to soften. Add the shallots, then cover with the chicken stock. Cook until the artichoke is soft.

While the artichokes are cooking, pan-fry the bacon rashers until crisp. Remove rashers from the pan but leave the bacon fat. Chop the bacon into little tiles and reserve.

In a dry pan, toast the hazelnuts until golden but not burnt. Reserve. Drain and dry the water chestnuts and cut into a small dice (2 mm). Dice the cooked chestnuts (5 mm). Toss in the hot pan with the bacon fat until golden. Remove to paper towel to drain any extra fat.

When the artichokes are cooked, blend the soup until smooth with a stick blender or in a food processor. Pass the soup through a fine sieve. Wipe out the pan and pour the soup back in. Add 300 ml of cream and stir it in. Season to taste and reserve.

Put the bacon and hazelnuts into a mortar and give them a quick pestle-pounding, to make a nutty bacon crumble. Toss this gently with the chestnuts and a tablespoon of thyme leaves.

When ready to serve, warm the soup and blitz with the blender again. This will aerate the soup and make it more velvety. Pour the soup into warmed bowls. Swirl with a little of the remaining cream. At the table, add a dessertspoonful of the crumble to the middle of each bowl.

NOT A TIP: if you don't soak the artichoke slices overnight before making the soup, expect high winds and noisy outbursts an hour after eating. This can be quite funny if you have posh guests but it is not advised. They may leave in red-faced embarrassment. If you are entertaining a rampaging Viking horde they will probably think it very funny.

SERVES 6–8

2 kg Jerusalem artichokes
juice of 2 lemons
100 g butter
200 g French shallots, thinly sliced
1 litre (4 cups) chicken stock
2 rashers smoky bacon
75 g (½ cup) skinned hazelnuts
1 × 225 g can water chestnuts
90 g (½ cup) cooked chestnuts
   (thaw if frozen)
600 ml (2⅓ cups) cream
salt and freshly ground black pepper
1 bunch thyme, leaves picked

AJO BLANCO

75 g (3–4 slices) stale white bread,
   crusts cut off before weighing
450 ml (just under 2 cups) iced
   water
220 g (1 cup) blanched, peeled
   almonds
2 large garlic cloves, peeled
3 tablespoons Spanish extra-virgin
   olive oil
3 tablespoons Spanish sherry
   vinegar
salt and freshly ground black pepper
20 seedless green grapes, halved
   (or quartered if they are larger
   than an olive)
½ rockmelon

ANCHOVY, GREEN OLIVE
AND ALMOND FRITTERS

1 cup reserved almond paste
   (from making the soup)
10 pitted green olives, cut into
   quarters
5 pink anchovy fillets, cut roughly
   into 5 mm tiles
40 g (¼ cup) self-raising flour
60 g (1 cup) panko breadcrumbs
   or cornflake crumbs
500 ml (2 cups) sunflower oil
freshly ground black pepper

TIP: If you *really* love your guests, peel the grapes. The slippery jellied texture of the peeled grapes is wonderful with the smooth, creamy texture of the soup.

Eating this soup as a kid in Andalucia with my Dad is one of my fondest memories of him. I remember him being so excited by the little courtyard restaurant we stumbled across. This made eating what is now one of my favourite soups as much a revelation about how good food could be, as about how food could change someone's mood.

Make the fritters just before serving, so they can be a hot contrast against the icy soup.

Tear the bread into hunks and pour a cup of iced water over them. Let it soak.

Blitz the almonds and garlic to make a paste. The almonds should become a fine texture. Moisten with some of the iced water (about 100 ml or so) until the paste falls in on itself when the blender blades are spinning slowly.

Squeeze any water out of the bread that you can. Then add the sodden bread to the almonds. Pulse to combine. Blend slowly and drizzle in the olive oil. Add 2 tablespoons of vinegar. Now add iced water until the soup is the consistency of runny cream.

Season with salt and a little extra vinegar if needed, so you can taste it but it doesn't dominate; the garlic and the almonds must be prominent.

Strain the soup. Reserve the almond paste you'll be left with to make the almond and anchovy fritters to serve with the soup.

Chill the soup in the fridge for a couple of hours at least. This will help the flavours meld and develop. Chill the grapes and the melon too.

ANCHOVY, GREEN OLIVE AND ALMOND FRITTERS Mix the almond paste, green olive pieces and anchovy pieces.

Mix in the flour bit by bit until the mixture just holds together. This will take about ¼ cup of flour, depending on how wet your almond paste was initially. Add more if needed but the less flour you use the better.

Form the resulting dough into balls of that big fat-olive size and coat each one in the crumbs.

Deep-fry in enough hot (160°C or above) oil so they are fully submerged. Do these in batches but don't crowd the pan. Grind a good whack of black pepper over them!

TO SERVE Reserve 20 halves of the grapes for garnishing. Then, if you have one, use a small melon-baller to make balls of the melon roughly the same size as the grapes. Toss the melon balls with a good grind of pepper and a little salt. Put the grape halves and melon balls into the middle of each soup bowl. Pour on the *ajo blanco*. Top with little eyes of olive oil and the reserved grape pieces and enjoy with the anchovy fritters and a nice glass of sherry, like a fino or a manzanilla.

SERVES 4

CORN FRITTERS, BACON JAM AND VARIOUS MEXICAN ACCOMPANIMENTS

oil for frying

2 avocados, sliced

½ bunch coriander or chives, chopped, to serve

2 limes

120 g (½ cup) sour cream

FRITTERS

3 fresh corn cobs, stripped (about 400 g kernels)

125 g plain flour

1 level teaspoon baking powder

1 teaspoon ground cumin

2 teaspoons salt flakes

lots of freshly ground black pepper

4 spring onions, whites only, finely chopped

½ bunch coriander, leaves and a bit of stem, finely chopped

3 eggs, 2 lightly beaten and white of the other, whisked

BACON JAM

500 g rindless smoked bacon, cut into 2 cm batons

1 tablespoon vegetable oil

4 garlic cloves

1 brown onion, quartered then finely sliced

6 sprigs thyme, leaves picked

1 chipotle chilli in adobe hot sauce, chopped and mashed (optional)

125 ml (½ cup) maple syrup

55 g (¼ cup) brown sugar

80 ml (⅓ cup) apple cider vinegar

250 ml (1 cup) strong black coffee

lots of freshly ground black pepper

water to keep moist

MAKES 440 G OR 1 ½ CUPS

This dish is like putting together two great soul singers with a mariachi band. It's crazy but it works. The corn fritters are sweet, soft and crunchy in all the right places and the bacon jam is rich, dark and dangerous, with depths of flavour from the salty and sweet to porky. Sure, it's not the prettiest thing in the pot but it's oddly addictive so don't be surprised if you find yourself lured back to the fridge over the next few days to eat it straight from the jar – and furious to find that your son or partner has beaten you to it and scoffed the lot.

BACON JAM

Make in advance. Fry the bacon in batches until browned, set aside on paper towel. In a large pot over low–medium heat, add the oil, garlic, onion and thyme and cook until soft. Add the bacon along with all other ingredients and cook for about 50–60 minutes. Allow to cool a bit before blitzing for a couple of seconds in a food processor or with a stick blender.

FRITTERS

Put all the fritter ingredients in a large mixing bowl and stir to combine. Add whisked egg white last and fold it in gently.

Heat a non-stick frying pan over medium heat, add a touch of oil and use a spoon to spoon the batter into the pan. Cook for 2–3 minutes on each side – the corn should still be crunchy. Fry in two batches, adding a bit more oil between batches. Keep warm while the other fritters cook.

Serve the fritters with a scoop of bacon jam, some avocado, herbs, lime wedges and a dollop of sour cream. Hard to beat!

Or simplify things and top each fritter with a poached egg and a good dollop of bacon jam to anchor. This is the perfect breakfast.

SERVES 4

CHICKEN DUMPLINGS

These simple pot stickers need no introduction but do come with a lot of tips.

TIP 1: If you don't want to do all this chopping, you can pulse the ingredients in the processor but try to keep some texture there. I reckon the chopping and retaining the wet bite of the bits of water chestnuts makes it worth it.

TIP 2: If you have some mince left over, you can always form it into little balls and then drop into chicken broth to poach as little chicken balls. Dress with finely shredded parsley. For golden chicken balls, roll them in cornflour and shallow fry them first.

TIP 3: If you want to get more veg into the kids, wilt some finely shredded Chinese cabbage in a wok. Cool and mix into the chicken mince.

TIP 4: If you want to cut the fat, steam the dumplings in a bamboo steamer over (but not touching) simmering water for 8 minutes, or until cooked.

TIP 5: For prawn dumplings, replace the chicken mince with 400 g of chopped prawns and add 1 tablespoon of fish sauce to your mix. These are ace served with the bacon jam on page 104 or the lemongrass–chilli sambal on page 61.

TIP 6: Can't find wonton wrappers? You can always use fresh lasagne sheets.

TIP 7: There is some debate over cooking pot stickers. Some prefer to start them off in a pan containing a couple of tablespoons of vegetable oil and ½ cup of hot water cooking over medium heat. Cover the pan for 5 minutes (or until the water has evaporated and only the oil is left). Remove the lid and cook for a couple of minutes until the bases of the dumplings have tanned up.

Mix together all the ingredients – bar the wonton wrappers obviously – in a ceramic or glass bowl. Do not overwork, just pull it all together. Now place in the fridge and leave the filling's flavours to develop for a couple of hours.

On a floured board, lay out 6 wonton wrappers and place a heaped teaspoon-sized dollop of the filling in the middle of each square. Gather up the opposite corners of the wrappers and pleat the dumplings so the filling is fully encased and the pasta tightly wraps around it. If you leave air in there you risk the dumplings bursting. This is more of an issue when you poach the dumplings in a broth.

Boil the kettle. Place a high-sided frying pan on the heat. You need one that you can fit a saucepan lid over to contain steam. Splash in some vegetable oil.

To cook the dumplings, place them in the hot oil with their bases sitting on the bottom of the pan. Leave for 2 minutes until golden. Pour in the boiling water and pop on the lid. Reduce the heat to medium. Cook for 5 minutes. While the first batch of dumplings is cooking, make the next batch. Now check the dumplings. If they are cooked, remove them and repeat the process.

Serve the dumplings immediately with the chilli sauce, Chinese brown vinegar mixed with a little water and caster sugar, or soy sauce with finely julienned ginger.

SERVES 6

400 g chicken mince
1 × 227 g can water chestnuts, drained, rinsed, finely diced
4 spring onions, finely sliced
1 garlic clove, finely grated
3 teaspoons light soy sauce
1 tablespoon lemon juice
3 teaspoons fresh ginger, finely grated
40 fresh flour wonton wrappers (these are also sold as gow gee wrappers in some supermarkets)
vegetable oil
1 cup boiling water

TO SERVE
sweet chilli sauce
soy sauce with fresh ginger, finely julienned
Chinese brown vinegar with a little caster sugar (optional)

SPANISH OMELETTE

3 potatoes
sea salt and freshly ground
  black pepper
3 tablespoons olive oil
1 red onion, quartered and sliced
6 rashers streaky bacon, cut into
  5 cm strips
1 small red capsicum, sliced
1 small green capsicum, chopped
2 garlic cloves, finely chopped
1 large green chilli, chopped
9 fresh free-range eggs
2 tablespoons cream
1 handful chopped coriander,
  to garnish
100 g cheese – Manchego is best
  but local tasty is fine

TIP: Keep things in theme with
the Spanish omelette for the best
results. Spanish sheep's Manchego
cheese from La Mancha is very good,
especially if you toss some grilled
chorizo over the top as well! The
piquancy of the cheese and the tang
of good chorizo resonate beautifully
together.

Before there was frittata, there was Spanish omelette. That was back in the
days when TV was in black and white, and grilling meant putting food *beneath*
flames or glowing hot electrical elements. You used what was known as the grill
or the griller; not to be confused with a gorilla … which is $1000 in professional
gambling circles – apparently.

Now grilling is something done with the heat *underneath*, usually on the
BBQ. One thing that hasn't changed is this recipe, which will require you to
finish the top of the omelette by giving your grill a long-awaited work out.

Peel and cut the potatoes into 10 cm cubes, season with salt and pepper.

In a large, heavy, non-stick frying pan, heat the olive oil on medium heat. Add the
potatoes and give a quick stir, toss in a tablespoon of water and cover. Leave the
potatoes to cook for about 5 minutes. Add the onion and cover again for about
10 minutes until the potatoes are beginning to soften but not brown. Remove
the lid.

Add the bacon to the pan, then add the capsicums, chopped garlic and chilli.
(Leave the chilli out if you are feeding smaller kids the omelette.) Give it all a gentle
stir and continue to fry until the potatoes are completely soft and the rest
of the ingredients are cooked.

Turn on the grill inside the oven and place the rack on the second highest level.

Break the eggs into a large mixing bowl, add the cream, and beat by hand with a
whisk or fork. Pour the egg evenly over the potato and onion mixture and allow to
cook for 4 minutes. The omelette should start to come away from the side of the
pan when pushed with a knife. At this point place the pan under the grill and cook
until the rest of the egg is just done. Be careful not to overcook the eggs.

Remove from the oven, place a large serving plate or clean wooden chopping
board over the pan and flip upside down so the omelette comes out onto the
plate. You could just serve it directly from the pan, if you like.

You can garnish with chopped coriander and the grated cheese. This is how
I would do it. Obviously it's not how an austere food stylist would do it.

SERVES 6

4 WAYS AND MORE WITH CANNED PULSES AND BEANS

I'm sitting on the terrace of a grand hotel in Bangalore with a dozen small saucers in front of me. On each of them is a little pile of jewels – golden, green, amethyst, milky-white, jet black. I am getting an impromptu lesson on dahl from an Indian chef. The largest ones are chickpeas – both dried (and slightly bitter) or roasted with a nutty crushable texture that doesn't require cooking. His knowledge is encyclopaedic and goes on in a similar fashion across all the saucers.

I am a little embarrassed to admit that I use few pulses, legumes and beans in my cooking. He shoots me the sort of pitying look you'd give someone who never had red pencils in his colouring set and dismisses my baulk about the hurdle of having to soak putting me off in the past with the typically polite but pointed Indian question, 'but is the soaking hard?'

He has a point, plus the presence (and ever-ready convenience) of good canned pulses and beans also helps overcome this objection when I get home.

Now I pan-fry chickpeas in a little olive oil with spinach and garlic for a simple base for grilled chicken, or mix **2 × 400 g cans rinsed cannellini beans** with **425 g can tuna**, **100 g whole blanched almonds**, **½ diced red onion**, **parsley leaves**, **thyme** and **200 g diced celery**. I dress this 'insalata' with a good glug of **olive oil**, a splash of **white wine vinegar** and a sprinkling of salt flakes. I love this recipe because it is so flexible. You can add radicchio, rocket or baby spinach to make it go further. Or cooked asparagus, a **bulb of fennel,** or a handful of **chopped green beans** can add the fresh or crunchy element to this beany party instead of celery. In summer, swap the thyme and parsley for a punnet of **quartered cherry tomato**es and a **handful of fresh basil**.

If cannellini beans creamily recall summer for me, then lentils are all about the darkness of winter, even when used in a salad where the earthiness of lentils pairs with the matching earthiness of beetroot and their leaves. This salad is as simple as roasting **600 g small firm beetroots** individually wrapped in foil in a 180°C oven for 45 minutes, or until a skewer easily pierces them. Wearing rubber gloves, peel the warm beetroot and quarter. Toss through **a 400 g can rinsed and drained lentils** with **200 g crumbled good Greek feta** and **100 g beetroot leaves**. Dress with **thyme leaves**, a generous handful of **sunflower seeds** and some **warm balsamic vinaigrette**. Heat **¼ cup balsamic** with **2 tablespoons brown sugar** until it melts together and reduces a little. Pour this into a little jug with **3 tablespoons olive oil** so the balsamic marbles the oil. Serve the dressing on the side so people can take to their liking.

The one area where I *can* be bothered to soak is when it comes to making dahl. The 2 hours soaking **yellow split peas** (aka *toor dahl*) or **red lentils** (aka *masoor*) and then a slow simmer with a baby's finger of **ginger** and **3 whole garlic cloves** gives you a base into which you can stir pretty much anything. A flavour base of **onions** fried with **tomatoes**, **curry powder** and **turmeric** is a great starting point but **sweet potatoes**, **cauliflower** and **carrots** will all be welcome too.

The main thing about dahl, and here I am casting back to the advice on that grand Bangalore balcony, is about the tempering. It is the addition of two final waves of flavouring that take this rich, lentil stew into another realm. A salsa-like dice of **tomato, chilli and red onion** now always tops my dahl, and then as a final step, I throw **mustard seeds** and **curry leaves** into **hot oil** and pour the pan's contents over the dahl as the seeds pop and the leaves release their perfume. This contrast of the fresh and the fragrant lifts this stolid lentil porridge to angelic heights. And that's why I love you, dahl.

FOUR-BEAN MIX – FIVE-BEAN SALAD

This is a wonderful country classic made special by the textural differences between the beans and the sweetness of the vinegar-driven dressing. To make this, drain and rinse a **large (750 g) can four bean mix** with **200 g green beans** that have been blanched/just and cut into 3 cm lengths. Toss though with a finely **diced red onion**. Top with loads of chopped **fresh parsley** and dress with a sweet **garlicky vinaigrette** made with a clove of **crushed garlic**, **1 tablespoon red wine vinegar**, **3 tablespoons olive oil** and **a teaspoon runny honey** whisked together. This is one of the few salads that improves if you dress the beans a little before eating but save putting on the parsley until you serve it.

BRAISED LENTILS WITH SAUSAGES AND GREEN OLIVES

Fry **half a dozen pork sausages** – pork and fennel are nice – for 5 minutes in a little oil under they start to brown in a pan suitable for stovetop and oven cooking. Then add a sliced **brown onion** and 2 minced **cloves of garlic**. When the sausages are nicely browned on all sides, remove them with the onions and keep warm. They don't need to be cooked all the way through as we'll finish cooking them in the oven. Pour **a cup of sherry** and **a cup of beef stock** into the pan. Let it sizzle and spit in the pan. As it bubbles away use the liquid to scrub off any of the tasty brown bits in the pan. When the sherry and stock are reduced and thickened to a sauce that doesn't taste boozy, pour in your drained and washed **400 g can lentils**, a cup of **pitted, crushed green olives** and the browned snags and onions. Stir and season if needed. Cover and cook for 15 minutes over a low heat until the lentils are warmed and the sausages fully cooked. Serve with **Dijon mustard** and **mashed potato**. If you can't be bothered with the mash, then just add a second can of lentils to make it more of a lentil braise.

CHICKPEAS – CHEAT'S HUMMUS

Peel **2 cloves of garlic** and pour boiling water on them. Leave for 5 minutes to moderate their heat. Rinse a **400 g can of chickpeas** and drain. Chop the garlic and blitz it with the chickpeas and **¼ cup warm water** using a stick blender. When blended, add the **juice of ½ lemon** and a **good pinch of salt**. This will give you the most basic and healthy hummus. If you want more richness and smoothness blend in **1 tablespoon olive oil**. Depending on the bitterness of the oil you might want to re-address the seasoning with more salt. On set at *MasterChef* we eat this as a mid-morning snack with sticks of peeled carrot and de-stringed strips of celery. If you add a little more water and lemon juice to make it looser, it makes a marvellous light dressing for salads and grilled fish too. Add **tahini** or **sesame seeds**, to taste to be correct.

CANNELLINI BEANS

Slow-baked cannellini beans with sage, tomato and bacon. Oh my, comfort food doesn't come any more comfortable than bean stew and few people cooked beans as well as the late Rose Gray of the River Café in my old manor of Fulham in London. I suspect it was a skill she learnt living in Tuscany – that area of Italy where they love legumes and pulses so much that they are known as the "bean eaters". This recipe is adapted from one of hers and plays with the fact that cannellini beans love the brightness of tomatoes and the sharp saltiness of bacon (although I think she would have used salted anchovies instead).

First preheat the oven to 160°C. This dish is all about long, slow cooking to break down the resistance of the beans and coax the best flavours out of the other ingredients.

Now, in a heavy-based pot or casserole dish, fry **4 slices of smoked bacon** (diced). Remove and reserve the bacon. Deglaze the pan with **½ cup white wine**.

Return the bacon to the pan. Pour in the **480 g drained cannellini beans**, **6 vine-ripened tomatoes** (green calyxes removed) and a good **frond or two of fresh sage**. Cook for 90 minutes uncovered, so that the top gets a little crusty but feel free to keep going for longer if you aren't ready to eat yet.

When you are ready, serve in a bowl with fresh sourdough bread. Drizzle with the **best olive oil** you have and a sprinkle of **salt flakes**.

TIP: If you want to make this dish fancier, buy one of those bunches of small tomatoes on the vine. Drizzle olive oil over them and roast them in the oven until soft and still brilliant red. About 10 minutes or so at 250°C or as hot as your oven can go. Then serve the beans with these toms for bite with gammon/ham steaks.

ONION AND GOAT'S CHEESE TART WITH ROCKET SALAD AND CANDIED WALNUTS

200 g (1¼ cups) plain flour
100 g butter
¼ teaspoon salt
2 egg yolks
1 tablespoon water
1 egg

FILLING
350 g brown onions
25 g butter
2 eggs
200 g crème fraîche
200 ml milk
salt and freshly ground black pepper
100 g goat's cheese (feta can
  be substituted)
8 sprigs thyme, leaves picked

ROCKET SALAD WITH
CANDIED WALNUTS
50 g sugar
35 ml water
60 g walnuts
¼ teaspoon salt flakes
1 tablespoon good red wine vinegar
3 tablespoons vegetable oil
1 French shallot, sliced
100 g rocket

First make the pastry. Combine the flour, butter and salt in a food processor and pulse until the mixture resembles course breadcrumbs. Add the egg yolks and pulse again. If the dough is a little dry, add some of the water until the dough leaves the edge of the bowl. Tip the dough onto a floured bench and quickly bring together to form a ball. Wrap in plastic wrap and chill for at least 1 hour.

Preheat the oven to 170°C. Butter and flour a rectangular 35 cm × 12 cm, loose-bottomed tart tin.

Roll out the dough to a thickness of 3–4 mm, then quickly place it in the tart tin and lightly press into the sides, mending any cracks along the way. Trim the edges with a knife, cover with foil or baking paper, and blind bake, using baking weights or rice to weigh down the pastry and prevent bubbling, for 20 minutes.

Remove the pastry case from the oven. Mix a little of the leftover dough with some egg or water and seal up any cracks that may have appeared during the blind-baking. Beat the egg and paint over the tart case with a pastry brush to patch any cracks. Leave to cool.

Preheat the oven to 160°C.

For the filling, slice the onion thinly and cook over low heat with the butter for about 30 minutes, stirring often to prevent burning. The onion should be very soft and a rich caramel in colour with no black bits. Whisk together the eggs, crème fraîche and milk with salt and pepper. Spread the onion evenly along the bottom of the pastry case and sprinkle the goat's cheese on top with half of the thyme. Place into the hot oven and pour the egg mixture into the tart to prevent the mixture spilling (be careful not to burn your arms). Bake until the centre of the tart does not wobble, about 35–40 minutes.

CANDIED WALNUTS Line a baking sheet with baking paper. Put the sugar into a small saucepan and pour the water around the edge. Place over medium heat but do not stir. When the sugar starts to bubble give the pan a quick swirl to make sure all the sugar has dissolved. Leave without stirring for about 3–4 minutes. As soon as the sugar begins to colour, add the walnuts. Stir and let caramelise for about 2 minutes. Take the pan off the heat when the sugar has turned golden brown. Pour the nuts onto the prepared baking sheet. Spread out and cool. When cold, you can break them up and add to your salad.

ROCKET SALAD Put the salt and vinegar in a bowl and let the salt dissolve. Add the oil and give a quick toss with a fork, then add the shallot. When you are ready to serve, add the rocket, and mix thoroughly with the dressing. Sprinkle the candied walnuts over the salad.

Garnish the tart with the rest of the thyme and serve warm with the rocket salad.

SERVES 6

3 WAYS AND MORE WITH ZUCCHINI

Zucchini is the most Aussie of veg – green on the outside and gold on the inside. It's also among the most popular veg when we celebrate Australia's quartet of national pastimes – cricket, the beach, the BBQ, and teasing Tigers supporters about their fervent belief that this is the year their football team has a real hope of winning a premiership.

Unlike Tigers' forwards, zucchini really is the most versatile of vegetables. It is lovely steamed over boiling water so it's still a little squeaky but has lost its raw snap, or even sliced into batons as a crudité to dredge in any number of dips. Pick your zucchini, like your men, young, firm and unmarked, though when it comes to stuffing them, larger zucchini are probably better and easier to work with.

Those same young and firm **zucchini** are also perfect for cutting into ribbons with a potato peeler to make a simple salad. Just dress the ribbons with **lemon juice** – zest the lemon first – a little **olive oil** and a splash of **salt flakes**. This will break them down slightly. Then tear over some **good ricotta**, a handful of **toasted pinenuts**, curls of **parmesan** (roughly a curl for each zucchini ribbon) and chopped **parsley**.

For me zucchini are always associated with ratatouille, that delicious stew of Med veg like **eggplant**, **capsicums and zucchini** all sautéed — ideally separately — with **onions and garlic** and then doused with a **rich tomato sauce** fragrant with **thyme, basil and a little fennel seed** (if you like). My mum used to turn this into a meal for us ravenous kids by poaching **eggs** in this simmering Mediterranean-veg stew on the stove. Delicious – assuming you cook the eggs so the yolks are still runny and the white poached firm by the hot tomatoey sauce.

Zucchini love eggs whether they are grated, drained and then mixed into a **frittata of whisked eggs** and **parmesan or feta**, as in the recipe overleaf, thinly cut into ribbons and curled through the soft **savoury custard** filling of a quiche, or even grated as the bulk of fritters.

Zucchini love seafood. No, I don't know why as there seems no logical answer for this other than the subtlety of both allows each to state their intent clearly. Toss strands of fresh grilled or pan-tossed **squid** with similarly sized strands of **pan-wilted zucchini** and serve it dressed with **lemon juice**, **olive oil** and **pepper**. A little chilli is nice whether as fried flakes or a **fine dice of fresh long red chilli** flesh.

Another interesting trick is to finely **dice zucchini** and blanch them very quickly – dip into boiling water, count to 20, and out – to make a sort of zucchini couscous. Toss with **slivered almonds** and serve under fillets of **steamed white fish**.

Zucchini love basil too. Try frying **6 zucchini** cut into rounds with **2 finely diced onions** in a little **butter** and **olive oil**. Once softened, pour in a cup of **chicken stock** for every cup of zucchini. When cooked through, blitz into a soup with basil. About a handful of **basil leaves** for every 4 cups of zucchini is my ratio, but let your palate decide. Add the leaves to the blender bit by bit, tasting all the way. To add some salty savour to your soup, stir in a cup of **finely grated** parmesan before serving. For a healthier alternative BBQ the zucchini in plump strips rather than frying them. While you won't get that brilliant green colour that comes with the fried zucchini, you will get a lovely woody BBQ'd note in the soup.

Alternatively, make a beefed-up zucchini soup by frying equal quantities of **chopped broccoli** with the **zucchini**. Blitz when cooked and then stir in most of a **200 g block of blue cheese** – reserve some for garnishing.

You can also continue zucchini's love affair with basil by adding long golden-fried **batons of zucchini** to cooked **spaghetti** and then dressing both in **pesto**. This is a great way to bulk up your pesto pasta without the carbs – and get some veggies into any pesto-mad kids.

Another cracking zucchini pasta dish is to mix cooked short **penne or farfalle** with **cubes of zucchini** flash fried in a good **glug of hot olive oil** with **nuggets of prawn tail** and a couple of cloves of grated **garlic**. Finish off this combo by cranking up the heat at the end of cooking – when the prawns are still springy and juicy – and throwing in **half a glass of wine** to bubble away and cook out its winey-ness. Throw the drained pasta, with a little of the pasta cooking water, into the pan with the prawns and zucchini. Toss the pan so the pan's oil emulsifies with the water and juices to make a sauce to lightly coat the pasta. Serve dressed with a handful of **chopped mint** and a little of your good olive oil. Remember zucchini loves mint almost as much as it loves seafood.

Also, with any seafood dish and any **zucchini dish** as well for that matter, **diced fried bacon** thrown into the **prawns** adds some welcome porky saltiness. Zucchini loves anything bacony, whether it's rashers of grilled middle or strips of prosciutto.

1. ZUCCHINI AND PARMESAN FRITTATA

Preheat the oven to 190°C.

Grate **3 medium zucchini** with a box grater, sprinkle with **a little salt** and leave in a colander with a side plate resting on top. This will draw out both the excess water and any bitterness from the zucchini.

Thinly slice another **2 zucchini** lengthways using a vegetable peeler and set aside. In a large bowl, mix together **6 eggs, 1 cup thickened cream, ¼ cup vegetable oil, 1 cup grated parmesan, the sliced white part of 4 spring onions, the zest of 1 lemon and ½ cup each chopped mint and basil**.

Push down on the grated zucchini to free any drained liquid and now add it to the egg mixture. Next slowly add **½ cup plain flour** to incorporate. Season with salt and pepper.

Line the base of an ovenproof frying pan (or baking pan 20 cm × 25 cm × 4–5cm deep) with a sheet of baking paper. Line the sides with a long strip of baking paper. Lay the slices of the 2 zucchini over the base and sides. Pour the mixture carefully over the slices. Place in the oven and cook for 30 minutes, or until firm and set.

Remove from the oven and allow to sit for a few minutes to cool slightly. Gently slide from the pan and remove the baking paper from the base. Serve slices of warm frittata with fresh mint gremolata sprinkled over the top. To make the **gremolata**, finely chop a handful of **mint leaves** and a **garlic** clove. Toss with the zest of a **lemon**.

TIP 1: Customise! Don't be scared to play with other herbs like dill, oregano or thyme, or even to use other flavourings like smoked paprika, cayenne pepper or ground coriander and cumin instead of the mint and basil. If you decide to use dill, think about using feta instead of the parmesan. The mint and lemon gremolata will really sing with this combination.

TIP 2: Some children have an irrational hatred of green flecks in food so if you intend to feed this very kid-friendly dish to children who are foreign to you, perhaps leave out the mint and basil. Or be prepared to reassure them that you actually haven't puréed grasshoppers to flavour the frittata, as your kids will have told them.

TIP 3: For those looking for a slightly healthy option, you could use a firm, fat-reduced yoghurt in place of the thickened cream but, of course, you will lose some of that yummy silkiness.

2. BBQ ZUCCHINI AND SQUASH SALAD

Slice **a good-sized zucchini** finely into long strips with a vegetable peeler. Mix **1 teaspoon caster sugar** and a **1 teaspoon sherry vinegar** together so the sugar dissolves. Pour on the raw zucchini ribbons. Mix a paste made from crushing **2 garlic cloves** with **2 tablespoons olive oil**. Slice **another zucchini** and **4 yellow squash** into wide 8 mm slices. Toss the slices in a little **olive oil** and slap on the hot BBQ grill. Cook quickly until they soften and get good bar markings; we want these little burny bits to add complexity. This will take about 5 minutes a side. Toss the well-grilled squash and zucchini in with the pickled zucchini. Throw in the garlicky olive oil. Garnish with salt flakes and then a handful of **torn mint**. This is perfect with any seafood, as a bed for grilled chicken and lamb from the BBQ. It also goes really well on warm flatbread spread with hummus. (See page 111 for a simple recipe)

TIP: Alternatively, dump the pickling and take strips of **3 hot zucchini** straight from the BBQ grill and interleave them in **warm bread** with thin **strips of mozzarella** that you've already sliced and **seasoned with salt flakes** while the zucchini are cooking. Feel free to add **some dill** or even a **sizzling strip of bacon** from the BBQ because zucchini does love bacon!

3. ZUCCHINI, SCALLOP, PANCETTA, AVOCADO AND TARAMASALATA WITH FLATBREAD

This is a pretty dish that could have stepped from the tables of a fancy $200 a head restaurant but that's really easy to make at home. My mate Pete, who tested this for me, loved it and that should be endorsement enough for you to make it!

Cut **2 zucchini** into 5 mm dice. Spread half the zucchini dice across four plates. Put the other half in a bowl and pour boiling water over them. Leave for 1 minute. Drain and pat dry on paper towel. When cool, spread between the raw dice to give you two subtly different 'expressions'* of the zucchini in terms of both taste and texture.

Dry **24 scallops** (without roe) on paper towel. Season the upper side of them with the tiniest amount of **salt**.

Heat a heavy skillet, frying pan or BBQ griddle as hot as you can. Fry **8 pancetta slices**, torn into strips the size of a pinky finger, in a little **olive oil** on high until crispy and salty.

Warm **4 pieces of flatbread**, until slightly crusty but not brittle.

Dice ½ **avocado** into roughly 1 cm cubes. Split this dice over the four plates. Dollop 12 × ½ teaspoon-sized dollops of creamy, **taramasalata** randomly on each of the plates.

Remove the pancetta from the pan or hotplate. Wipe out the pan, very lightly oil it and reheat until it's really hot. Place the scallops salted-side down on the hot metal with good space between them, in batches. They should sizzle. This tells you the pan is hot enough. Season the other side of the scallop very lightly with salt. Leave until the pan-side tans up, then flip your scallops over. This final cooking stage will take only 30 seconds or so (in all about 90 seconds).

Arrange **sprigs of dill** and **shards of crispy pancetta** on each plate. Place 6 scallops between the sprigs. Using ½ **lemon** squeeze a **few drops of lemon juice** on each plate. Drizzle with the very best olive oil you have.

*('Expressions' is a very wanky, cheffy phrase, which rather embarrassingly, I seem to have picked up. It should be used whenever you are expressing the 'philosophy' behind how you cook – or perhaps even better … never used. Feel free also to use other trendy cheffy words like 'seasonality', 'passion' and 'lucrative ambassadorship'!)

EGGPLANT, FETA AND FELAFEL

Wordsworth found inspiration around the lakes of Cumbria, Lord Byron in exotic adventures in Constantinople and Greece and John Donne in the bed of his mistress. Their works as poets are epic, romantic and have stood the test of time. Rather less impressively, inspiration hits me in the aisles of my local supermarket and thus expectedly my recipes have the froth and uncoordination of a newborn foal about them. I expect the prognosis for their survival past the first few months is poor but I hope you try this crunchy, creamy, salty and soft jumble of flavours more than once as it is great on its own, tossed through a simply dressed cos lettuce salad or even stirred through buttered penne. On second thoughts, just like all these great poets, my inspiration came while away from home so maybe there is hope for me yet!

I wandered lonely as a shopping trolley
That floats on high o'er vales and hills,
When all at once I saw a cauli,
Some peas, baked beans and check out tills

Make the felafel mix according to the packet instructions. It will need 15 minutes to soak so you have tasks to do while this is happening.

Cut the eggplant into 3 cm chunks.

Blitz the cumin seeds with the coriander seeds and the garlic cloves in a food processor or crush using a mortar and pestle.

Mix the yoghurt with the diced cucumber. Season.

Fry the eggplant in 2 batches in a little hot oil until golden on each side and creamy in the middle. This will take a few of minutes for each batch. Eggplant can be a sponge for oil, so make sure the oil is very hot when you add the eggplant each time – and make sure you regularly shimmy the pan so the eggplant doesn't stick when it goes in or as it is cooking. As always, when cooking with hot oil – be careful.

Add the red onion to the second batch. Throw in the garlic and spice seeds at the end of cooking and toss through for a minute. Reserve the first batch of the eggplant and spiced eggplant.

Shape the felafel into golfball-sized balls using your hands.

Add more oil to the pan. When hot and sizzly, cook the felafel in batches. Drain on paper towel.

Now toss the eggplant mix with the fresh chopped herbs in a large bowl, crumble over the feta and add the felafels.

Season to taste and throw over a little lemon zest. Serve with the yoghurt and cucumber dressing and wedges of lemon on the side.

SERVES 4

1 × 200 g pack felafel mix
2 large, heavy eggplants (about 1 kg)
1 teaspoon cumin seeds
2 teaspoons coriander seeds
4 garlic cloves
260 g (1 cup) Greek yoghurt
1 Lebanese cucumber, peeled, seeded and diced
salt flakes and freshly ground black pepper
vegetable oil, for frying
½ red onion, diced
bunch oregano or mint, chopped
bunch flat-leaf parsley, chopped
200 g feta
lemon zest of 1 lemon
1 lemon, cut into wedges, to serve

TIP: Can't be bothered with the felafel? This eggplant and feta mix is delicious stirred through cooked pasta like rigatoni or penne. Add some crunch by tossing through some fresh breadcrumbs, fried lightly golden with 2 cloves of very finely diced garlic, and a handful of chopped parsley. Good times!

FIGS, BLUE CHEESE AND PROSCIUTTO. OOH-ER, MISSUS.

This is a sexy dish for loads of reasons – most of which I am too much of a gentleman to discuss. Suffice to say, if you come round to my house and these beauties are baking in the oven cancel all tomorrow's meetings or leave quickly with your virtue intact.

Cut the stems from the end of the figs to about three-quarters of the way up the length of the fruit, keeping the lid. Using the handle of a wooden spoon, edge the flesh away from the centre to create a space. Stuff this space with the cheese and top with the lid.

Wrap 1–2 slices of prosciutto around each stuffed fig, then place the figs in a small baking dish. Chill in the fridge for an hour or so.

Preheat the oven to 180°C.

Bang them in the warm oven for 15 minutes, or until the prosciutto goes crispy and the figs soften.

Cooked like this they will create a suitably sexy explosion in the mouth when eaten.

SERVES 6

6 large ripe figs
100 g mild blue cheese such
  as White Costello
12 slices good prosciutto,
  thinly sliced

MARNIE'S SWEET CHILLI CRAB

3 tablespoons roughly
  chopped garlic
2 tablespoons fresh ginger,
  roughly chopped
1 teaspoon lemongrass,
  white part only, chopped
½ brown onion
2–3 small red chillies
375 ml (1–½ cups) water
4 tablespoons peanut oil
210 g (¾ cup) tomato sauce
140 g (½ cup) sweet chilli sauce
1½ teaspoons salt
6–8 blue swimmer crabs, cleaned
1 egg, beaten (optional)
coriander sprigs, to serve
extra chillies, to serve (optional)

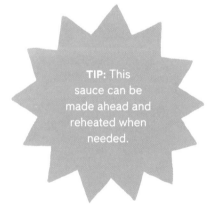

TIP: This sauce can be made ahead and reheated when needed.

One of the things I love about this whole book thing is sharing friends' recipes that we've eaten and enjoyed together.

Really this book reflects my own food interests but also the culinary smarts of so many great home cooks I respect and whose recipes I now cook for my family and for other friends.

Their names pop up throughout the book, but Marnie is special. Not only is she a good friend but she has also acted as my culinary muse and sounding board through the whole book's process, sometimes being brutally honest about my more stupid ideas – thankfully. She has also been kind enough to test the majority of these recipes. This book is far, far better because of her help. I wanted to make sure that a little of her is recognisable in the book and asked her to create her own recipe using one of my favourite flavours, sweet chilli, so you can see why I think she's so good. Just like Marnie, this recipe is bright and vibrant, sharp and sweet, saucy and spicy but far more crabby than its creator.

Blitz the garlic, ginger, lemongrass, onion and chillies to a paste in a food processor using ½ cup water. Alternatively, chop finely and pound in a mortar and pestle, leaving out the water.

Heat the oil in a wok or large heavy-bottomed, high-sided frying pan over medium heat and sauté the blitzed ingredients for a few minutes just until fragrant, taking care not to burn the garlic. Add the tomato sauce, chilli sauce and water and bring to the boil, stirring.

To prepare the crabs, remove the top shell of the crab and clean out the innards (the clear sac that covers the flesh), then chop in half down the length of the crab.

Add the crab pieces and toss through the sauce. Cover with a lid and simmer until the crabs are cooked, about 15 minutes. Make sure you toss several times while the crabs cook.

Turn off the heat and stir through the beaten egg (optional). Finish with the sprigs of coriander and more fresh red chillies, if you like it hot.

Serve with steamed rice or just eat straight from the pan!

SERVES 4–6

PASTA
AND RICE

PASTA SECRETS

Fate is a funny thing. Almost as funny as the woman you love booking an Italian hotel online and then discovering that the hotel she booked wasn't overlooking the ancient cathedral in an arcaded Medieval town that has my favourite food in Italy, but in a faded spa town an hour up a dowdy valley loaded with depressing autumn mist. Almost as funny as then realising that the silver lining was that this was the town where one of my greatest culinary heroes, Mario Batali, learned to cook pasta.

The first night in that little spa town, everything Batali had talked about, every rule that he'd shared, was there to see in two bowls of pasta in a cracking little local canteen. The pasta cooked in loads of water, as salty as the sea (and not rinsed!). The sauce acting almost as a condiment to the pasta, not dominating it. The flavours direct and linear, not overcomplicated.

Who would think that a simple, fresh tomato sauce over small envelopes of supple, yolk-yellow pasta stuffed with snowy fresh ricotta could taste so bright, so perfect? Who would have thought that fresh tagliatelle with little more than butter-fried slices of fresh porcini mushrooms, picked from the wooded slopes outside the little town that morning, would taste so rich and funky? But then, two of the essential rules of Italian pasta cookery had been met – the person cooking knew that pasta loves salt almost as much as pasta loves fat.

MAKING FRESH PASTA

The basic ratio for fresh pasta is 1 egg for each 100 g of flour; ideally Italian 00 flour. If you want a richer, yellower pasta, increase the quantities of egg yolks in the mix so it is 1 egg and 3 yolks for every 200 g of flour. Mix the ingredients in a food processor until the mix changes from looking like breadcrumbs to looking like little balls and isn't sticking to the bowl. Turn out, pull together and knead until the pasta feels smooth and your thumb comes out clean when pushed into the dough ball.

Rest the dough, wrapped in plastic wrap for at least 60 minutes, to relax the dough before working. Oh, and don't forget when rolling fresh pasta dough to make sure you keep it moist, and remember to repeat folding over the dough and rolling it out a few times to ensure the pasta is strong and well-laminated. Also remember fresh pasta cooks more quickly and absorbs more liquid than dried pasta, so pull it out earlier to toss, cook, and soak in your sauce.

Don't ever feel that fresh pasta is always superior to dried. Sure, I like fresh pasta for filled shapes and cut thinly for delicate flavours like white truffle and butter, but I reckon the strength and bite of dried pastas like spaghetti, rigatoni, bucatini or penne are perfect for most peasanty meat and tomato sauces, or anything with a bit of fieriness about it. This is good, as making those last three as fresh pastas is a pain in the bum anyway.

PERFECT PASTA CHOICE

There is one main rule and then countless regional rules, which it would take a Vatican Council to sort out. That main rule is that the chunkier the sauce, the chunkier the pasta. So, for a pesto a thin spaghetti is the go, while a robust chunky meaty ragù is best paired with a thick, ribbon-like pappardelle. In fact, pappardelle is pretty much always the go-to pasta when game like boar, hare or rabbit are central to the sauce. There are a few other unspoken rules that you deduce over various visits to Italy but none are definitive. Flat linguine is often favoured for seafood dishes. While it is usually flat and wider tagliatelle for Bolognese and not spaghetti. Spaghetti is more often seen with dishes like the rich, salty, funky riot of olives, capers and anchovy that is a classic puttanesca. Carbonara and Amatriciana might both come with spaghetti, although bucatini, which is like a thick spaghetti with a tiny hole running through it, or rigatoni, which is like a bigger-gauged penne, usually lined or ribbed, are also popular in Rome. These holes catch more sauce and the rigatoni can also cradle lumps of guanciale, the cured pork jowl that's the classic meat in these dishes. When it comes to shapes, any dish with zucchini seems to demand butterfly farfalle or corkscrew fusilli pasta and Sicilian pasta, like the aubergine, ricotta, tomato and basil of their *Norma* sauce is classically served with those pretty pasta wheels called *rotelle*.

PERFECT SAUCE

I'd argue that pasta sauces can largely be divided into four distinct groups defined by whether they are centred around cheese, cream, tomato and oil and butter.

CHEESE SAUCES

The smallest of the four groups, carrying the flag for cheese sauces is macaroni cheese – one of my top classics and known in Naples as *maccheroni al gratin* (see page 133 for my family's version that's a few hundred years old as well as my modern take on it). But there is also the wonderful Rome workers' dish of spaghetti or rigatoni with no more than black pepper and grated pecorino (see my *Cacio e pepe* recipe on page 134). I think you could also class pesto – that pounded green mass of parmesan, basil, oil, garlic and pine nuts as another cheese classic. Of course, if you follow Marcella Hazan's advice you pretty much dress all your pasta with a little finely grated cheese before combining it with the sauce for extra richness, and that would allow pretty much every sauce other than seafood to claim some affinity to the cheesy clan.

CREAMY SAUCES

You could argue that fettuccine Alfredo is really a creamy sauce but you'd be wrong (cream sauces usually are!). My immediate reaction when asked for a cream sauce recipe for pasta is to shout, 'No, don't! That's the sort of thing that Americans do that makes Italians laugh at them as porkers and tourists.' My opinion tends not to be too popular and it forgets that pasta loves fat, and cream is most definitely that.

Try cooking mushrooms and peas in a cream sauce hit with a little crumble of a veggie stock cube, which is an old staple from London Italian restaurants. Try gently frying diced red capsicum so it sweetens and reduces its blush into the oil. Add some diced mushrooms to cook, then stir in some cream to make a delicate pink sauce for mushroom, game or even plain ricotta ravioli. Other creditable creamy pasta sauces include one Stefano de Pieri used to make for pappardelle with sage, chicken livers, cream and butter; the simple combination of cream, parmesan and prosciutto; or the eighties stalwart of smoked salmon, dill, lemon, vodka and a splash of cream over farfalle. While I'd claim that the Piedmontese dish of leeks in a creamy sauce loaded with parmesan over *maltagliata* (rags of fresh pasta squares) is really leeks in a cheese sauce, anything with chicken or avocado in a creamy sauce over pasta isn't either creditable or credible, with or without cheese.

RED SAUCES

These are tomato sauces based on the most basic of sauces, the Napoli, which is little more than tomatoes cooked with oil and sometimes, if you are from the north, butter. A Napoli can be easily customised adding cured pork (pancetta, bacon or classically guanciale) to the hot oil at the beginning to make an Amatriciana (see page 140) or chilli-spiked to make its angry cousin, *arrabbiata* to be tossed over ridged penne. Add fried onion and garlic to the oil before adding the tomatoes and you have the perfect foundation for chunks of pork and fennel sausage, or ground pork and veal meatballs, to be added.

While many of the Italian seafood sauces like marinara, crab, *cozze* (mussel) or *vongole* (clams) built on skinny pastas, like linguine, rely on tomato to provide some pep, fashion dictates that while their sauces might have fresh tomato, they are really more about amping up the flavour of the seafood with white wine, garlic and good olive oil, so perhaps they belong in our next category.

OIL OR BUTTER SAUCES

Red sauces used to be seen in Italy as a wee bit bogan and so oil-based sauces became more popular, like something as simple as Rome's *spaghetti alla gricia*, which is just fried local bacon made from pork jowl and the fat that it has been slowly fried in, tossed with spaghetti, a bit of the cooking water and grated Pecorino which is tangy from sheep's milk.

I find this a fertile area to play, whether it's making a primavera sauce combining loads of spring veg like asparagus, beans, peas, zucchini, sugar snaps or snow peas to toss through penne; pairing zucchini with prawns and mint or pine nuts, garlic and parsley, rocket with prawns, or tuna with black olives, lemon and parsley. Then there are those meatier sauces, such as rabbit and green olives. These sauces are given some liquidity to carry the ingredients' flavours by splashing in pasta water, reduced white wine, stock or a combination. This liquid is then tossed with the oil that has been the cooking medium, so it emulsifies into a sauce and clings to the pasta it is dressing. This is an essential part of making pretty much any modern pasta sauce these days.

While *Norma* is probably Sicily's main contender as one of the classic pasta sauces, the south has much to boast about, such as the Calabrian dish of broccoli, anchovies and chilli coating ear-shaped orecchiette (page 129). Cross the water back to Sicily and their 'pasta for bad times' has salted anchovies, and sometimes broccoli, fried with green olives, garlic, breadcrumbs and chilli to be tossed through spaghetti; or bottarga (pressed fish roe) shaved over spaghetti with lemon zest and perhaps some fried breadcrumbs.

Solely butter-driven sauces tend to be from the north and the combination of burnt butter and sage, dressing filled pasta like ravioli or tortellini, or on pumpkin gnocchi, does the job so perfectly it has to be one of my pasta classics. Similarly, Italy's white truffles need little more than hot butter poured over their thin slices to make fresh pasta dance.

Interestingly, it was a Roman restaurant run by Alfredo di Lelio that came up with *fettuccine al triplo burro* in 1914. This sauce of reduced cream, butter and nutmeg into which grated parmesan has been steadily stirred. This is the pasta that Douglas Fairbanks and Mary Pickford raved about after their Italian honeymoon – quite something, a pasta that got the silent movie stars talking – and formed the basis for Italian–American kitchens' most famous pasta dish, fettuccine Alfredo that forgot its butter 'burro' roots.

While I don't subscribe to the view that all oil sauces and butter sauces should be finished with a fresh glug of oil or knob of butter, I do think they benefit from a final flourish with something like chopped herbs, lemon zest or a crunchy sprinkling of *pangrattato* (fried breadcrumbs) for added texture.

THE TEN RULES OF PERFECT PASTA COOKING

1. ALWAYS CHOOSE A LARGE, LIGHT POT.

You want the pasta to have lots of water to dance in and a lighter pot will conduct heat more quickly and be easier to carry to the sink when you want to drain the pasta.

2. ALWAYS SEASON YOUR PASTA WATER WITH LOTS OF SALT.

It should be as salty as the sea. Remember a minimal amount of that salt will make it into your pasta. Most will whirl down the plughole.

3. NEVER ADD OIL TO THE WATER.

4. ALWAYS ADD YOUR PASTA WHEN THE WATER IS BUBBLING FURIOUSLY.

Immediately stir in a glass of cold water, which will stop the pasta sticking, and then return the water to the boil.

5. ALWAYS SERVE YOUR PASTA *AL DENTE* OR WITH A LITTLE BITE TO IT.

This is for two reasons: first, you want the pasta to cook in the sauce a little and soak up some of the sauce; second, when *al dente* the pasta tends to taste more of cooked dough rather than soggy, waterlogged dough.

6. ALWAYS DRAIN YOUR PASTA A LITTLE BEFORE THE *AL DENTE* STAGE.

So you allow for the extra cooking in the sauce before it is eaten. This doesn't mean taking the pasta out when it is even a little chalky or still snaps.

7. ALWAYS HAVE YOUR COLANDER IN THE SINK READY TO GO.

I usually place my plates or bowls under it so the hot discarded pasta water can warm them before heading down the drain.

8. ALWAYS SAVE A CUP OF THE PASTA COOKING WATER

from the bottom of the pot to use when thinning and emulsifying the sauce.

9. ALWAYS HAVE THE SAUCE READY FOR THE PASTA BEFORE THE PASTA HAS FINISHED COOKING.

Like a true diva, pasta doesn't like to be kept waiting around.

10. NEVER RINSE COOKED PASTA.

TIP: You can always swap things around and use the anchovies with the cauliflower and the broccoli with the pancetta. The pangrattato goes well with both too.

3 WAYS WITH BRASSICA PASTA

Salt kills the perception of bitterness. Don't believe me? Compare two glasses of tonic but stir a good pinch of salt into one of them and see what happens. ('Salty tonic' is not the answer). Here the bitterness of brassicas, such as broccoli and cauliflower, is perfectly balance by the saltiness of anchovies or cured pork in the most simple and tasty way.

1. CAVOLFIORE, PANCETTA AND PANGRATTATO PENNE

400 g cauliflower (*cavolfiore*) florets
400 g penne
250 g pancetta
olive oil
40 g butter
80 g (1 cup, loosely packed) fresh, coarse breadcrumbs
3 garlic cloves, finely chopped
bunch fresh thyme, leaves picked (optional)
1 teaspoon ground cumin (optional)
150 g parmesan, finely grated

Bring a large pot of salted water to the boil.

When the water is bubbling madly, drop in your pasta. Add a cup of cold water and stir. This will stop the pasta sticking. Return to the boil, throw in the cauliflower florets, and then reduce to a gentle simmer. Cook the penne for as long as it says on the packet instructions and, miraculously, the cauliflower will be cooked too.

In a separate pan, fry the pancetta until a little crispy. Remove to a plate covered with paper towel. Splash about 1 tablespoon of olive oil and the butter into the same pan and heat. Throw in the breadcrumbs and fry until lightly golden. Toss in the garlic and soften – when this is done the pangrattato (aka fried breadcrumbs) will be a lovely, golden nutty colour. Toss with the thyme leaves or cumin, if using.

Drain the pasta and cauliflower. Toss with the pancetta. Sprinkle with the parmesan and the pangrattato and serve.

SERVES 4

2. RENEE'S BURNT CABBAGE TAGLIATELLE

One of my favourite cabbage recipes was given to me by the soulful, and slightly terrifying, singer Renee Geyer – a simple touchstone recipe that her mum always made for her when she needed comfort. It's as simple as cooking **ribbons of cabbage** in **butter** until they start to catch on the bottom pan and get browny and scorched. Then add **a little salt** and **sugar** and stir. Next add the same amount of **cooked tagliatelle**. You want as much cabbage as there is tagliatelle. Finish with a little more butter and season. Yum!

3. CALABRIAN ORECCHIETTE

400 g broccoli
500 g orecchiette pasta
6 anchovy fillets
2 garlic cloves, crushed
4 red chillies, seeded, deveined and finely chopped
olive oil
dried chilli flakes, to taste
150 g pecorino (or parmesan), finely grated

Bring a large pot of salted water to the boil. When the water is bubbling madly, drop in your pasta. Add a cup of cold water and stir. Return to the boil and then reduce to a gentle simmer. Cook for 4 minutes until firm and definitely not mushy.

Put half the broccoli in the pasta water, the other half can steam above the water in a steamer or colander covered with a saucepan lid.

Drain the pasta and remove the slightly mushy broccoli florets. Fry the anchovies, garlic and chilli in a pan with a little olive oil and add the broccoli. Mash together. Taste. Add a few pinches of dried chilli if you want more heat. Cook down this broccoli purée for a couple of minutes, then toss in the pasta. Stir to coat. Finally add the steamed broccoli, which will be firmer than the boiled broccoli. Toss.

Serve loaded with the grated pecorino.

SERVES 4

with 1/2 lb of Rough Carroway
Jits, bake them in tin pans,
plates ———— ————

For an Ague
====================================

Two ounces of Bark powder One
Spoonfull black pepper, One __
moist Sugar One Nutmeg, to
be mixed with brandy to Con-
-tency, the size of a nutmeg
to be taken Every hour ———

Eye Water
====================================

2 ounces of Rose water & 6 drops
of Extract of Saturn ———

To make Gingerbread

... a p.d fresh butter D.o fine sugar
... ff of Treacle, warm the Treacle
... four spoonfuls of Cream add
... quarter of a pint Brandy 1/4
... of an ounce Mace One ounce
... Ginger beat & sifted as much
... Flower as will make a stiff
... paste Roll it in what shape
... you like & bake it on tins

To dress Mackaroni

Wash your Macaroni very well,
boil it a quarter of an hour, then
stir it over the fire with some
Parmesan or Gloucester Cheese
half a pint of Cream, & a little salt
after it is done, you must brown it

MACHERONY

My family have been cooking macaroni cheese for over 250 years and I thought it might be fun to share that original recipe (written by my great x 7 grandmother) with you as well as a slightly more detailed version from my kitchen today.

MACHERONY 1765 (PROOF: SEE PHOTOGRAPH ON PREVIOUS PAGE)

Wash your macaroni very well, boil it a quarter of an hour, then stir it over the fire with some Parmesan or Gloucester Cheese, half a pint of cream & a little salt after it is done, you must brown it.

MACHERONY ABOUT 250 YEARS LATER (PROOF: SEE THIS PAGE)

Bring a **large pot of salted water** to the boil. Pour in 400 g macaroni when the water is seething furiously. Stir and bring back to the boil. Cook the macaroni for 2 minutes less than it says on the packet so the macaroni is still firm.

Preheat the grill.

Drain and throw the pasta into a pot over low heat with **300 ml cream** and **300 g finely grated parmesan**. Stir until the cheese is melted and the cream is reduced, take off the heat and stir. Be careful NOT to overheat at this stage or the cheese will go like chewing gum. Taste and season with **salt and pepper**.

Place in a flat casserole dish and throw under the hot grill. Remove when the macaroni has got lovely dark burn marks on its surface and some of the edge of the macaroni starts to crisp up.

Don't be afraid to top the macheroni with a little grated tasty or a **sprinkling of breadcrumbs** (not historically correct, but good).

SERVES 4-6

CACIO E PEPE

old rinds from parmesan or
  pecorino (if you haven't got old
  rinds, an extra 100 g cheese
  will do)
freshly ground black pepper
400 g thin spaghetti
60 g unsalted butter, cut into
  1 cm cubes and chilled
120 g (1½ cups) finely grated
  pecorino (or the best parmesan
  you can afford)
salt flakes, to taste

Rome is the city that lays claim to three of the best pasta dishes ever: rich tomatoey *Amatriciana*, oozy *carbonara* and their lesser known brother, *cacio e pepe*. This is simply spaghetti, or perhaps rigatoni, served with cheese and pepper. While it might be a simple combo, when made with precision these simple ingredients take on a true nobility.

This version is a little more complex because the acidity and bite of the parmesan/pecorino water really adds to the dish but if you can't be pfaffed with the first two steps ignore them and just toss the spaghetti in butter, pepper and cheese. I won't judge you … in fact, instead I might join you!

Collect your old rinds of parmesan and pecorino. Ask your friends to save theirs too.

Finely grate all the rinds so you have about 100 g fluffy cheese. Pop the cheese in a small pan with any bits of rind that were too hard to grate, cover with 500 ml (2 cups) warm water and slowly heat. Stir. Slowly the water will go milky as the cheese surrenders its flavour. The solids will start to coagulate at the bottom of the pan. Stir the pot to encourage all the flavour to leave this oozy mess.

Drain and put the cheesy water back in the pan on a very gentle heat and leave it to reduce for about 20 minutes. Keep an eye on it to ensure that it doesn't reduce too much or boil. It should get to around 125 ml (½ cup) liquid.

Grind the pepper into a fine sieve so the dust of the most finely ground pepper can be removed from the more robust grounds. You need a good, heaped teaspoon of the sieved pepper grinds.

Now it is time to cook the pasta. Salt a large pot of water until it is as salty as the sea – taste, don't just guess. Bring the water to the boil. Add the spaghetti. Stir in a cup of cold water. Return to a simmer. Cook for 2 minutes less than the packet instructions say and drain, saving the last cup or so of the spaghetti's cooking water.

In the warm pasta pot, melt half the butter over medium heat. Add the ground pepper and toast it in the melted butter for a minute. Add ½ cup (125 ml) starchy reserved pasta water and the reduced parmesan rind water. Bring to a simmer.

Now throw in the cooked spaghetti and the remaining butter. Reduce the heat to low. With a sinuous, circular motion roll the pan away from you and back tossing the pasta over and over. What you are doing is coating the pasta in buttery, peppery cheesy goodness and emulsifying a sauce from the pan contents. Tossing encourages the butter and pasta water to emulsify together and the pasta to finish cooking to al dente.

Sprinkle in half the cheese. Season with a good grind of salt. Stir through the pasta. When this cheese is melted, remove the pan from the heat, stir in the rest of the cheese and gently mix together. Moisten with a little more pasta water if the spaghetti seems dry. It really needs to be glistening. Serve immediately in warm bowls with extra pepper.

SERVES 4 AS A LIGHT MEAL

PAPPARDELLE WITH CORN, HAZELNUTS, PEPITAS AND CHEDDAR

1 tablespoon salt

400 g wide ribbon pappardelle pasta (if you can't get that, the widest gauge tagliatelle will do)

2 red onions, chopped

olive oil, for frying

320 g (2 cups) frozen corn kernels

105 g (¾ cup) skinned hazelnuts

80 g (½ cup) pepitas

50 g butter

120 g mature cheddar or vintage tasty, in 1 cm cubes (you could used smoked cheddar if you like)

1 tablespoon fresh thyme leaves

IDEAL SIDE SALAD

¼ head red cabbage

½ red onion

60 ml (¼ cup) red wine vinegar

35 g (¼ cup) currants

This is one of the dishes I lived on when separated from my family for eight months of the year filming *MasterChef* in Sydney. I get depressed throwing away all the fresh stuff that would go off each weekend when I nipped back to Melbourne. So I came up with this dish that uses ingredients that have a long life in the freezer, fridge or store cupboard.

It's all about the crunch and nuttiness of burnt butter, seared corn and hazelnuts, while the long-lived red cabbage would bring some relieving acidity, freshness and crunch. It's also a beautiful dish singing of the joys of autumn and perfect comfort food. Like most comfort food it will willingly also cosy up with chestnuts, mushroom or bacon as occasional guests.

Bring 4 litres of water to a rolling boil with the salt. The water should taste salty like the sea. (Try it *before* the water boils – I tend to forget and end up with either burnt fingers or burnt lips.)

As the water is heating, and sticking to the theme of things that last in your pantry, we'll make a small pickled red cabbage salad. Finely shred the red cabbage and red onion. Pour over the red wine vinegar. When you drain the pasta, also drain the cabbage and onion and mix in the currants. Reserve.

Drop the pasta into the boiling water so it is completely submerged. Add a couple of cups of cold water and stir. This will help the pasta from sticking. Return to the boil and then simmer until the pasta is *al dente*; basically so it still has a little resistance when you bite into it – but it shouldn't be crunchy.

While the pasta is cooking, fry the onion until golden in an oiled pan. Throw in the frozen corn and cook. It's good if the corn gets little burnt edges. Leave it over a low heat to keep warm.

In a separate pan, toast the hazelnuts. Remove them and then fry the pepitas until they colour. Remove. Drop the butter in the pan and cook until it froths and starts to smell nutty. The solids in the butter will turn a golden brown. Watch because you don't want it to go past this 'brown butter' or *noisette* (French for hazelnut) stage. Remove from the heat.

Drain the pasta. Don't rinse it. Immediately toss it through the hot onion and corn. Stir through the cubes of cheese so the heat of the pan and the pasta starts to melt it. (Now is the time to drain your cabbage too.) Mix the hazelnuts and pepitas with the pasta.

To plate, tip the pasta mix into a warm bowl, drizzle with a little of the burnt butter and a good sprinkling of thyme leaves.

Serve with the crunchy pickled cabbage or, alternatively, a small raddichio salad dressed with lemon and salt.

SERVES 4

AGLIO, OLIO E PEPERONCINO
(GARLIC, OIL AND CHILLI DOESN'T SOUND NEARLY AS ROMANTIC)

For me the best Italian food is all about simplicity and this dish proves it. It's all about little things done perfectly. Salting the water; not overcooking the pasta; using fresh lively flavours that happily swing hands around the strands of spaghetti but never drown out the taste of the pasta. Better yet, to cook this dish takes only as long as it takes to cook the pasta.

Bring a large pot of water with lots of salt to the boil.

Add the spaghetti to the boiling water, submerge and then pour in a glass of cold water and stir. This will stop the pasta sticking. Return to the boil and then reduce the heat to a simmer. Cook until *al dente*.

While the pasta is cooking, grab yourself a large sauté pan, big enough to toss all the cooked spaghetti in.

Heat the olive oil and then add the chilli, pepper and garlic in that order over a low-ish heat. Cook them until the garlic is starting to take on a tinge of colour. This should only take a couple of minutes. Take care not to burn the garlic for this will bring unwelcome, bitter charry notes instead of the toasty, caramelly sweet garlic tones that we want. Add the parsley and stir through.

Tong the pasta straight from the water into the pan with the garlic, chilli and oil, toss the pan to coat all the strands of the pasta with little pieces of chilli, garlic, parsley and their oil. Season to taste.

SERVES 4

1 × 500 g packet spaghetti
140 ml (a little over ½ cup) good-quality extra-virgin olive oil
8–10 long red chillies, seeds and veins removed, slightly less finely diced
loads of freshly ground black pepper
12 garlic cloves, finely diced
1 bunch flat-leaf parsley, chopped

TIP: Alio aglio peperoncino is simplicity at its best: it needs no help. But if you are someone who just has to dress things up, then a scatter of finely grated parmesan cheese or pangrattato are your best accessories. Pangrattato is known as poor man's parmesan. It is just bread, torn in small pieces and pan-fried in a touch of oil, salt and pepper. Yes, you can add little shards of leftover prosciutto to this when frying.

PASTA ALL'AMATRICIANA

500 g dry bucatini or rigatoni pasta
splash of extra-virgin olive oil
walnut-sized knob of butter
300 g guanciale (or bacon), cut
  into cubes
4 garlic cloves, peeled
2 × 400 g cans tomatoes
200 g pecorino (or the best
  parmesan you can find and afford)
2 long red chillies, finely sliced in
olive oil, to serve

TIP: If you can't get guanciale – and
let's face it this Italian bacon made
from pig's cheek is hard to track down
unless you live near an Italian area –
then try thick cut pancetta or a slab of
bacon cut into cubes. You can even
use speck. The main thing is you need
fatty pigginess for this recipe.

My grandfather was born in Rome but looking at him you'd never have known it. Ramrod straight, bristling moustache, an army man, he looked like the Scot he was; that is, until he started to speak Italian. Then that military bearing dissolved into a windmill of gesticulation and arm waving. Needless to say he was bullied at school for his thick Italian accent and when that happened he tended to break people's noses. I think that's why this Roman nature seldom was put on show. Plus the War changed his relationship with Italy forever. He was on the other side. Given his ambivalent attitude to the country of his birth, it is ironic that my go-to pasta sauce comes from a village just outside Rome.

My recipe has been a work in progress over twenty years but two bits of advice have been key to shaping my Amatriciana. One famous; the other infamous. My friend Fay's AWOL Roman boyfriend advised that the sauce was about getting the flavour from the pork into the oil and it was this oil, emulsifying with the reduced tomatoes, that was the soul of the dish; that you could throw away the bacon and just keep the oil and the dish would be little impaired. The advice of world-famous Italian chef, Mario Batali, was that the pasta should be the rugged hero and the sauce just the diverting comedy sidekick. This is an Amatriciana of which my strict traditionalist grandfather could approve (just don't tell him anything about the Aussie carbonara – or how I added chilli on the side).

Bring your largest saucepan filled with water to the boil. Season the water with enough salt so that it tastes as salty as the sea. Drop in your pasta. Add a large glass of cold water and stir the pasta. This will stop it sticking. Bring the water back to the boil and then simmer the pasta until cooked but still with a little bite. This is usually 1 minute shorter that it says on the packet.

Now to make the sauce. Place the butter and a splash of olive oil in a high-sided, heavy frying pan. Heat. Fry the pancetta or guanciale cubes over medium heat so the meat cooks and releases some of its fat.

Crush the garlic cloves. Add to the pork and fat. When the meat is starting to tan up but still juicy and the garlic is cooked, add the canned tomatoes and mix them in. Cook the sauce until reduced by about a third. The fat and the tomato juice will combine to make a rich, but still quite light sauce. This is not a sauce that needs much cooking – it is a quick peasant sauce designed to give some flavour to pasta for those on a tight budget.

Drain your al dente pasta, saving a cup of the pasta cooking water. Toss into the sauce. Leave the pan on the heat while doing this and the sauce will not only coat the pasta but the pasta will also suck up or absorb some sauce. This is another reason to slightly undercook the pasta.

Serve sprinkled with grated Pecorino and the little bowl of chilli slices covered in olive oil on the side for those who like things spiced up.

SERVES 4

PERFECT RICE 4 WAYS

Every day more than three billion people eat rice. Australians eat an average 10 kg of the white stuff themselves every year, and that's no surprise when you see how versatile it is. But the thing is far too few of us know how to cook it properly.

Rice has so many more uses than anchoring your curry to the plate. Look around the world and you'll find it's the central ingredient of so many national dishes, whether it's Japanese sushi, Korean bibimbap – rice topped with veg – and, of course, the Chinese breakfast staple congee (rice porridge). Indonesia is famous for its coconutty *nasi lemak* and fried egg-topped *nasi goreng*, while from their time as colonisers, the Dutch adopted the '*rijsttafel*' or rice table, a sort of feast of many little dishes served with rice.

Then there are those rices that are cooked with stocks or other flavourings, such as Spanish paella, the Hyderabad delicacy biryani, and that Aussie suburban Chinese favourite, special fried rice.

Rice seems to have an affinity with chicken, whether it is Lebanese chicken and almond rice, the barberry-strewn delight of buttery *zereshk polo* served in Iran, or Singapore's Hainanese chicken served with rice made extra delicious by the addition of a little chicken fat. The ability of rice to bind together, as seen so beautifully in nigiri sushi, is also used wonderfully by the Italians to make the crunchy fried bar snacks *suppli* and *arancini*. The Japanese hide similar surprises in their *onigiri*.

Poverty and African heritage have also ensured that rice and pulses have become natural bedfellows, whether in the red beans 'n' rice of the Caribbean, or 'Moors and Christians', which is eaten in Cuba but originated in the Moorish rice-growing region of Valencia in Spain's south. In the US south, they eat Hoppin' John, a similar stew of rice and cowpeas. In Puerto Rico they take this one step further for their national dish, *arroz con gandules*, by stewing rice with pigeon peas, pork, stock, cumin and bay leaves. This is vaguely reminiscent of the Cajun dishes gumbo and jambalaya, which also feature rice in a stewy situation.

My favourite rice dishes sit in that territory of rich and cooked with stock. In Valencia, Madrid and the Basque country they make a simple, delicious dish called *arroz negro*, which is black rice made with fish stock and cuttlefish ink. While in Argentina they make a richer stew of rice, sticky with reduced stock and popping with the intense flavours of chorizo, caramelised onions, peas, cubes of fried yam and little pieces of rump steak. Delicious.

Interestingly, sweet rice dishes are far less common, being limited mainly to the rice puddings of Latin countries, India, the UK and parts of South East Asia. Italians make a texturally interesting ice cream with rice, and Indians make rice cakes called *pongol*.

When it comes to rice in Australia, risotto is the dish we most request. I love it for two reasons. It was always one of the best things my mum used to make us when we were growing up – risotto with chicken livers – although, as she used long grain rice and chicken livers, it was more of a pilaf as it wasn't creamily gooey from the rice's starch like a good risotto. The second reason I love it is its versatility, which means risotto can be a carrier for pretty much any seasonal produce.

PERFECT BOILED RICE

Covered or uncovered? Wash or soaked? Simmer, steam or boil? Brown or white? Basmati, jasmine, bomba or arborio? Absorption or draining? For such a simple thing there are a lot of decisions to be made when it comes to rice. Here are my thoughts.

Use long grain rice like jasmine and basmati when you want the rice to soak up curries and sauces on the plate or when you want any dish where the rice grains are separate and fluffy.

Use short grains when you are looking for creamy dishes or dishes that revolve around the rice soaking up flavours, like arborio or vialone nano for a risotto or bomba for your paella.

I like the nuttiness of brown rice for salads but note that this will take twice as long to cook, needs to be simmered slowly and should be cooked with more water.

For perfect fluffy white rice, rinse the rice a couple of times to remove any starch or talc used in processing. Throw **1 ⅓ cups rice** into a big pot with **1 ¾ cups water** and a **good pinch of salt**. Bring to the boil and then immediately drop the heat to a bare simmer. Cook covered for 12 minutes until the water is absorbed. Remove from the heat, leave covered, and let the rice sit for 5 minutes to steam out, or until needed. The rice will hold its heat like this for about 20 minutes in normal conditions. Fluff with a fork before serving.

PILAFS

One of my grandmothers was taught to make pilaf by Elizabeth David in Egypt during the War. This is how she used to make it – I think – although by the time I could ask her she was quite old and in the sort of addled state where she'd pour milk on her toast for breakfast – and then laugh about it.

Heat **a tablespoon grapeseed oil** in a large saucepan until sizzly. Throw in a 5 cm length of **cinnamon**, **3 cardamom pods** and **2 cloves**. Shake until fragrant. Gently cook ½ **finely diced onion** with the spices until translucent. Add **2 fresh** (or 1 dried) **bay leaves** and **a cup basmati rice**, washed until the water runs clean. Stir and fry until the rice smells toasty. Sprinkle in **a teaspoon salt** and **375 ml water**. Bring to the boil, then drop the heat for 10 minutes. Cover the pot with a clean tea towel (to stop condensation from the rising steam dripping back into the rice) and then the pot lid. Make sure the cloth is well clear of the flames! Remove the pot from the heat after 10 minutes and leave to steam for 10 minutes. Fluff with a fork and **dot with butter**.

To make your pilaf a little more sexy and Persian, cook the **rice** in the same amount of **chicken stock** rather than water and soak ½ **cup barberries** in hot water for 10 minutes to plump up. Drain and fry the barberries in **a little butter** with ½ **cup pinenuts**. Stir the barberries, butter and toasted pinenuts through the rice. Top with BBQ chook if you want.

For an Afghan twist, dump the barberries and bay leaves but stir through ½ **cup cashew nuts**, a few hunks of this weekend's **roast leg of lamb** (just re-fried) and top with **plumped raisins** and very slender matchsticks of **fried carrot**. You can use lamb stock if you have it to cook the rice.

SERVES 4 AS AN ACCOMPANIMENT

SIMPLE RISOTTO (PICTURED)

Place a large, heavy-based pan on the heat and melt **30 g butter** with a slug of **olive oil**. Cook a finely **diced onion** gently in this pan. Soften, but – and this is important – do not let it colour.

Put **1 litre stock** on the heat to warm up. Hot stock is vital to risotto success. Cold stock will shock the rice and screw with its correct cooking. Choose chicken, veg or fish stock, depending on your tastes and what you'll be topping the risotto with.

When the onion is softened, add a **garlic clove** and stir. Add **2 cups risotto rice** (carnaroli or vialone nano rice are best as they have a higher starch content than arborio. This means you can use the no-stir method below to get the required creaminess) and toss it in the pan. Keep it on the heat for a few minutes to toast the rice. The rice will subtly change colour and start to smell a little toasty. Turn up the heat and add ½ **cup white wine** to the rice. It will sizzle and steam. Simmer until the rice and onion mix looks slippery rather than wet. It should move in the pan like wet sand. Add **4 cups of your hot stock** and stir through the rice.

Pop a lid on the pot and turn down the heat. Don't touch it. After 10 minutes, check the rice. To do this, crush a grain of rice with your thumb on the back of a wooden spoon. If it squidges outwards leaving a little white star at its centre then it needs to cook longer. Add ¼ cup of stock and stir until absorbed. Use the squidge test again and continue adding more stock if needed. If you see three tiny white stars, then the rice is ready. Cooking the rice usually takes about 12 minutes.

Take **100 g cubed cold butter** and **100 g grated parmesan**, stir half of each into the rice vigorously with a wooden spoon. And I mean vigorously. Show your enthusiasm! This will help knock some starch off the rice, making the risotto creamy. Keep doing this, adding the rest of the cheese and butter until it's all incorporated. The texture you are looking for is oozy. Add a little more warm stock if it needs some help.

Taste, season and top with whatever you want. I love **scallops, dill and finely shredded fennel**, but throw the fennel in to soften with the rice at the end of cooking. **Roast corn kernels and roast prawns** are also good, but cook the kernel-stripped cobs in the chicken stock before making the risotto to intensify the corn flavour. **Braised mushrooms or roast duck and chestnuts** also fly but instead of white wine use muscat or sherry with the mushrooms and Amarone or pinot with the duck.

SERVES 4

VEGETABLE RISOTTO

Put on a small pan of boiling, lightly salted water and prepare a large bowl of iced water. Blanch a **small bunch of asparagus** after you've snapped the woody ends off. Then add **150 g sugar snaps**, **150 g green beans** and **150 g broad beans** to the boiling water. You are blanching them to intensify their green colour and just take the rawness off them. When each veg has just lost its rawness (about 1 minute), remove from the water with a slotted spoon and plunge into iced water to stop them overcooking.

Do the same with **200 g frozen peas** but refresh them in a sieve so they don't escape. Don't throw away the cooking water, as it has now become a basic vegetable stock, but instead measure it out. Add vegetable stock to make the total liquid 5 cups. Then return the stock to the pan and keep warm.

Cut **2 zucchini** into 3 mm thick strips; peel and trim **8 spring onions** but leave the roots on. Brush both with **olive oil** and grill them so that they bar-mark, soften and intensify in colour. Cut the blanched asparagus, beans and sugar snaps into 2 cm lengths.

Make a simple risotto, as left, but use the vegetable stock you have made.

When cooked perfectly and creamy from the **butter and parmesan**, stir through the peas, sugar snaps, beans and asparagus. Taste and season.

Top with a nest of zucchini slices, spring onions, broad beans, a sprinkle of herbs like **dill, parsley or mint**, and a grate of **lemon zest**. Season with **salt flakes**. Serve the risotto with **wedges of lemon** and a **black pepper** grinder.

SERVES 4

EGG IN NEST WITH ITS FUTURE BREAKFAST
(AKA CARBONARA REVISITED)

Carbonara is like, you know, really popular and I really wanted to put a recipe in this book but I did my usual recipe in the last book and I was told I wasn't allowed just to cut and paste as that apparently would be 'contrary to the terms of my contractual obligations', whatever that means.

A conundrum. What recipe to use.? Obviously my Roman-born grandfather would not be impressed with any smart-arsed additions to this classic like onion, garlic, cream, mushroom or rabbit and olive meatballs, and there is nothing I hate more than disapproval from beyond the grave – you know all those pictures falling off the walls and levitating beds.

So maybe I could play with the form. A nice Italian chef in the Barossa showed me how to make a sort of zabaglione of egg yolks, white wine and parmesan, which was delicious under some batons of speck and a tumble of spaghetti. It certainly had all the flavours of carbonara in a new form but my conscience (which comes in the shape of two feisty women when it comes to food) pointed out that it sounds like it would be more work than the classic method, and that it would require something called 'technique'. I am not, or so Ms and Ms Conscience suggested, Mr Technique when it comes to food, or pretty much anything really. I'm more the 'artistic type', which I suspect is their shorthand for inept or impracticable.

So I get creative, which these days means 'conceptual'. How about frying long skinny strips of bacon and then reserving them in their stringy, porky goodliness while I toss spaghetti in the bacon-fatty pan and then add a cup of finely grated parmesan or pecorino? Then I take these cheese-flecked, bacony pasta strings and curl them in a nest in the bottom of each of four warmed bowls. Into each nest I drop a poached and rather runny egg. Top that with the bacon 'worms' and there we have it: *Egg in Nest with Its Future Breakfast.*

Slightly pretentious yes, but also rather tasty and built on strong authentic Italian foundations as it references the classic Campania pasta where they top their spaghetti with runny, pork lard–fried eggs.

Cook the spaghetti as per the packet instructions in lots of salty water. Drain well.

Meanwhile fry the bacon 'worms' over medium heat until brown and crispy.

While the bacon is cooking, poach the eggs. Take a saucepan filled with boiling water, lightly salted. Create a 'whirlpool' in the water with a wooden spoon. When the water is swirling, gently lower in one egg at a time to the centre of the swirl. Turn off the heat and leave to sit for 3–4 minutes. Drain.

Toss the pasta with a touch of oil and half the parmesan to coat. Tong the pasta into a mound on each of four plates and make a shallow well on the top. Grate over loads of parmesan and black pepper, then gently lay 1 poached egg in each hollow. Finish with strips of the crispy bacon.

SERVES 4

500 g spaghetti
6 rindless bacon rashers, cut into long thin strips
4 eggs
extra-virgin olive oil
200 g parmesan cheese, freshly grated
freshly ground black pepper

CHICKEN BOLOGNESE WITH CORKSCREW PASTA

2–3 tablespoons olive oil

90 g (3 rashers) bacon, finely sliced
  into batons

1 onion, finely diced

3 garlic cloves, peeled and chopped

3 stalks celery, finely diced

1 carrot, finely diced

1 fresh bay leaf

3 sprigs fresh thyme

500 g chicken mince

100 g (⅓ cup) tomato paste

500 ml (2 cups) chicken stock

250 ml (1 cup) white wine

2 punnets cherry tomatoes,
  cut in half

½ bunch flat-leaf parsley, chopped

salt flakes and freshly ground
  black pepper

500 g fusilli pasta

parmesan cheese

When you tie yourself to writing cookbooks that feature recipes that you cook for your family, it means that you are catering for the toughest critics of them all: your kids. Amazingly, they loved this lighter version of Bolognese; one even called it 'super-delicious', which is about the highest praise you can get in my house. Well, other than 'it's almost as good as Nanna's'. Yes, it's fiddly browning off the ingredients in three batches but it is well worth it for the taste.

In a large heavy-based pot over medium heat, add 1 tablespoon of oil and fry the bacon until brown. Remove from the pot and drain off any excess fat.

Add the onion, garlic, celery, carrot, bay leaf and thyme sprigs to the same pot and cook until caramelised, about 15–20 minutes.

Remove the vegetables from the pot, add 1 tablespoon of oil and brown the chicken mince, don't overcook. When the chicken mince is browned, put the vegetables and bacon back in the pot along with the tomato paste, stock, wine, cherry tomatoes and half the parsley. Bring to a simmer and cook until the sauce has reduced, about 25–30 minutes. Taste for seasoning.

Meanwhile, cook the corkscrew pasta as per instructions in lots of salted boiling water.

When ready to serve, stir the pasta and the remaining parsley through the sauce. Serve with the parmesan, for grating, on the side.

SERVES 6

12 WAYS WITH OLD BREAD INCLUDING 4 WAYS WITH TOAST

Times are tough and every little bit helps but there is nothing new about this. Most of our forebears lived in perpetually straightened times where nothing could go to waste, whether it was using all the beast or eating everything in the pantry no matter how far past its best it was.

As so many countries have bread at the centre of their peasant food cultures, it is no surprise that there are lots of ideas of what to do with the inevitable stale bread.

So what can be learned that is of value today? Sure, we all know that stale bread can be blitzed into breadcrumbs for binding meatloaf or rissoles. Stale breadcrumbs are ace for crumbing thumb-sized and kid-friendly nuggets of chicken breast, which can then be spritzed with oil and baked in a 180°C oven for 15–20 minutes; or they can coat a fillet of schnitzel or fish to be pan-fried or baked to a crunchy, golden conclusion. Just remember to drop whatever you are crumbing in flour and then egg wash before the crumb. The crumb sets better if refrigerated before cooking. In all cases you can make the crumb more adult by adding grated parmesan and some fine-diced herbs like thyme, tarragon or parsley.

Heck, breadcrumbs are great saved frozen and can even be fried in very hot olive oil with some minced garlic, fresh herbs and perhaps a little bit of porkiness, like chips of jamon or prosciutto, to make Spanish *migas* or Italian *pangrattato*. This can top scallops to go under the grill or add firecracker pops of texture to pasta.

Keep your breadcrumbs more like little pepita-sized lumps than crumbs and they can be tossed with salted butter to make a delicious crunchy 'Brown Betty' topping for anything from a fish pie to a macaroni cheese. This can even replace the usual topping on an apple crumble to delicious effect – just add some brown sugar with butter to the rough crumbs.

There are also lots of examples of breadcrumbs being used as a sauce – in the Middle Ages bread rather than flour was used to thicken sauces. In Catalunya their *picada* is famous for this. To make a picada, blitz **24 toasted almonds** with **4 cloves garlic** and **3 slices stale or dry bread** until combined. Moisten with **hot stock** or hot water and add to your sauce a few minutes before serving.

In the UK, any fowl – chicken, turkey, even partridge – is classically matched with a **bread sauce**. This is as simple as infusing **hot milk** with **a bay leaf** and **a small onion studded with 5 cloves** then cooking this spiced milk with the breadcrumbs until the crumbs swell to make a velvety sauce. In Sicily they make a similar sauce by pounding **bread, almonds and anchovies** together.

While a British bread sauce was an essential part of my Sunday lunches growing up, the day habitually ended with a plate of eggy bread – **2 de-crusted slices of last week's loaf** dipped in a wash of **2 eggs** beaten with **1 tablespoon milk**, seasoned, and then **fried until golden**. Simple and perfect just with **a squirt of HP**. Here are twelve other ways that I love to use up the inevitable stale bread that clogs the bread bin these days.

1. SAMATYA BREAD SAUCE

I discovered this wonderfully simple sauce in a little shack in an old fishing village on the outskirts of Istanbul. Its tart creaminess goes wonderfully with the crunch of crumbed calamari, ensuring a double use of breadcrumbs!

Take **4 (300 g) cleaned tubes of calamari** and cut into rings. Dust in **cornflour** then dunk in a bowl of loosely **beaten egg** and finally coat with **coarse fresh breadcrumbs**. Pop these in the fridge while you make the sauce.

Soak **4 thick slices stale sourdough** (crusts removed) in a cup of **warm water**. Squeeze free of the water and process the bread with **3 garlic cloves**, which you have peeled. Add **300 g Greek-style yoghurt** and work until the bread is combined in a sauce. Add **3 tablespoons water** or so to make the sauce smoother and season with a **little salt**. Fry the calamari rings in batches until just golden, place on a paper towel-lined baking tray and keep warm in the oven. When all the calamari is cooked, sprinkle the rings with a little salt and serve with a **crisp green salad**, **wedges of lemon** and the bread sauce to dollop on.

2. TURKISH TARATOR

Across a wide swathe of the Muslim Mediterranean and the Balkans they also make sauces using stale bread. Foremost of these are the tarator sauces that are usually served with fish or lamb. These usually partner the breadcrumbs with garlic and pounded nuts, like walnuts in Azerbaijan and Lebanon, or pine nuts in Turkey. To make a simple Turkish tarator, soak a **couple of slices of day-old bread** in water, squeeze and then blitz with a **cup pinenuts**, a **couple cloves minced garlic** and the **juice of a lemon** (about ½ cup). Then you just drizzle in about **½ cup olive oil**, but do it slowly with the processor turning so the oil emulsifies. Serve on fish or chicken.

3. PEARA

How clever is this? Medieval Venetians used to make a sort of poor man's polenta using just old bread and 500 ml beef stock. This *peara* is wonderful with the simple boiled meats so typical of Italy's north.

To make this sauce, toast **2 cups breadcrumbs** in a dry pan; in another pot gently cook **120 g unsalted butter** and **½ cup bone marrow**, that has first been soaked free of any redness in salted water overnight, then dried and then finely chopped. When the bone marrow has largely melted away, stir the combined fats into the breadcrumbs over low heat. Cook for 2 minutes to combine. Now stir in **½ cup beef stock**. Season with **salt and lots of freshly ground black pepper.** Slowly cook the stock and crumbs, stirring as if it was a polenta. Add another **½ cup stock** when the first is absorbed and the crumbs start to swell. Repeat, cook and stir. After about 20 minutes, you'll end up with a wonderful rich, peppery side that goes perfectly with beef, veal or chicken and still has some texture.

Classically, Venetians use minimal butter (if any) and instead loads of bone marrow. However, if you are a little squeamish about bone marrow you could just use 250 g butter. The end result won't be as satiny but it will still be delicious.

4. BREADCRUMB SOUP

Venetians would also use more stock and cook the *peara* longer to make a silky sauce. This gave me the idea to zap another **batch of peara** (made as above) with another **couple of cups of beef stock** to make a soup. It's a slow process but you just keep adding the stock bit by bit until the bread gets so saturated its molecules seem to burst open. Keep adding stock and stirring until you have a creamy consistency.

The end result is a wonderful flavour strangely like a cream of mushroom soup but made for a far, far cheaper price. To fool people further you could garnish this dish with a dice of **fried mushrooms**, a few drips of **brown butter** and a couple of **thyme leaves** or strings of **orange zest**.

5. KNÖDEL

In Europe breadcrumbs have also always been used to make dumplings or gnocchi-like *gnudi*, where the crumbs are paired with ricotta to keep them light. These *knödel*, however, are robust enough to make a light dinner and were taught to me by my very particular German friend, Caroline from the Barossa, who manages to give them an Italian lightness.

Fry until translucent **100 g very finely diced onion** with **200 g diced speck** in a slow pan with no oil; the speck should release some of its fat. Don't let anything brown. Leave it to cool. Warm **½ cup milk** and whisk in **2 eggs, ½ cup cream** and **salt and pepper**. Pour over **750 g stale bread** cut into small (1.5 cm) cubes and mix in the cooked onion, a cup of finely chopped **curly parsley** and **75 g any old cheese** (diced). Mix together and then leave it to rest for 20 minutes.

Now knead your knödel dough thoroughly. If too wet, add a little flour but try to minimise this by using stale bread as this sucks up more liquid and flour can make for bullety knudel. Using wet hands, roll into balls between a squash ball and a tennis ball in size. Roll them in flour. Steam for 15 minutes resting on baking paper punched with holes. Then rest in the steamer off the heat for a further 15 minutes. Serve with a blizzard of **finely grated parmesan, olive oil, pepper and salt** or to soak up the sauce of your goulash or sauerbraten.

These knudel can be frozen on baking paper on metal racks and then transferred to a zip-lock bag. Or wrap each one individually in baking paper and then wrap in plastic wrap, if you are a very particular German woman!

6. PAPPA AL POMODORO

Italians love bread soups made from *panada* or *pancotto* – basically bread soaked in liquid. The simplest use of stale bread is perhaps for the Roman dish of 'bathed bread', where a slice of stale bread is placed in each bowl and then thin stock or brothy soup is poured over it and left to soften the bread for 10 minutes before eating. In Piedmont they add milk and onions to stale bread.

In Lombardy they keep the bread untoasted and whip in egg and grated parmesan but the summery combination of silky bread and super-ripe tomatoes in this Tuscan tomato soup is perhaps the most classic.

Gently cook **3 finely sliced garlic cloves** in a small pan with **100 ml olive oil** until the garlic softens. Cut **2 kg tomatoes** in half. Remove and reserve the seeds and spilt juice. Process three-quarters of the tomatoes into a purée and add to the oil. Increase the heat and simmer for 20 minutes. While this is happening tear up the leaves from **1 bunch basil**, chop the remaining tomato halves into chunks and process the flavoursome tomato seeds by blitzing the reserved tomato seeds and then straining out the bits of seed in a fine sieve. You'll be left with an intense tomato water.

After 20 minutes, bring the soup to the boil and then gently stir in **200 g stale sourdough**, free of crusts and torn into thumb-sized pieces. With a very gentle heat under the soup, let the bread soak up all the tomatoey juices. When the bread looks silky and sodden, stir in the remaining tomato pieces, the torn basil and **100 ml of the best olive oil** you can afford. Sit off the heat for 10 minutes to let the flavours combine and the soup to cool slightly. It's good to serve this soup lukewarm and dressed with the fresh tomato water, some more olive oil and a sprinkle of salt flakes.

7. BREAD SALADS

Torn bread salads, like Italian panzanella and Middle Eastern fattoush, make stale bread the hero, partnering it with herbs and the bread-staining juiciness of good ripe tomatoes and olive oil.

Making a panzanella salad is as simple as taking **300 g dense sourdough**, cut into 2 cm cubes. Toss the bread with **5 tomatoes**, chopped into hunks along with any seeds that slipped out when cut. Sit for 30 minutes. Just before serving mix in a **thinly sliced red onion**, a minced **garlic clove** and **120 ml good olive oil**. Splash this on the bread and tomatoes. Now splash on **40 ml balsamic vinegar** and season with **salt and pepper**. Toss. Finally, toss through **20 leaves of basil** torn roughly into pieces. You can add **capers, anchovies** and **fat black olives** if you like some salty sexiness. Just remember to season after adding these (not before) as they will reduce the additional salt requirement.

In Sicily they make an even simpler bread and tomato salad: **500 g cubed stale bread** is dipped into warm water to soften and then tossed with slices of **ripe plum tomatoes** and **a cup olive oil** shaken with a couple of crushed **garlic cloves**, **some salt, pepper** and **dried chilli flakes**. Here you might want to use the best heirloom tomatoes you can find as Sicily's plum tomatoes have an amazing flavour thanks to the sun, maritime climate and the salinity of the soil.

8. BROWN BREAD ICE CREAM

Don't be trapped into thinking that stale bread is just for savoury dishes. Don't forget a custardy bread and butter pudding, French toast, French *pain perdu*, or something my Grandmother excelled at 40 years ago – this now very modern and on-trend ice cream.

40 g butter
75 g fresh brown breadcrumbs
125 g soft, light brown sugar
6 egg yolks
1½ teaspoons cornflour
450 ml semi-skimmed milk
1 teaspoon vanilla extract
150 ml cream

Melt the butter in a large frying pan. Add the breadcrumbs and stir until evenly coated in the butter, then sprinkle 50 g sugar over the crumbs. Fry gently for another 4–5 minutes until lightly browned. Remove from the heat and leave to cool. The crumbs should be crispy at this point. When the crumbs are cold, rub them between your fingers to break up any lumps.

Fill the sink with very cold water. Make the custard by whisking the egg yolks, the remaining sugar and the cornflour together in a large bowl until thick and pale. Heat the milk in a saucepan until just before boiling point, then remove from the heat. Secure your bowl and gradually pour the hot milk over the egg mixture while whisking constantly. Pour the mixture back into the saucepan and return to the heat, continue stirring until the custard thickens and coats the back of a spoon. As soon as you can, run your finger along the back of the spoon and leave a line, the custard is ready. At this point you must stop the cooking process. Remove from the heat and place the pot into the cold water. Allow to cool completely.

Add the vanilla and cream to the custard and mix well. Transfer to an ice cream maker and churn until thick. Add the breadcrumbs to the mixture and churn until ready.

MAKES 750ML

4 WAYS WITH TOAST

Toast is another of the great uses of bread that's no longer the freshest – and how important it is! Imagine a world without toast and you'll see how vital it is to our happiness. Imagine a boiled egg without soldiers, or a whole pantry full of marmalade and jam jars forlornly waiting for the heart-warming pop of a toaster that will never come. We might be enamoured with more exotic bread concoctions but let's not forget the great Anglo-Celtic contributions to cuisine that is easily their equal – toast! Here are four great expressions of toast's nobility.

1. CHOCOLATE, OLIVE OIL AND SEA SALT TOASTS

200 g good-quality dark chocolate, chipped
  or roughly grated
1 sourdough loaf, cut into 8 × 1.5 cm thick slices
40 g unsalted butter
2 tablespoons olive oil
1 tablespoon extra-virgin olive oil (I like to use
  a green, unfiltered one), to drizzle
salt flakes

Sandwich the chipped chocolate between the slices of sourdough.

Heat 20 g of butter and 1 tablespoon of olive oil in a heavy-based frying pan over medium heat.

Cook 2 sandwiches for 3 minutes each side, or until golden and the chocolate is melting.

Wipe the pan clean and repeat with the remaining butter, oil and sandwiches.

To serve, drizzle the sandwiches with best-quality green olive oil and sprinkle with a few flakes of salt.

SERVES 4

2. AVOCADO ON RYE BREAD TOAST

a loaf of the moistest, darkest rye bread you
  can find (or else good crusty sourdough)
2 ripe creamy avocados
100 g feta (best quality, such as Dodoni)
3 limes, cut into wedges
good salt flakes, such as pink Murray River or Maldon

Lightly toast 4 slices of rye bread on each side. Spread each slice by pressing a skinned half of avocado down on to it. This will heavily load each slice and leave the toast as little more than a textural and nutty contrast to the acidity of the lime, the bite of the salt and the creamy green flavour of the avocado. The look of the avocado on the toast should be chunky rather than smooth. (That's so the lime juice and the salt/feta have loads of places to pool and hide, giving you different bursts of flavour as you eat.)

Sprinkle each piece of toast with feta (about 25 g is good).

Serve with lime wedges that you should squeeze over the top of the avocado before eating and some salt flakes on the side for a textural and saline contrast.

SERVES 4

TIP: While shooting this dish our guilty pleasure was thickly spreading the rye toast with a little Vegemite before pushing on the avo. Sounds weird but it works really well. (Remember that the Vegemite is salty so don't add salt on top at the end; but lime is fine, when using Vegemite.)

3. WELSH RAREBIT

1 leek, white part only, very thinly sliced
180 g (1½ cups) grated cheddar or mature
  tasty cheese (good-quality, not pre-grated)
375 ml bottle hoppy ale or stout
½ teaspoon dry mustard powder
½ teaspoon paprika or cayenne pepper
Worcestershire sauce, to taste
4 slices square white bread

Place the leek in a small bowl and refrigerate while you prepare the toast. This will help soften the flavour.

Meanwhile, mix the grated cheese with 2 tablespoons of beer, the mustard powder, paprika or cayenne and a couple of shakes of Worcestershire. Give it a good stir – it will clag together nicely. Drink the rest of the beer from the bottle while toasting.

Heat the grill to medium–high and toast the bread on one side until golden.

Divide the cheese mixture among the untoasted sides of bread, spreading it to the edges. Grill for 3 minutes or until golden brown and bubbly.

Meanwhile, rinse the leek in cold water and pat dry with paper towel.

Serve the toasts, uncut, with a sprinkle of freshly ground black pepper and a little pile of leek on the side as a refreshing garnish and to remind you of this toastie's essential Welshness.

SERVES 4

4. THE ULTIMATE CHEESE TOASTIE

Once, in the USA, I saved a man's life. Back then he was a cheese man. This toastie is close to his heart!

1 small leek, trimmed and sliced into 5 mm rounds
1 red onion, diced
1 perky spring onion, sliced up until
  just before the green ends get sloppy
2 French shallots, finely diced
1 garlic clove, very finely diced
125 g best-quality English cheddar
butter, at room temperature
4 slices good artisan-baked sourdough bread,
  cut into 1.5 cm thick slices

Warm up your sandwich maker or sandwich press. Pop the leek slices in a bowl and cover with just-boiled water. Let them sit for a minute, then drain thoroughly and place the leek on sheets of paper towel to dry out. Mix the leeks together with the diced red onion, spring onion, shallot and garlic. Grate the cheese. Butter one side of each slice of bread.

Lay 2 slices, butter side down, on the hot sandwich press plate. Push your fist into the bread to make a small depression. Place a little of the leek mixture in the indentation. Add a generous handful of grated cheese, then top with some more leek mixture. The ratio is up to personal taste but I like the cheese to outnumber the leek mix at least two parts to one. Add the second slice of bread, butter side up. Close the sandwich press and toast until gooey.

Repeat until either a) the cheese, bread or leek mix runs out; b) you are full; c) you find the perfect ratio between leek mix and cheese for your taste, then get a pen, amend this ingredient list and write your name over the top of this recipe.

SERVES 2

ROASTS
AND
BRAISES

MEATY...

TOWNSVILLE TAXI DRIVER'S ONE-POT SCREAMER CHINESE CHICKEN AND RICE

2 brown onions, finely diced

100 ml (just under ½ cup) peanut
   or vegetable oil

1.5 kg chicken thigh fillets, halved
   if large

75 g (½ cup) cornflour

salt and freshly ground black
   pepper

1 tablespoon five-spice powder

2 teaspoons grated fresh ginger
   and its juice

4 stalks celery, cut into
   2 cm × 1 cm dice

8 garlic cloves, halved

600 g (3 cups) jasmine rice

250 ml (1 cup) sherry or
   shaoxing rice wine

1.5 litres (6 cups) chicken stock

2 oranges

2 × 230 g cans water chestnuts

2 × 225 g cans bamboo shoots

sesame oil

8 spring onions, sliced

2 long green chillies, sliced

1 bunch coriander

soy sauce

TIP: If you want to play with this dish, take inspiration from those classic Chinese claypot chicken rice dishes and add mushrooms like shiitake for some umami or even a little Chinese lap cheong sausage for a burst of porky sweetness.

You never know where inspiration will hit you . . . but in the front seat of a taxi at a shopping centre on the outskirts of Townsville is one of the more unlikely locations. Our 75-year-old taxi driver's conversation ranged from the familiar – that is, the Cowboys' chances in the finals – to the unusual – the recipes of Donna Hay. This recipe apparently started out as one of the lovely Donna's but he'd customised his version by adding spices and water chestnuts. As I love both water chestnuts with chicken and the ease of one-pot cookery I played with his idea by adding bamboo shoots, spring onions and green chilli slices for more colour as well as crunch. And this is what emerged.

Fry the onions with 2 tablespoons of oil until soft over medium heat in a large, wide saucepan or casserole. Remove and reserve.

Toss the thighs in the cornflour seasoned with salt, pepper and 3 teaspoons of five-spice powder. Turn up the heat, add the remaining oil, and then add the chicken thighs to brown on both sides. Do this in two batches. When golden, remove the chook and keep warm.

Throw the ginger into the pan and fry for a minute. Throw in the celery and garlic and stir over the heat until fragrant. Now stir in the rice and toast the rice in the rendered chicken fat with these aromatics for a couple of minutes, moving it around the pan all the time.

Deglaze the pan with the sherry or Chinese wine stirring it through the rice and celery until it thickens.

Add the stock, the final teaspoon of five-spice powder, and 2 finger-long lengths of orange zest. Bring to the boil over that same high heat.

Add the onions, chicken, water chestnuts and bamboo shoots. (If making this dish with full quantities for 8 people you may need to split everything between 2 pans, which isn't a disaster.)

Cover the pan and reduce the heat to very low. Stir every 5 minutes to stop the rice from sticking. Cook for about 20 minutes, or until the rice has absorbed the stock and the chicken is tender. Add more stock if you think the dish is looking too dry.

Sprinkle the finished dish with a little sesame oil. Doing this at the end of cooking ensures that the sesame oil stays wonderfully fragrant. Garnish with slices of spring onion, fine strips of fresh orange zest from the oranges, green chilli slices and fronds of coriander and cover with the lid again.

Serve at the table in the covered pot so that when the lid is removed your guests are assailed by the smell of the chook, sesame oil and fresh herbs.

Have some soy sauce on the side to splash on each serve.

SERVES 8

TIP: This dish goes really well with a simple, crisp salad of sliced wombok, orange segments (from the 2 zested oranges – natch) and fresh mint. Dress this with a vinaigrette of a minced garlic clove, a good squeeze of lemon juice, sesame oil and rice wine vinegar in roughly a 1:2 ratio.

SLOW-ROASTED PORK SHOULDER WITH APPLES AND LEEKS

1.25 kg pork shoulder, boned
  and rolled
1 teaspoon salt flakes
150 ml (just over ½ cup) apple cider
310 ml (1¼ cups) chicken stock
1 garlic clove, crushed
½ brown onion, sliced
freshly ground black pepper
sugar, to taste
30 g butter
1 tablespoon chopped sage leaves

THE APPLES AND LEEKS
2 tablespoons olive oil
2 tablespoons apple cider
1 tablespoon honey
1 tablespoon chopped sage leaves
2 large leeks, white and tender
  green parts
2 Golden Delicious apples
salt and freshly ground black pepper

This dish is inspired by various Garden of Eden stories. The presence of the apple is obvious but what's far less well known is the ancient myth that when Satan left the Garden, onions and garlic appeared respectively wherever his right and left foot fell. This leads me to suspect that leeks sprouted up wherever he sat. The pig, of course, was central to *The Simpsons* telling of Adam and Eve's fall from grace. This dish tastes like paradise, too.

Preheat the oven to 160°C.

Score the skin of the pork and season with the salt. Place the pork on top of a rack in a roasting pan – this will prevent the pork from burning on the bottom. Place in the preheated oven and leave for 1 hour before basting with the fat. Baste again after the second hour. The pork can then be left to cook for another 2 hours without basting, allowing the skin to crisp up and become crackling.

For the apples and leeks, whisk together the oil, cider and honey. Add the chopped sage. Wash the leeks, cut in half lengthways and then into 5 cm pieces. Peel and core the apples and cut into wedges. Add the leeks and apple to the cider dressing, season with salt and pepper, and toss to coat. Add the leek and apple to a baking dish and bake in the oven with the pork for the last 30 minutes of its 4-hour cooking time.

When the pork is ready, remove from the oven. Give the leeks and apple a stir in their dish, and leave them in the oven for another 15 minutes until they are golden and the apple is soft.

Leave the pork uncovered to rest for 15 minutes.

To make the cider gravy, remove the excess fat from the pork roasting pan and place the pan on the stovetop. Add the cider, chicken stock, garlic and onion and stir over a medium–high heat. When the liquid has reduced by half, season with salt and pepper. If your cider is very dry you might need to add a little sugar for sweetness. Whisk in the butter, strain through a fine sieve and add the sage.

Remove the crackling from the pork and break it into pieces. Carve up the pork and arrange on a serving plate along with the crackling and the cider gravy. Serve with the apples and leeks.

SERVES 4 GENEROUS PORTIONS

ROAST CHICKEN WITH FUDGY SWEET POTATOES AND MAPLE BUTTER

This will be the best roast chicken you've ever made but that may just be the supreme sugar hit of those sweet potatoes talking. Baked in the oven, their flesh turns into a sort of moist, slightly caramelly candy; something that a spritz of salt and a dollop of rich, sweet maple butter can only make better. You see, roast chicken loves baked sweet potato like lawyers love money. Once tried, I suspect that these orange-fleshed beauties will become a staple for every roast chook dinner.

Preheat the oven to 200°C. Remove the chicken from the refrigerator at least 30 minutes ahead of time.

Rinse the chicken in cold water, pat dry and season the cavity with salt and pepper. Halve the lemon, place one half of the lemon with the thyme inside the chicken. Squeeze the remaining lemon over the chicken, rub all over with 20 g of butter, and season well.

Place on a rack, breast-side up, in a roasting pan. Roast for 15 minutes. Turn the heat down to 160°C and roast for a further 45 minutes.

Remove the chicken from the oven, check that the juices are running clear, and rest breast-side down for at least 30 minutes. You can reheat the chicken briefly just before serving.

For the sweet potatoes, wrap each sweet potato in foil and place in the oven on a rack alongside the chicken. They will take about 1 hour to cook, depending on their size. When you take the chicken out of the oven, remove the sweet potatoes. Remove them from the foil, cut them in half lengthways, take a fork and rake it over the flesh to mess it up a bit, put them into an ovenproof dish and place the potatoes back in the oven until you are ready to serve.

For the maple butter, blend 100 g of butter, the maple syrup and Dijon mustard until combined.

Remove the sweet potatoes from the oven and serve with a large dollop of maple butter on each half and serve with the roast chook.

SERVES 4-6

1.8 kg chicken
salt flakes and freshly ground
   black pepper
1 small lemon
½ bunch thyme
120 g butter
4 small sweet potatoes (about 1 kg)
2 tablespoons pure maple syrup
1 tablespoon Dijon mustard

BAKED CHICKEN WITH THYME, POTATOES AND CAPSICUM

6–8 chicken thighs on the bone with skin (you can use any cut of chicken on the bone)

1½ heaped teaspoons dried thyme

3 teaspoons salt flakes, plus more to season

lots of freshly ground black pepper

100 ml (just under ½ cup) olive oil, plus extra

12 smallish potatoes (allowing 3 per person), skin on

30 g butter, melted

5 red onions, cut into 8 wedges

2 heads of garlic, cloves separated, skin on

3 red capsicums, seeds and veins removed, cut into thick strips

10 sprigs thyme

½ bunch flat-leaf parsley, roughly chopped

2 tablespoons red wine vinegar

TIP: Try this sometimes with green capsicums instead of red to add an elegant, bitter herbaceous edge to the dish.

This dinner is perfect for those lazy nights when inspiration is snoozing by the fire. It's so simple it almost throws itself together and lets the oven do all the really hard work. It's also even better as a dish to take to a bring-a-plate dinner. With dried thyme, capsicum and chook all together, a fancier cookbook would call this *Provençal poulet* but at my home we just call it *delicious*.

Preheat the oven to 200°C.

In a bowl or plastic bag, put the chicken, ½ teaspoon of dried thyme, 2 teaspoons of salt, lots of black pepper and 50 ml of oil. Massage the ingredients into the chicken and allow to sit while you par-boil the potatoes.

Par-boil the potatoes until the skin just starts to split. Drain and allow to cool long enough to handle. Break in half with you hands to get a rough edge on the potatoes. Don't worry if they break apart. Toss in the melted butter, 50 ml of oil and 1 heaped teaspoon salt flakes.

Put the potatoes in a very large baking dish or two smaller ones (divide the ingredients between the two trays). Arrange the onions, garlic and capsicum among the potatoes. Scatter over another teaspoon of dried thyme and toss all the vegetables with a touch more oil.

Lay the chicken on top of the vegetables and scatter over the sprigs of thyme. Bake in the oven for 1 hour. At the 30-minute mark, baste with the pan juices and sprinkle over a bit more salt.

Remove the chicken from the oven when an hour is up and the chook is cooked.

In a small bowl, toss the parsley in the red wine vinegar and scatter over the hot dish.

SERVES 4

LAMB, APRICOT AND PRUNE TAGINE

1.3 kg lamb shoulder, 1 kg after
  fat is trimmed off a bit
3 teaspoons ras el hanout
1 teaspoon ground cumin
1 teaspoon sweet paprika
100 ml extra-virgin olive oil
3 garlic cloves, finely chopped
6 French shallots or 1 large brown
  onion, peeled and cut into
  8 wedges
1 tablespoon fresh ginger,
  finely chopped
1–2 red bullet chillies, split open
1 cinnamon stick
1 teaspoon salt flakes
freshly ground black pepper
500 ml (2 cups) chicken stock
1 sweet potato, peeled and chopped
  into large chunks
6 little kipfler potatoes, peeled
2 carrots, peeled and each one
  cut in 3
150 g (1 cup) dried apricots
3 strips orange peel
1 tablespoon honey
1 × 400 g can tomato purée
250 ml (1 cup) water
150 g pitted prunes
60 g almonds, blanched
sprigs coriander and mint leaves,
  to serve
couscous and plain yoghurt, to serve

TIP: To make your own ras el hanout
spice mix (if you can't find ras el
hanout ready-made) toast and then
grind together to a powder ¼ teaspoon
of cumin seeds, half a blade of mace,
a cardamom pod, ¼ teaspoon of black
pepper, ½ teaspoon of coriander
seeds and ¼ teaspoon of cinnamon.

'*How many ingredients?*' I can hear you exclaim as you turn from my pal Mark's gorgeous picture of the tagine and see that this recipe may not be as simple as buttering toast. Immediately let me reassure you that while the ingredient list might be long, the method is short and very simple – more like making buttered toast with peanut butter and jam. Basically, you just throw different sets of these ingredients into the same pot at different points in the cooking and then go back to the hookah. Oh, and if you are still carping about the length of the ingredients list, just remember I could have given you a complex recipe to make your own ras el hanout spice mix and sent you out searching for such esoteric ingredients as chufa, orris root, grains of paradise, dried rosebuds and monk's pepper to name but a few. This would have doubled the number of ingredients – and then you'd have to find them!

Trim the lamb of excess fat, chop into large chunks and add to a bowl or large zip-lock bag with the ras el hanout, cumin, paprika and 3 tablespoons of oil. Toss to coat the meat. Set aside in the fridge to marinate for at least 1 hour or overnight if possible. Allow the meat to return to room temperature before cooking.

Preheat the oven to 160°C.

Heat a tagine or ovenproof pot with a lid over medium heat on the stovetop with a tablespoon of oil and brown the meat in batches. Set the meat aside and add the garlic, shallots or onion, ginger, chilli, cinnamon stick, salt and pepper to the same pot, along with 2 tablespoons of oil. Fry for a couple of minutes, stirring occasionally. If the pot becomes too dry add a splash of the stock.

Add the meat back to the pot along with the sweet potato, potatoes, carrot, apricots, orange peel and honey. Toss before adding the stock, tomato purée and water. Bring to a gentle boil, stirring occasionally. If you are using a tagine, reduce the heat to low and either cook on the stovetop or in the oven. If you are using an ovenproof pot, place in the oven with the lid on.

At about the 45 minute mark, add the prunes and almonds, and return the pot to the oven. Cook for a further 60 minutes. If at any time it looks dry, you can add water and stir.

Remove from the oven or cooktop. Scatter with the coriander, mint and plain yoghurt and serve with plain couscous.

SERVES 6

NEAPOLITAN LAMB PUTTANESCA

The whores of Naples have been betrayed. For years spaghetti puttanesca was *their* invention – a quick dish to bolt down between clients. Then culinary smarty pants pointed out that the name came from the Italian word *puttanata* which means rubbish, and was actually thrown together first by either a nightclub owner or an artist on the island of Ischia off Naples in the fifties. Having spent a bit of time in Naples I believe this fine city of Sophia Loren, Enrico Caruso and Diego Maradona deserves better and so I have created this dish to dedicate to the hard-walking women of Piazza Garibaldi. I think they'd like this braise, which partners chunks of meaty lamb shoulder with the rich umami hit of stewed tomatoes and the olives, capers and anchovies that traditionally always shone alongside lamb … but then for 80 euros, I suspect they'd say they liked anything.

Preheat the oven to its max (approximately 240°C).

Season the lamb with salt and pepper and a little olive oil and place in a roasting pan. When the oven has reached its full heat, add the lamb and roast for 30 minutes. Turn the oven down to 130°C, cover the lamb with foil and cook slowly for 1½ hours.

While the lamb is cooking, make the puttanesca sauce. Fry the onion in olive oil. Once it is translucent, mash in the anchovies, add the garlic and cook through. Pour in the wine and cook down, scraping any caught bits in the pan back into the sauce. Add the tomatoes, olives and 50 g of capers. Stir and cook on low heat for 15 minutes. Stir in the lemon juice and adjust the seasoning with salt and a little sugar so it is in balance (but only if needed – those capers and olives will add lots of salt). Stir in half the chilli (if using) and half the parsley. Cook for 10 minutes or so longer to combine the flavours.

When the lamb has been cooking for 1½ hours, pour the sauce over the lamb and return it to the oven for 30 minutes. When the lamb has been in the oven for 20 minutes, cook the pasta in well-salted boiling water until *al dente* – or still a little firm to the bite. Drain and toss with a little olive oil.

The lamb should be almost ready now, so dry the remaining capers on paper towel and then fry in a little olive oil until they are crispy. Drain again on paper towel.

Serve the dish at the table with little pasta grains and garnish with the crispy capers, lemon zest, the remaining chopped parsley and diced chilli (if using). Do use it as it's jolly nice!

SERVES 6

1.5 kg lamb shoulder
salt flakes and freshly ground
   black pepper
olive oil
1 large brown onion, diced
25 g anchovy fillets (best and
   pinkest you can find)
3 garlic cloves, crushed
125 ml (½ cup) red wine
1 × 400 g can whole tomatoes
150 g (1¼ cups) black olives,
   drained (ideally choose olives
   without stones, but even if they
   are pitted do check them before
   you add them to the sauce)
200 g (1 cup) capers, washed
   and drained
zest and juice of ½ lemon
2 long red chillies, seeded and
   deveined, chopped (optional)
sugar
bunch flat-leaf parsley,
   finely chopped
1 × 500 g pack pasta (orzo or
   risoni are ideal, or failing that,
   egg tagliatelle)

TIP: If you want to be fancy, you could top the lamb and pasta with a fine tangle of kataifi pastry and bake it at 180°C until it's golden. This would add some crunch to the dish.

TIP: The puttanesca sauce is delicious without the lamb. Use normal spaghetti instead of small pasta though and just top with a little finely grated parmesan to add an extra layer of savouriness before sprinkling on the crispy capers, fresh chilli and chopped parsley.

TRADITIONAL 3-HOUR STEW WITH LIGHT HERB DUMPLINGS

4 rashers bacon, diced

400 g (about 3) brown onions, sliced

3 celery stalks, string removed and cut into crescents

olive oil, for frying

1 small head garlic, peeled and crushed, and chopped

1.5 kg stewing steak

160 g (1 cup) plain flour

1 teaspoon salt flakes

freshly ground black pepper

250 ml (1 cup) sherry

1 good tap of Worcestershire sauce

1 litre (4 cups) beef stock

1 × 400 g can whole tomatoes

3 fresh bay leaves

1 heaped teaspoon Vegemite (or 3 anchovies if you aren't Australian)

140 g tomato paste

500 ml (2 cups) apple cider

400 g sweet potato, peeled and cut into large chunks

400 g carrots, topped, peeled and cut into rounds

400 g parsnips, topped, peeled and cut into 3 pieces (top cut in half and end by itself)

400 g swedes, topped, peeled and cut into 8 pieces

HERB DUMPLINGS

½ teaspoon salt

grind of black pepper

200g (1¼ cups) self-raising flour

100 g frozen butter

125 ml (1½ cups) milk and a splash more

¼ cup chopped herbs – any will do, like parsley, chervil, thyme, oregano, chives, even sage

This is my mum's stew. Although the picture only has half the dumplings that my mum or this recipe requires due to the crew eating them before the picture was taken.

Fry the bacon, onion and celery in a little olive oil in the largest flameproof casserole you have. Add the garlic. Soften. Then remove everything from the pan and reserve.

Now brown the beef for the stew. Toss the meat in seasoned flour. To do this easily, take a clean but evil plastic bag (with no holes mind) and fill with the flour, salt and a very good grind of black pepper. Throw in your meat, hold the mouth of the bag shut (yes, this is important) and shake. Remove the floured meat from the bag, shaking off any excess.

In four or five batches, brown the meat in the onion pan with the rendered bacon fat and some extra oil. Remove when each batch of meat has turned brown. Reserve with the onions.

Now deglaze the pan. Pour in the sherry, which will sizzle. Using a wooden spoon, scrape away all the tasty brown stuff thus 'deglazing the pan. When the sherry has bubbled away to half its volume add the Worcestershire sauce, the beef, the onion mixture, the stock, the tomatoes, the bay leaves, Vegemite (or anchovies), the tomato paste and the cider. Stir as you bring this to the boil.

Preheat the oven to 160°C.

Stir half the veg into the pan. Once the stew hits the boil, reduce the heat to a gentle simmer, cover and cook in the oven slowly for 90 minutes. After 90 minutes, throw in the other half of the veg and stir. This will knock some of the soft edges off the cooked veg and thicken the sauce more. Return to the oven. We do this in two batches because the first batch will break down into a magnificent gravy with a rooty sweetness. The latter batch adds texture. Cook for another hour or so. Add your dumplings 20 minutes before you want to eat.

HERB DUMPLINGS Season the flour, then grate in the frozen butter which is another trick I picked up from the wonderful Rose Gray at the River Café. (I think it was an Aussie pastry chef who first showed her this!) Rub these together gently with your fingers so the flour and butter gets a texture like pale breadcrumbs. Splash in the milk a little at a time until the mixture becomes a pillowy soft dough. I find you usually need a splash (about ⅛ of a cup) extra to bring all the crumbs together into a sticky mass. Remember, a wetter dough gives softer results. Like when making scones, I use a blunt knife to 'cut in' the milk at first. Don't overwork it. Roll the dough into 13 dumplings and pop them on top of the stew. The dough is quite sticky so flouring your hands will help shape it into balls – but this isn't essential. I usually can't be bothered or forget.

Cover and leave to cook until the dumplings have swollen to twice their size and are cooked. Eat the unlucky 13th dumpling to check if they are all cooked through.

MUM'S CABBAGE ROLLS

8 large white drumhead
   cabbage leaves
4 onions, finely chopped
1½ teaspoons ground cumin
   (depending on how much you like)
2 tablespoons olive oil
2 × 400 g cans crushed tomatoes
3 tablespoons tomato purée
1 lemon
300 g chook mince
300 g sausage meat
4 tablespoons packeted sage and
   onion stuffing (available in the
   supermarket)
80 g butter, and a little more
   for dotting
½ cup chopped flat-leaf parsley
salt flakes or sugar, to taste
70 g (about 1 cup) fresh
   breadcrumbs
120 g (1 cup) grated tasty cheese

TIPS: Separating the leaves from the cabbage without tearing them can be a challenge but there are a couple of tricks. Route one is to wash your cabbage, pat it dry, wrap it in plastic wrap and pop it in the freezer for a couple days. Thaw out the cabbage in the fridge the day before you need 'em. When thawed the leaves should pull way far more easily.

Another method is to microwave the cleaned cabbage head on a low heat setting for 10 minutes. Once cool enough to handle, peel the leaves off. If you find the cabbage leaves aren't as supple once you're down a few layers, reheat for a few more minutes as needed.

This is the dish that I crave when I go back to my mum's house in London. The sausage meat might not be traditional, or even very good for you, but this is a peasant dish that is all about maximum flavour for minimum price. Tasty but mean – that's me all over! This is the amount for four people but I'd usually make double as these rolls are also really very good the day after too.

Put a big pot of salted water on to boil.

Trim the cabbage leaves into squares and then dunk them in the boiling water for 1–2 minutes to soften. Drain, pat dry and leave them to cool.

Preheat the oven to 160°C.

Make a simple tomato sauce by frying off half an onion with the cumin seeds in half the oil. Then when they are golden throw in the cans of crushed tomatoes, a tablespoon of the tomato purée and a long strip of lemon peel. Season. Cook slowly to thicken.

Throw the remaining onion into the hot oil in a large frying pan. Cook at a low heat until translucent and then mix in the meats. Stir, breaking up the meat with a wooden spoon. Cook until they start to change colour – about 3–5 minutes.

Boil a kettle. You'll find out why in a moment.

Now stir in the stuffing, ½ tablespoon of tomato purée, half the butter and half the parsley. Mix into the meat. Pour in boiling water to bind this filling. You'll need about a cup but start off slowly stirring it in and watching it absorb. Cook for a few minutes, adding boiling water as required. You want the meat and stuffing to be malleable and not too dry.

Use the remaining butter to grease a baking dish that will hold the cabbage rolls snugly.

Spread out a cabbage leaf and fill with an eighth of the filling. Roll up the cabbage leaf and place in the baking tray join-side down, so the plump, filled face gazes up at you. Repeat seven more times.

Check the seasoning of the tomato sauce and adjust with lemon juice, salt or a little sugar if required. Pour the hot tomato sauce over the cabbage rolls and cover with foil. Bake for 25 minutes.

Remove the foil. Check with a metal skewer or meat thermometer that the rolls are cooked through. Return to the oven sprinkled with the breadcrumbs, cheese, the remaining parsley and a few dots of butter. Bake until the topping is golden and bubbly in places. Serve with potatoes baked in their jackets.

SERVES 4

MINI MEATLOAF

A brilliant tip for making the perfect creamy mash with hardly any butter and without any cream, plus Australia's most desired recipe revised into a cute, handy size that the kids will love. Quick too. 'Nuff said.

Preheat the oven to 180°C.

To make the potato topping, peel and cut the potatoes into large chunks. Keep the peel aside. Place the potatoes in a large saucepan of cold water and bring to the boil. Reduce the heat just a bit and when cooked, turn off the heat, drain the potatoes and return them to the hot dry saucepan to steam dry.

While the potatoes are cooking, place the milk and potato peelings in another saucepan and bring to a gentle boil. Reduce the heat to a low simmer for about 10 minutes to release the starch from the skins but most of all flavour the milk. Turn off the heat and leave to sit.

Mash the potatoes with the butter, salt and pepper, strain the milk and add to the potatoes a bit at a time until you have a smooth consistency. Keep warm until ready to use.

To make the meatloaf, mix the mince, onion and garlic together. Stir in the oats, then add the egg and mix. Stir in the milk. Pull mixture together but do not overwork it. Season with salt and pepper.

Lightly spray a 6-hole giant muffin tin with oil. Press the meat mixture into each hole until about three-quarters full. Bake in the oven for 10 minutes.

To make the glaze, heat all the glaze ingredients in a small saucepan over medium heat until it looks thick and syrupy. Taste and adjust the seasoning. Add a little extra Worcestershire sauce if it is too thick.

Take the tin out of the oven and brush each mini meatloaf with a generous layer of glaze. Return to the oven and bake for a further 10 minutes.

Remove the tin from the oven and change the oven setting to grill.

Top each little meatloaf with lashings of warm mashed potato. Run a knife around the edge to prevent the potato sticking to the edge of the tin. Brush the butter and/or sprinkle grated cheese over the top, slide under the grill for a couple of minutes until a golden crust forms.

MAKES 6

1 kg beef mince
½ red onion, finely chopped
3 garlic cloves, peeled and finely chopped
125 g (1 cup) rolled oats
1 large egg
125 ml (½ cup) milk

POTATO TOPPING
750 g (5 medium–large) washed potatoes
200 ml milk
20 g butter, melted
salt flakes
freshly ground black pepper
40 g butter
60 g grated cheese, to top

GLAZE
125 ml (½ cup) tomato sauce
1 tablespoon Worcestershire sauce
2 tablespoons brown sugar (the darker the better)
1 tablespoon mustard (Dijon is best)
½ teaspoon cayenne pepper (optional)

CHICKEN, LEEK
AND THYME PIES

1 kg chicken thigh fillets
2 carrots
2 celery stalks
1 onion
2 tablespoons olive oil
8 sprigs thyme
salt flakes and freshly ground
   black pepper
3 small leeks, white part only,
   trimmed and washed
1 tablespoon butter
250 ml (1 cup) white wine
3 tablespoons plain flour
150 ml (just over ½ cup) cream
grated zest of 1 lemon
100 g (about ¾ cup) fresh or frozen
   baby peas
2 sheets ready-made shortcrust
   pastry for the base
1 egg, beaten to seal and glaze pastry
2 sheets of ready-made puff pastry
   for the top

If chickens loved leeks anymore they'd probably all spontaneously turn into plumbers and start wearing low-slung jeans to go out on jobs. It's probably also why this recipe calls for double thyme.

Trim the chicken thighs of excess fat and cut into small chunks.

Finely chop the carrots, celery and onion.

Heat about 1 tablespoon of oil in a large frying pan and add the chopped vegetables, along with the thyme, and cook for a few minutes, then add the chicken and cook for another 5 minutes. Pour enough water into the pan to barely cover the chicken, season with salt and pepper and bring to the boil, then turn down the heat and simmer for about 1 hour.

Meanwhile, finely chop the leeks. Heat the remaining oil and the butter in a non-stick frying pan, add the leeks and gently cook for about 5 minutes. Add the wine and continue to simmer until reduced by half. Add the flour and cook for 1 minute. Pour in the cream, then remove 200 ml of the chicken cooking stock and add to the leeks. Add the lemon zest, season well with salt and pepper, and continue cooking for another 10 minutes.

When the chicken has finished cooking, remove the sprigs of thyme, and add the leeks. If the mixture is too watery, continue to simmer until you have a thick and creamy consistency. Add the peas last, check the seasoning, turn off the heat, and leave to cool completely.

Preheat the oven to 180°C.

When the chicken has cooled, line 6 individual pie cases with the shortcrust pastry. Divide the chicken between them and brush the edges of the pastry with the beaten egg. Cover each pie case with the puff pastry. Trim away the excess pastry around the edges and crimp with a fork. Brush each pie top with the beaten egg, place on a baking tray in the oven, and bake for about 25–30 minutes until the pastry is golden brown.

MAKES 6 PIES

CHICKEN, CAPSICUM, CHICKPEA, CHILLI AND CRUSHED TOMATOES ON COUSCOUS
(WITH CORIANDER)

olive oil, for frying
1 kg chicken thigh fillets
1 large red onion, sliced
2 red capsicums, seeded and
    chopped into large pieces
2 × 400 g cans crushed tomatoes
1 × 60 ml bottle Tabasco sauce
1 bunch coriander, chopped
2 × 420 g cans chickpeas, rinsed
    and well drained
3 long red chillies (add to taste,
    depending on how spicy you
    like things), split
salt flakes
couscous, to serve

Just like Skyhooks, we're living in the 7Cs and the seven C words that make up this dish create a really tasty and really healthy braise that will feed up to eight pretty darn cheaply. I also call this dish C7s because it's an even more explosive dish than C5. That's a Dad joke. I'm sorry. I can't help myself. My sister came up with this recipe. She's that sort of overly virtuous woman, at least when it comes to cooking. She refuses even to fry the onions when making the base for a braise like this. This dish has become her party piece and even though I am partial to more than my fair share of animal fats I'm a bit addicted to the textures that make this dish fun to eat – and I don't even notice it's healthy. I do use a little oil to fry the onion because, well, I'm fallible and human. So fallible that if you count carefully you can find eight ingredients beginning with C in this dish!

Heat a heavy-based pot with a splash of oil. Throw in the chicken to get a lot of colour before adding the onion, capsicum and tomatoes. Fry until the chicken is opaque but still a little soft.

Splash in a good glug of Tabasco, the amount depending on your chilli tolerance. This will add a funky tangy edge to the braise, as well as heat. Stir in half the coriander. Simmer gently for 20 minutes.

Add the chickpeas to the pan and cook for a further 10 minutes. This step maintains some texture in the chickpeas.

Season to taste with more Tabasco and salt before serving.

Garnish with the red chillies and the remaining coriander leaves. Serve with that bottle of hot sauce and loads of buttered couscous – just make sure you don't tell your sister you've buttered it or else you'll be in *sooooooo* much trouble.

SERVES 8

TEATIME

SOME THOUGHTS ON FAMILY, RECIPES
AND WHY TEATIME IS THE MOST CONSERVATIVE OF MEALS

Nations have museums and history books, families have dining traditions and family recipe books.

The food that we cherish has often been part of the DNA of the family passed along the branches of the family tree, whether through dishes from the old country recreated with the ingredients of the new, or a very direct link to a loved and lost relation. Few things are more precious than that recipe for gnocchi just like Nonna used to make, or baking the cake that your grandmother used to recall making with her own grandmother when she made it for you.

These dishes and foods offer the most tangible connection, one that engages all five senses, plus that final and most evocative of senses – our memory. (While we could argue long and hard about whether memory really is a sense – and goodness knows I have – I am sure we can all agree that memory can intensify what we perceive with our senses, hardwiring them into our emotions.)

Ask me what I would save in a fire? Well, other than the kids, the woman I love and the photos, it would have to be the family recipe books. I am lucky to have family recipe books that date back centuries. The printed ones complete with fading handwritten copperplate pencil 'notes to cook' in the margin, the ones on scraps of torn-out and yellowing newsprint splattered and stained with cake mix and batter from over fifty years ago.

Most precious of all is a little leather-bound volume full of hand-written 'receipts' dated on the first page, '1765'. There is something quite moving and very intimate about reading through recipes for beef à la mode and lemon pudding, imagining the flickering lamp light, the hustle of a Georgian household and wondering at the love of food that demanded that this heirloom be crafted.

The world then was on the cusp of great change. While Catherine II of Russia was revolutionising vodka production, Europe's first restaurant opened in Paris and Dr James Baker opened the first chocolate factory in the US. Politically these were uncertain days. The storm clouds of revolution were gathering in France and the Americas. In that year the British Parliament enacted the Quartering Act and Stamp Act that would lead to almost immediate insurrection and to the famous war cry of the 13 colonies – 'no taxation without representation'.

I've drawn on a few of these recipes through the book but it is here in Teatime that they seem most appropriate, which isn't necessarily a surprise given that teatime is perhaps the most conservative of the seven main meals of the day. While what we eat for dinner and lunch seems to change beyond recognition every generation, and whole mealtimes may appear, like brunch, or disappear, like high tea, teatime remains stiffly unyielding; a time of cake and biscuits, crumpets and biscuits and always a lovely cup of tea. These four biscuits (on pages 187–188) all go wonderfully with a nice cuppa.

JENNIFER'S FLAPJACKS

100 g demerara sugar
200 g butter
3 rounded tablespoons
  golden syrup
300 g rolled oats

TIP: Feel free to experiment by adding nuts, fruit or ginger (powdered or preserved) to your flapjacks. Or why not substitute more molasses, rich brown sugar or honey for the demerara or the golden syrup?

Now here's a controversial family recipe and all thanks to the confusion of the name. My mother scarred a generation of teenage American girls by offering them flapjacks for tea when what turned up weren't the pancakes they were expecting but a sort of Shakespearian muesli bar. While some Australian guests were expecting a plate of Balmain bugs, such is their nickname. It could have been worse, they could have fled fearing that my mum would turn all Mario Milano or Double H on them and face-slam them into the canvas. You see, the flapjack is a wrestling throw that is also, rather confusingly, known as the pancake slam. The fact is the name 'flapjack' predates all of these by a good couple of centuries and refers to a flat baking tin in which this perfect sweet and chewy oatcake was made in Britain, the Isle of Man and Newfoundland. Shakespeare loved flapjacks so much he even had Pericles offer them as an inducement in his play about the long-suffering Prince of Tyre. You see, this book is more than just recipes and mawkish sentiment. There are edifying facts here too.

Preheat the oven to 160°C. Grease and line an 18 cm × 27 cm slice tin.

In a saucepan over medium heat, combine the sugar, butter and golden syrup. Stir in the oats. Press the mixture into the tin and bake in the oven for 20–25 minutes, or until golden brown.

Let the slice cool off a bit before cutting into tiles or triangles, which are my favourite shape. Please note, however, that in some parts of Britain triangular flapjacks are banned at schools due to concerns about their sharp corners. True.

MAKES 15 SLICES

4 WAYS WITH BISCUITS

1. STORING BISCUITS 1765

When my grandfather died he left me the family cookbook that was handwritten in 1765. Among the 'receipts', for everything from oyster ketchup to worming powder, is the curious recipe for 'storing biscuits'. The sugar and coriander combination is intriguingly moreish and the part-bready, part-cakey texture might hint at where the US got their use of the word 'biscuit' for their crusty scone-like creations.

4 eggs
250 g sugar
50 g coriander seeds
150 g (1 cup) plain flour
sugar for sifting

'Take 4 eggs and beat them an hour, strewing in sugar till you have put in half a pound. Put in 2 ounces of coriander seed. Stir in 5 ounces of flower (sic). Put in buttered paper pans. Sift a little sugar on the top. Cook in ovan (sic) rather quick.'

The recipe is reproduced word for word but I'd suggest using an electric whisk for 10 minutes rather than a hand one for an hour. The coriander seeds we get today are much fresher and more potent so best reduce the quantity of seeds to 50 grams. I use a small muffin tin filled about one-third to half, rather than 'paper pans' and bake in a moderate (170°C) for 15 minutes.

MAKES 36

2. TARA'S MACAROONS NOT MACARONS

Macaron or macaroon? What is it with biscuits and language? The main differences are that these –oons are quicker to make, use coconut and don't have a filling made from something weird and trendy like black olive, kaffir lime or ocelot.

2 egg whites
100 g (scant ½ cup) caster sugar
160 g (1¾ cups) desiccated coconut

Preheat the oven to 180°C (160°–170°C for fan-forced ovens).
Whisk the egg whites to firm peaks, then fold in the sugar and coconut until they lightly come together. Using two dessertspoons shape the mixture into small balls the size of walnuts. Place on a lightly greased baking tray and bake in the centre of the oven for 12 minutes, until very lightly golden. Transfer to a wire rack to cool.
Store in an airtight container for up to one week.

MAKES 18

TIP: If you are making these with little kids you can whisk the egg whites, sugar and coconut all together and then shape the mixture into balls using wet hands but I find this has a slightly heavier and less consistent outcome.

3. GINGERBREAD 1765

Gingerbread was brought to France in 992 by an Armenian monk but this was more a spiced bread rather than the gingerbread biscuits that the English and Germans preferred. The Germans made houses out of it for Christmas; the English reached back to their pagan roots by shaping it into gingerbread men, which was something of a craze in the reign of Good Queen Bess. The Virgin Queen, more than anyone in the kingdom, knew that good men were hard to find – and at least a gingerbread man wouldn't plot to return England to the Catholic fold. This family recipe dates from the reign of Mad King George the Third. Perhaps that's why the biscuits are to be shaped 'into what shape you likes'. The original 1765 recipe is published here in full – or more accurately 'in short' as old recipes tend to assume you know stuff!

1½ lb (680 g) of flower
½ lb (225 g) of butter (at room temperature obviously, cos in 1765 they didn't have fridges)
½ lb (225 g) of sugar
1 lb (450 g) of treacle
½ ounce (14 g; 1 tablespoon) of powdered ginger (or a quantity that pleases you)
1 teaspoon bicarbonate of soda

'Mix them all well together then form them into what shape you likes and bake them on iron sheets.'

I reckon the best interpretation of this recipe is to beat the butter and sugar together until light and creamy, then beat in the treacle. Next fold in the plain flour sifted together with the ginger and bicarbonate of soda. Shape into walnut-sized balls and press onto baking trays greased with butter. Bake in a preheated 180°C oven for about 15 minutes, or until cooked so the middles are still moist.

MAKES 60

4. CHOCOLATE AFGHANS

Are we allowed to call them that? Or more importantly why are they called that? Did Afghan cameleers have a thing for cornflakes and chocolate? And are these biscuits really originally from New Zealand? And if so, why? Did they have cameleers there too? No biscuit poses as many questions, but one thing I do know is that my friend, Jen, is an inspirational baker. She gave me her chocolate Afghan recipe on which this recipe is based. It is bit more effort than other recipes but it is also very forgiving. Is the extra work worth it? The answer has to be yes – or more accurately, check out that empty biscuit tin!

60 g (2 cups) cornflakes
220 g butter, softened
110 g (½ cup) caster sugar
1 teaspoon vanilla extract
150 g (1 cup) self-raising flour
75 g (½ cup) plain flour
3 tablespoons cocoa powder
2 tablespoons desiccated coconut

ICING
15 g (2 heaped teaspoons) butter
125 g (1 cup) icing sugar
1 level tablespoon cocoa powder
few drops vanilla extract
1 tablespoon boiling water (you could add a further ½ teaspoon to make the icing more workable)

Preheat the oven to 180°C.

Using a rolling pin or other blunt instrument, lightly crush the cornflakes in a plastic bag.

Cream the butter, sugar and vanilla together until light. Sift the flours and cocoa together and add the lightly crushed cornflakes and coconut. Add to the butter/sugar mixture and mix thoroughly. Form into walnut-sized balls and place on baking trays lined with silicon or baking paper. The mixture may be a little crumbly but it holds when baked.

Bake for about 12 minutes. Remove the biscuits from the trays and leave to cool on a wire rack. Ice when cool.

To make the icing, first melt the butter. Sift the icing sugar together with the cocoa. Add the melted butter, a few drops of vanilla and then the boiling water. Beat well. Use while still warm. (This icing will thicken as it cools so to make it more workable warm the mixing bowl gently before you start. If you prefer a thick dollop of icing, allow to cool more before using.)

MAKES 18

LIME CORDIAL AND SUMMER

Summer seems to bring back some of my most vivid memories from the past. There's something about the longer days and the sunshine that also makes these memories rosier. Maybe it's all those 'happy' endorphins that sun helps your body release.

Those endless warm days of summer that, combined with the longest holiday, seemed to promote the formation of gangs and reduced the attention of those who were looking after us. It didn't seem to matter whether this was hanging out with your mates on the beach until dusk turned the blue waters inky, or batting in endless games of park cricket where the innings seemed realistically epic for those with dreams of being Bradman, Botham or Brian (Lara, of course, not Booth or Close). These days all seemed to be punctuated by large groups of kids running just a little bit feral. And of memories of crushed sandwiches eaten too late in the day, now compressed and soggy; tomato oozing through the bread so that we'd laugh at how it looked like our skinned knees after the inevitable stacks that came from living in the saddle of a beaten up Malvern Star, Chopper or BMX.

The other fondest memories of food that I have vividly of those summer times are sweet. Of fruit 'scrumped', as we like to euphemistically describe our short-panted, daylight robbery. Of ice lollies melting stickily down fist and into tight little hands – the sort of tight little hands that could take a full-length, high-speed sprawl on the cheese-grater rough tarmac of the playground and still come up having not let go of your Splice.

In fact, I seem to recall everything being done at only two speeds – full-speed ahead or shambling. Normally the pace was decided by how many of you there were … Two of us would always lope; perhaps back from some stream in that particular honey-warm light at the end of the day with caught sticklebacks in jam jars, sucking at fingers pricked from the briars along the banks. Get over five kids together, however, and everything was done at a pell-mell pace with a siren roar of shouting to accompany it. I think that the only times we stopped were to career into someone's kitchen for a refuel of cordial. Sweet but tart homemade cordial, with large bergs of ice cubes that we'd suck like cut-price gobstoppers bulging our cheeks like bullfrogs. The cordial was always drunk out of scarred, plastic beakers that skilled eight-year-olds could dropkick more than eight feet after they'd drained 'em … twice. Sure, OK, it wasn't always homemade but that was when it was best.

I largely remember it was pulled from where it hid in the dark in the cupboard under the sink, invariably and irresponsibly left next to the bleach and Drano, like a silent natural selection test. This whole forbidden, 'danger Will Robinson' nature of homemade cordial was heightened by the fact it always seemed to be in old whisky bottles with faded, partially scraped off, labels like something out of an illegal Irish poteen still.

CONTINUED OVERLEAF →

LIME CORDIAL AND SUMMER (CONT.)

My mum bought her lurid cordial from the supermarket in plastic flagons. No, I don't remember feeling any shame. She liked convenience but while there is a long list of things that are generally too much of a fag to make oneself – such as balsamic vinegar, puff pastry, oyster sauce, Vegemite and kids' baked beans – cordial is a cinch. And making it comes with three big benefits. First, you can make it far more tart than most of the commercial ones; second, it actually tastes like the fruit you've made it from; and, finally, you get to see quite how much sugar goes in to making the cordial which means you'll be more cautious about how much you use. The other big excitement is that you get to throw in loads of spooky white powders like those trendy modern chefs do, which will make you feel bang up to date even though this recipe is about forty years old!

So, here's how to do it. Happy summer!

Oh and remember … make this cordial when the citrus you want to use is in season, like when limes are 30 cents each and not $1.90. This recipe will work with lemons, oranges or a combination of citrus.

Using a clean potato peeler (if you have one – if not, wash it you dirty thing, or use a knife) peel long strips of the zest off just five of the limes.

Juice all the limes and keep the juice (obviously).

Bring the water to the boil with the lime zest.

Mix the sugar and powders together.

Now pour the combined sugar and crazy white science powders into the boiling water. Stir until dissolved. Boil for 3 minutes. Remove from the heat. Pour in the lime juice, ideally pouring it through a fine sieve to remove any little bits of flesh that might make your cordial cloudy.

Bring the cordial back to the boil and then gently simmer for 2 minutes. Remove from the heat and leave to cool.

Remove the zest. Now bottle in sterile containers – ideally 2 old Johnny Walker bottles if you want to keep with tradition.

Allow to settle for a day before using.

MAKES ABOUT 2 LITRES

10 limes
1 litre (4 cups) water
1.32 kg (6 cups) sugar
2 teaspoons citric acid
1 tablespoon tartaric acid

HOT CROSS BUNS

200 ml milk
25 g fresh yeast
50 g (a scant ¼ cup) caster sugar
500 g (3⅓ cups) strong
  white bread flour
100 g butter, diced
1 teaspoon salt
1 teaspoon ground ginger
3 teaspoons mixed spice
¼ teaspoon ground allspice
2 eggs, lightly beaten
200 g sultanas
50 g mixed peel

PASTE
60 g plain flour
60 ml (¼ cup) water
pinch of salt

GLAZE
2 tablespoons caster sugar
2 tablespoons boiling water

Like doing a marathon or making a quilt, making hot cross buns is about the journey as much as the self-satisfaction of reaching the destination. Yes, these hot cross buns are better than the ones you buy from the shops – especially when warm from the oven – but do it for the joy of the bake rather than to save money, or to have something that's revelatory compared to the best supermarket HCBs. Oh, and never underestimate the line 'yes, I baked these hot cross buns myself'!

Bring milk up to blood temperature, then mix with the yeast and 1 teaspoon of the sugar.

Tip the flour into a large mixing bowl and add the butter. Rub in with your fingertips, or process in a food processor, until well mixed, then add the rest of the sugar, the salt, ginger and spices.

Make a well in the centre of the flour mixture, and add the beaten eggs and the yeast mixture. Mix together to make a soft dough. Tip onto a well-floured benchtop and knead for 10 minutes until smooth and elastic, keep adding flour as required.

Lightly grease another bowl and put the dough into it. Cover with plastic wrap and leave in a warm place until it has doubled in size – this will take 2–3 hours.

Tip the dough out onto a lightly greased work surface and knead for a minute or so, then flatten it out and scatter over the sultanas and peel. Knead again to spread the fruit evenly, then divide into 16 equal pieces. Roll into round balls and using your thumbs smooth out the top of each ball, pushing the dough underneath with your fingertips until you have a smooth top surface.

Place into a short-sided roasting dish about 1.5 cm apart, and leave covered for another 3 hours.

Preheat the oven to 200°C, 20 minutes before using.

PASTE
Mix the plain flour and water with the salt to make a smooth paste. Using a piping bag or teaspoon, draw a thick cross on the top of each bun. If the buns have joined together you can do this in a continuous line. Place into the hot oven and bake for about 25 minutes until golden.

GLAZE
Meanwhile, mix the sugar with the water. Brush the buns with the glaze as soon as they come out of the oven. Eat hot with lashings of butter.

MAKES 16

SALTED-CARAMEL BANANA BREAD CUPCAKES

250 g (1⅔ cups) plain flour
1 teaspoon bicarbonate of soda
1 teaspoon baking powder
pinch of salt
¼ teaspoon mixed spice
125 g butter, at room temperature
220 g (1 cup, firmly packed)
   brown sugar
2 large eggs
1 teaspoon vanilla extract
100 g sour cream
2 over-ripe bananas, mashed

SALTED CARAMEL

225 g sugar
2 tablespoons liquid glucose
60 ml (¼ cup) water
130 ml pure cream
30 g butter, cubed
½ teaspoon salt flakes

CARAMEL BUTTER ICING

250 g butter, softened
700 g icing sugar, sifted
225 g salted caramel (recipe
   above – save the rest for
   a treat in your fridge)

TIP: Leftover caramel sauce can be stored in the refrigerator and is delicious over ice cream or puddings.

All the virtuous, waste-saving goodness of banana bread but in a handy lunchbox-sized cupcake; and more good news, because they are cupcakes you also get some delicious buttery, salty caramel icing.

Preheat your oven to 170°C.

Sift together the flour, bicarb soda, baking powder, salt and spice.

Cream the butter and sugar in an electric mixer until light and fluffy, scrape the bottom of the bowl with a spatula to make sure all of the butter and sugar are combined.

Turn down to medium speed and beat in the eggs one at a time, and the vanilla extract. Add half of the flour mixture, the sour cream, banana, then the rest of the flour. Stir the mixture by hand with a spatula to ensure everything is completely combined and divide between 12 cupcake cases. Bake in the oven for about 20 minutes until done.

SALTED CARAMEL

In a medium-sized saucepan, combine the sugar and glucose, then pour the water around the edge of the sugar. Carefully stir the sugar to combine the ingredients, ensuring that the dry sugar does not touch the side of the pan. Bring to the boil and stop stirring, just give a little swirl once in a while to even out the cooking. Continue to cook until the caramel turns a dark amber colour, then remove from the heat and let stand for about 30 seconds. Pour the cream into the mixture. The mixture will bubble up significantly and is very hot. Return to the heat and continue stirring while adding the butter bit by bit. Add the salt, remove from the heat and allow to cool.

CARAMEL BUTTER ICING

Beat the butter in an electric mixer until very soft. Add three-quarters of the icing sugar to the butter and beat until it is light and fluffy.Begin adding the cooled salted caramel. Add the rest of the icing sugar until the frosting is at the desired consistency.

MAKES 12 CUPCAKES

CHOCOLATE
CARAMEL MUFFINS

I love a surprise. Sorry, I should qualify that statement. I like a *nice* surprise, like flowers or a kiss when you least expect it, rather than discovering a snake in your sleeping bag or that the gun *was* still loaded. Those aren't nice surprises. These muffins are surprising for three nice reasons:

1   Unlike most muffins they don't taste of horse chaff but of really light chocolate cake instead

2   They might taste like really light chocolate cake but they've still got a wonderful crusty muffin top – no sniggering now

3   When you bite into them and they're still warm there's a little burst of chewy caramel in the middle, as if someone from the celestial re-engineering company has reinvented the doughnut for chocoholics who don't like dough!

Now here's the thing, if you are eating the cupcakes warm, the caramels will still be melty and oozy but the caramels will firm up as the cupcakes cool. So if you are going to eat all or some of the cupcakes cold, make sure you place something with soft caramel in the middle of those ones. Ideally, use a Caramello Koala buried Jimmy Hoffa-style in the middle of the cake mix. If the kids are helping, lose the mafia hit references and just say that Mr Koala is tired and having a little rest tucked up in his chocolate bed.

Preheat the oven to 180°C.

Cream the butter and sugar in an electric mixer and beat in the eggs one at a time.

In a separate bowl, mix together the flour, baking powder, bicarb soda, salt and cocoa and gently fold the dry ingredients into the butter and sugar, alternating with the cream and water until everything is combined. Do not overmix.

Divide the cake mixture into 6–8 giant muffin cases and push 3 of the caramel chews or chocolate pieces into the centre of each muffin, until they are completely submerged but not touching the bottom.

Bake the muffins for 20 minutes and serve warm while the caramel is still runny.

MAKES 6–8 GIANT MUFFINS

185 g butter, at room temperature
160 g raw caster sugar
2 eggs
230 g plain flour
3 teaspoons baking powder
½ teaspoon bicarbonate of soda
½ teaspoon salt
60 g good-quality cocoa powder
85 ml cream
85 ml water
18 caramel chews or 8 caramel-filled chocolates such as Caramello Koalas, broken in half

MEXICAN HAM
AND CORN MUFFINS

600 g (4 cups) self-raising flour
1 tablespoon caster sugar
2 teaspoons baking powder
1 red capsicum, diced
1 green capsicum, diced
1 × 225 g can corn kernels, drained
200 g gypsy ham, roughly sliced
  into lengths
100 g (1¼ cups) grated parmesan
  cheese
240 g (2 cups) grated tasty cheese
100 g feta cheese, cubed
1 teaspoon salt flakes
4 eggs, lightly beaten
375 ml (1½ cups) milk
250 ml (1 cup) olive oil
125 g (½ cup) sour cream

TIP: If you want to turn these
lunchbox snacks into something
more – without putting an old Colt
1851 Navy revolver in one hand and
the works of Francisco Madero in the
other – serve them with a salad of
cubed avocado, fresh lime, the finely
diced flesh of a green or jalapeno
chilli, a chopped bunch of coriander
and half an iceberg lettuce. Sweet
chilli sauce goes very well with these
muffins too, as does sour cream.

There are certain things I don't like – preserved lemon that tastes like toilet lollies, bigots, and above all muffins. In cafés, they serve the role of a guilt-free snack that tastes like windmill sweepings and that is obviously only guilt-free because eating them is a penance to rival walking to Rome on your knees along a very gravelly road. In kids' lunchboxes they fill the muffin-sized hole that all kids' lunchboxes are, by law, dictated to have. No wonder our teenagers give us so much trouble after six years of dusty apple, cinnamon and bran monstrosities.

There are, in fact, only two ways to make muffins fun – well, three if you use them for softball practice. The first is to overload them with too much, say, chocolate and salty caramel (see page 203). The other is to dress your muffin up in a poncho, sombrero and comedy Zapata moustache. If you can't find a sombrero small enough, then try this savoury muffin recipe.

Preheat the oven to 200°C.

Mix the first three ingredients together. That's the flour, sugar and baking powder. Now mix in the next five. That's the capsicums, corn, ham, cheeses and salt.

Mix together the eggs, milk and olive oil. They will look messy and don't need to combine just to marble each other.

Stir this wet combo into the flour and veg mix to make a sludgy mess.

Spoon the Mexican sludge into your favourite greased muffin tins, safe in the knowledge that this dish will resurrect itself from the sorry situation it seems to find itself in at this moment.

Now bake the soon-to-be-muffins for 25 minutes, or until the tops are brown and the middle is cooked but not dried out. Test with a skewer – or just break one apart and eat!

If you are using a giant or Texas muffin tin, drop the temperature by 20°C as it will take longer for the muffins to cook through and you don't want them over-browning before they're cooked.

Turn out the muffins onto a wire rack to cool or eat immediately, while they are still warm. Good times!

Repeat the tin-filling and baking process until all the mixture is used and your kitchen benches are covered with so many muffins it looks like Pancho Villa's División del Norte is attacking Zacatecas from all sides.

If you want to make the muffins more adult, add some fresh chilli rings, a little paprika and some finely crushed coriander and cumin seeds to the mix.

MAKES 12 GIANT OR 24 NORMAL-SIZED MUFFINS

LEMON LOVE NOTES
(AKA FRENCH LETTERS)

90 g butter, at room temperature
200 g icing sugar, plus extra to dust
150 g (1 cup) plain flour, sifted
lemon zest, to garnish

TOPPING

2 eggs
zest of 1 lemon
2 tablespoons lemon juice
220 g (1 cup) caster sugar
2 tablespoons plain flour
½ teaspoon baking powder

Pulling together the recipes for this book is a matter of gathering recipes for family favourites from my archives and from friends and family as well as writing some new stuff that I think you'll like. The trickiest part can be getting those recipes from friends. Trickier still when you tell the mate who is helping you, to ring your mother-in-law (and a very fine and upstanding mother-in-law she is, my M-i-L Jude) and ask for her recipe for 'French Letters' – especially when the recipe was actually called Jeanette's Lemon Love Notes! I'm probably not a very good son-in-law 'cos I laughed like a drain at this. I have also renamed this recipe accordingly. I'm sure she won't be offended – well, other than to point out that this was originally her friend Jeanette's recipe. Thing is, I'm not game enough to call it Jeanette's French Letters. Yes, I am a coward.

Preheat the oven to 180°C.

Cream the butter and icing sugar. Add the flour, mix well and press gently into a greased and lined slice tin. (The ideal size is a tin approximately 22 cm × 15 cm × 5 cm deep, and the size tin makes a big difference.) Cook for 20 minutes in the oven.

Remove from the oven.

TOPPING Beat the eggs then add the lemon zest and juice and the sugar. In a small bowl, sift the flour and baking powder together and gently stir in the lemon mix. Pour over the crust and bake again for 20 minutes.

Allow the 'cake' to remain in the pan for a while to cool before you remove to a wire rack. Allow to cool completely and dust with icing sugar and lemon zest.

MAKES 12 SLICES

NOTE: *Every recipe in this book is re-tested a few times and by different people. When testing this recipe we made it several times, using various-sized tins and paying careful attention to the timing. The dish size made a huge difference. Using a 30 cm × 25 cm tin, the edges ended up too brittle and the base was too tough. The second time we used a smaller, deeper 22 cm × 11 cm dish and while we got a much better result, the edges were still quite hard. The flavour was always divine so the measures were all correct but the texture wasn't.*

This is where the panic sets in with testing because there are so many variables, as well as the choice and size of baking dish, such as time and oven temperature, that can come into play. We even started questioning whether it would perhaps be better cooked in a thicker ceramic dish rather than the thin metal slice tins we were using.

While we were mulling this over, a lemon slice in a 22 cm × 15 cm slice tin came out of the oven and gave us just the right mix of softness and subtle differences between the layers. Success. Finally!

SALTED CARAMEL CHOCOLATE SLICE

If the title of this slice doesn't grab you then nothing I can say in this paragraph will help as you are either 1) iron-willed 2) strangely unmoved by the pleasures of the flesh 3) lacking in the English skills to decipher the joy that those three words – salted, caramel, chocolate – can bring when collided together in the same place.

Preheat the oven to 170°C. Line a 17 cm × 26 cm tin with baking paper.

SHORTBREAD CRUST

Sift the flour, baking powder and salt into a bowl, add the sugar and coconut and stir with a wooden spoon. Pour in the melted butter and combine. Spoon this mixture into the tin and very lightly press to make an even layer. Bake for 10 minutes.

CARAMEL

Place the butter, salt and sugar in a non-stick saucepan over low heat, add the condensed milk and bring gently to the boil, stirring continuously for about 8 minutes. Pour the caramel over the base and bake in the oven for another 10 minutes. Allow to cool completely in the refrigerator.

CHOCOLATE GANACHE

Put the chocolate and butter into a heatproof bowl and place over a saucepan of boiling water, being careful not to allow the water to touch the bowl. Leave until the chocolate has completely melted. Remove the bowl from the heat and stir until the chocolate and butter have combined. Spread the chocolate evenly over the caramel and leave in a cool place for about 4 hours.

Sprinkle with salt flakes before serving. The crystals will sparkle against the chocolate topping like stars against the black velvet of the night sky. They aren't just pretty as they make the chocolate seem richer too!

MAKES 15 SLICES

SHORTBREAD CRUST
100 g (⅔ cup) plain flour
½ teaspoon baking powder
pinch of salt
75 g (⅓ cup) soft brown sugar
70 g (¾ cup) desiccated coconut
90 g unsalted butter, melted

CARAMEL
80 g butter
½ teaspoon salt
95 g (½ cup) soft brown sugar
390 g sweetened condensed milk

CHOCOLATE GANACHE
100 g dark chocolate
30 g unsalted butter

salt flakes, to decorate

COLLAPSING FLOURLESS CHOCOLATE CAKE

5 eggs
280 g (1¼ cups) caster sugar
125 ml (½ cup) water
350 g bitter chocolate (min. 70% cocoa solids), roughly broken into pieces
225 g unsalted butter

The world is full of great flourless chocolate cakes – Nigella's Cloud cake; the River Café's famously flawed Chocolate Nemesis; the Tuscan chocolate tart from my last book (*whoa, rein in the ego there, big boy*) – but I like this one because it seems to get better, fudgier even, after a couple of days and is great for up to a week (if you can resist gorging on it for that long). It is not a pretty cake, however, and sometimes the crisp crust on the top will collapse in on itself. This can leave a crater. A crater that, conveniently, can be filled with pretty much anything you like: cubes of double-strength orange jelly, fresh orange segments and whipped cream kissed with orange liqueur for a sort of grandiose Jaffa cake; or, use nothing more than fresh, seedless segments of mandarins picked of all pith and then plumped and warmed in a little sugar and muscat syrup with cinnamon. Really, the possibilities are limitless! Note that you may need to use your cake forks to eat this delicately otherwise you'll ruin your ladylike, white-kid gloves.

Preheat the oven to 160°C. Line a 22 cm round cake tin with baking paper.

Beat the eggs in an electric mixer for 10 minutes, until they have quadrupled in size. Add one-third of the sugar to the eggs while they are beating.

Heat the remaining sugar with the water over medium heat until it has dissolved completely. Add the chocolate and butter and stir to combine. Remove from the heat and allow to cool slightly.

When the eggs are ready, reduce the speed to low and pour in the chocolate. Remove the bowl immediately and using a spatula make sure all the chocolate is incorporated into the eggs. Now pour the mixture straight into the prepared cake tin and place in the oven. Bake for 45–50 minutes.

Remove the cake and allow to cool completely in the tin – don't be tempted to take the cake out early. The centre of the cake will collapse – don't panic, the sides will soon come down to join it. This cake is best made a day ahead as it gets better over time.

SERVES 12

DATE AND HAZELNUT SLICE

240 g unsalted butter, chopped,
    plus 40 g extra, melted and
    cooled
110 g (½ cup) caster sugar
320 g plain flour
330 g (1½ cups) firmly packed
    brown sugar
125 ml (½ cup) pure maple syrup
2 teaspoons vanilla extract
pinch of salt
2 eggs, lightly beaten
240 g (1½ cups) pitted dates,
    thickly sliced
125 g (1 cup) roughly chopped,
    toasted hazelnuts
2 tablespoons thinly sliced
    glazed ginger
80 ml (⅓ cup) melted dark
    chocolate, to drizzle

It is my mother in law Jude's opinion that this slice competes with the Bus Driver's Mother-in-law's Slice in my last cookbook. Make it and tell me if you think it does. Let me know via twitter @mattscravat or on my facebook page. (Sorry, you sprung me! Yes, this is a sneaky way of getting the people who didn't buy the last book to buy it now.)

Preheat the oven to 170°C.

Line a 20 cm × 30 cm lamington tin with baking paper, leaving a bit of overhang on all sides for easy lift-out later.

In a food processor, whiz the chopped butter and caster sugar for 30–60 seconds until light and fluffly. Add the flour and pulse to form crumbs, not a ball. Press the crumbs into the base of the lamington tin and chill for 10 minutes.

Bake for 20–25 minutes until lightly brown. Cool for 5–10 minutes.

Meanwhile, mix the melted butter, brown sugar, maple syrup, vanilla, salt and eggs to combine, then pour over the base. Scatter over the dates, nuts and ginger. Bake for 30–35 minutes, or until set. Leave to cool completely before drizzling the melted chocolate on top. Allow the chocolate to set before cutting.

SERVES 16

DESSERTS

MAGNIFICENT 7 EASY CHEAT'S ICE CREAMS AND GRANITAS

Let's not beat about the bush, there are very few desserts that are not made better without the addition of ice cream. There are loads of good shop-brought ice creams in the supermarket freezer cabinet and I'm not afraid to use them or even customise them, but there is nothing quite like making your own ice cream. The thing is, too often this requires three things many of us don't have: time, freezer space, and an expensive ice cream machine. So I set myself the task of looking at ways that I could bring ice creams to the table while eliminating at least one or two, and ideally all three, of these.

The seven recipes that follow represent three different approaches to getting a chilly finish to any meal. Whizzing frozen fruit with egg whites to create a surprisingly creamy sort of sorbet is a very flexible technique that can be employed with any frozen fruit. Add cream for a creamier result or think about playing with additional flavourings. The rather neutral nature of tinned pears means that you can replace the coriander and lime of the following recipe for the zest and juice of lemons to create a very passable, no-hassle lemon sorbet – even if the pear, lime and coriander combo is almost too sexy to ignore.

Granitas are equally as easy to play with. Once you have mastered the two basic granitas here, feel free to play with other flavours or even infused liquids. Think about making a granita with coconut milk and some threads of kaffir lime or orange juice with some passionfruit. Remember – flavours become muted when frozen, so big flavours like this work best for granitas. For example, purée in-season raspberries with a little sugar and rosewater, then sieve the purée to remove seeds, and freeze. When needed, shave, scrape or blitz the resulting ruby ice for an easy dessert. I love the contrast of a granita's vibrant flavours and iciness with any creaminess, so partner the raspberry granita with whipped cream or vanilla ice cream and some crisp sugar biscuits for a warm crunch.

You can also be brave with how you use the granita idea. Watermelon cooked with a little sugar syrup that's spiked with fresh lime can make a fine granita or the beginning of a rather nice vodka cocktail too. While all of us working on this book were enamoured with an almond milk granita; to make this simply mix 500 ml of the best almond milk you can find with 2 teaspoons of soft brown sugar and freeze. Chop up the resulting ice block and then blitz this into crumbs. This granita is great with coffee ice cream, with the peaches ice cream here, or with vanilla ice cream and some dark ripe cherries garnished with toasted almond slivers. In fact, here is the perfect formula for turning a granita from a palate-cleansing full stop for a meal to a full blown finale. Just partner the icy granita with something for creaminess, something fresh, fruity and complementary but contrasting, and finally something for crunch! Now go forth and multiply these ideas!

1. PEACHES AND CREAM SOFT SERVE

The smell of Southern Comfort always rushes me backwards to being 16 and kissing girls. Although I'd never drink it now there is something wonderful about the way peaches and bourbon go together. Try it in this rather adult take on peaches and cream.

First drain, chop and freeze an **825 g can peaches**. When frozen, whiz these in a food processor or blender on high speed with **55 g caster sugar**. Add **1 egg white**. After a minute or so the mixture should start to turn paler and look smooth. If it doesn't, add a **second egg white**. Now add a splash of bourbon and mix. Add a little more if you want but note that you want to be able to taste it subtly and not let it dominate. Finally add ¼ **cup cream**. Then drizzle in **another ¼ cup cream** but stop if the soft serve is looking too soft! This is delicious as soft serve ice cream blanketed over fresh raspberries and vanilla-candied pecan nuts or crumbled almond biscuits like Italian amaretti.

MAKES 800 ML

2. MANGO GELATO

Blitz **500 g frozen mango pieces** with **50 g sugar**. Throw in **1 egg white** and continue to blitz at high speed. The mango ice will start to go pale and smooth as the egg white does its magic (if it doesn't just add another). Spike with the juice of ½ **lime**. Serve with a sprinkling of **a few green peppercorns** and a **handful toasted pinenuts**, which sounds weird but is actually very, very delicious. The idea is that the peppercorns should only pop up in every third spoonful or so. And if anyone asks why you are being such a rebel – green peppercorns and mango indeed, the very idea! – just tell them that Heston Blumenthal told you to do it. 'Cos in a roundabout way he did! It's one of his favourite 'odd' flavour combos. Can't wait for mango to freeze? You can make an ace mango slushie by puréeing the flesh of **5 mangoes** with **4 cups ice**. Spike with a little basil if the green peppercorns are still upsetting you.

MAKES 600 ML

3. PEAR, LIME AND CORIANDER SORBET

Not too sweet and with a lovely icy freshness, the flavours of pear, coriander leaves and lime are amazingly complementary as I discovered after a long night drinking them in cocktail form in the shady backroom of one of my favourite bars Ocho7Ocho in Buenos Aires. Hi, Mate!

To make, drain and freeze an **825 g can pears**. When frozen, chop the block of frozen pear with a big butcher's cleaver and throw the frozen pieces into a food processor or blender. Whisk on high speed adding **55 g caster sugar**, then **1 egg white** and finally the **zest and juice of 1 lime** and a handful of **chopped coriander** to taste. Serve immediately in little glasses, or freeze for 4 hours for a refreshing sorbet.

MAKES 800 ML

4. STRAWBERRY ICE CREAM

Blitz **500 g frozen strawberries** with **50 g sugar**. Throw in **1 egg white** and continue to blitz at high speed. The strawberry ice will start to go pale and smooth as the egg white does its magic. Add the juice of ½ **lemon** to help it. If it doesn't throw in another egg white. Serve immediately as a dollop of soft serve with **grated white chocolate**, **fresh strawberries** and **crumbled shortbread**. Or serve with cream and roasted strawberries doused with black pepper (page 233)!

MAKES 500 ML

5. CONDENSED MILK ICE CREAM

There's nothing better than when you discover that a long-running Aussie family favourite is popping up in cool recipe books. Such is the case with that old, country staple that I love – condensed-milk ice cream, which is as simple as first chilling your proposed ice cream container in the freezer. Now separate **3 eggs**. Keep both the whites and the yolks. First, use an electric whisk and beat the 3 egg yolks and **1 teaspoon vanilla extract** with a steady drizzle of the contents of a **400 g can sweetened condensed milk**. Beat for 3 minutes. Whip **300 ml cream** until thick; and whisk 3 egg whites until very stiff. Carefully fold the cream and then the egg whites into the condensed milk. Pour into the now-chilled container and freeze.

MAKES 800 ML

6. COFFEE GRANITA

I have a bit of a thing about granitas – not just for their flavour but also for the contrast in texture and temperature that they can offer to any dessert or ice cream dish. The secret is to use a robustly flavoured base to start with, as the cold of the icy granita masks all but the most strident of tastes. To make a simple coffee granita, freeze **400 ml strong espresso** into a block. When frozen, remove from the freezer and, using a fork, scrape the frozen espresso into granules and return to the freezer until needed. Work quickly as the coffee ice will melt quickly. Serve with a **dollop of good chocolate ice cream** and a **plume of soft whipped cream**. Granitas love the contrast of something creamy or rich!

MAKES 400 ML

7. PINK GRAPEFRUIT GRANITA

Squeeze **2 kg grapefruit** (about 4 grapefruit) and strain the juice through a fine sieve. It will give you approximately 750 ml juice. Mix the juice with **caster sugar**. Add the sugar bit by bit as how much you need depends on how sweet the grapefruit are. Think sweet but tangy … remember once frozen the flavours will be more muted. Stir until the sugar has fully dissolved. Pour the mixture into a metal ice cream tray or plastic tub with a large surface area and pop in the freezer. After 45 minutes take it out and mix the frozen edges through the slushie, un-set centre and return to the freezer. To serve, remove the now-frozen grapefruit granita from the fridge and scrape a cold metal spoon over the surface to get curls of pale pink ice. Pile a generous mound on a cold plate. Grate the top layer of **zest from ½ lime**. Serve with **a cheek of lime** and **splash of freezer-chilled Campari** if you are feeling Italian rather than austere and Japanese. Grated salty white chocolate is a more out-there alternative!

MAKES 750 ML

RASPBERRY CHEESECAKE

BASE
60 g unsalted butter
150 g plain sweet biscuits
40 g (¼ cup) brown sugar

FILLING
3 teaspoons powdered gelatine
60 ml (¼ cup) boiling water
500 g cream cheese, at room
   temperature
zest of 1 lemon
2 teaspoons vanilla extract
320 g sweetened condensed milk
2 egg whites
165 g (½ cup) raspberry jam

RASPBERRY JELLY
1 × 85 g packet raspberry jelly
   crystals, 1 teaspoon crystals
   reserved

TO DECORATE
¼ teaspoon citric acid
fresh raspberries, to serve

It is well documented that I have an obsession with two things: food history and the Aussie icy pole. This cheesecake combines them both, paying homage to one of my favourite ice creams – the last Raspberry Splice of summer – as well as the current childish obsession with extreme sourness in sweets like Sour Worms. I then took the idea of placing a layer of raspberry jam on the biscuit base from one of Henry VIII's favourite little cakes, called Maid of Honour tarts, rather than from the Argentine and Brazilian way of serving cheesecake with marmalade- or jam-smeared bases.

Knowing how the king with six wives was devastatingly attracted to lovely things I think he'd fall for this cheesecake. With its virginal and ermine-smooth, creamy filling topped with a glinting, glistening rubble of ruby jelly cubes, it looks more spectacular than any other cheesecake you've ever seen but the raspberry jam provides a suitably sticky end.

BASE Preheat the oven to 160°C. Line the base and side of a 22 cm springform cake tin with baking paper.

Melt the butter in a saucepan over medium heat. Finely grind the biscuits and the sugar in a food processor. Stir the melted butter into the crumbs until combined. Press the crumbs evenly and firmly into the base of the prepared tin and bake in the oven for 10 minutes. Allow to cool.

FILLING Dissolve the gelatine in the boiling water and allow to cool. Beat the cream cheese, zest and vanilla until combined, add the gelatine and mix through. Add the condensed milk and continue beating until smooth. In a separate bowl beat the egg whites to soft peaks and fold gently through the cream cheese mixture until combined.

Spread the jam over the cooled base leaving a 1 cm gap from the edge so the jam doesn't leach out and it remains a surprise, and carefully pour the cream cheese mixture over the jam. Leave the cake in the fridge to chill for at least 4 hours until required.

RASPBERRY JELLY Reserve 1 teaspoon of jelly crystals and set aside. Make the raspberry jelly according to the instructions on the packet, but using only half the amount of water required, so that your jelly is double strength and extra springy. Set in a shallow, narrow tray or plastic container in a 1 cm layer.

When the jelly is set and you are ready to serve, cut the jelly into small cubes and scatter over the top of the cake to decorate. Combine the reserved dry jelly crystals with a little citric acid and sprinkle over the top of the jelly for a zing in the mouth. Tumble on the raspberries and serve.

SERVES 8-10

LIME CHEATSCAKE

1 × 250 g packet plain sweet
  biscuits, crushed
50 g (½ cup) desiccated coconut
175 g butter, melted
250 ml (1 cup) cream
340 g (1⅓ cups) sweetened
  condensed milk
zest of 3½ limes
2 tablespoons lime juice
1–2 kaffir lime leaves *
  (use 2 tablespoons toasted
  flaked coconut if you can't
  find lime leaves)

*Honestly, the kaffir lime leaves really
add something, and are worth seeking
out from an Asian grocer or your
local Thai restaurant if you can. Save
any leftover leaves in the freezer for
next time.

TIP: Why not step up this cheatscake
by serving it with a little of the lime
and black pepper syrup on page 227.
Or add some more fiery South-East
Asian heat by using the same method
but spiking the lime syrup with a
couple of long red chillies.

This take on a Florida Key Lime Pie is so ridiculously easy it should be known
as a 'Cheatscake' as it delivers everything you love about no-cook cheesecake
in a manner so easy that even my laziest 'me' finds it's a breeze to knock
up. The topping is inspired by Christina Tosi's no-crust, spoonable New Age
cheesecake from New York über-hot Momofuku Milk Bar but without the
cornstarch and the cooking. I didn't dye the filling green with food colouring
but you can if you want to reference the Key Lime Pie's seventies heyday. If you
want to seem smart at dinner – even though you are serving about the world's
most simple dessert – note that this pie originated with Florida's sponge
fishermen in the mid 1800s as a scurvy-fighting, shipboard favourite whose
no-cook nature and storage-friendly staples of tinned milk and fresh limes were
perfect for a life at sea. So there!

Line a slice tin (22 cm × 16 cm or thereabouts) with baking paper. Leave some
paper to overhang the edge of the tin. This will help you when it comes to getting
the cheatscake out of the tin.

Whiz the biscuits to fine crumbs in a food processor or bash with a rolling pin in
a strong plastic bag. Mix with the coconut and melted butter and press firmly into
the base and just a little way up the sides of the tin.

Using an electric mixer, beat the cream to soft, stable peaks. Now gently – you
don't want to knock any of the air out of it – spoon into a large bowl and set aside.

Whip the condensed milk for 1 minute, then fold in the lime juice and lime zest.

Gently fold the condensed milk and cream together until just combined. Next, layer
this over the biscuit crumb so it sits like a billowy white and rather limey cloud.

Set in the fridge for at least 3 hours. To serve, zest a little more lime over the top
and finish with fine shreds of the kaffir lime leaf*, cut by rolling up the leaf and
then slicing as finely as you can so it looks like fine blades of grass. Alternatively,
you can top with a line of toasted, flaked coconut if you want.

SERVES 8-10

KATE'S PEAR AND ALMOND TART

There's always someone in your group of friends who inspires awe when it comes to baking. For us it's my friend Kate. She's lived in France and is a bit of a cake whisperer. Whatever sweetness she brings to any BBQ or dinner is always the first thing to be devoured. What's funny, though, is that when little kids pronounce her name it sounds like Cake. No wonder she has become my baking guru and helped me with lots of the sweet stuff in this book. This tart is the first thing of hers that I ever ate. It's a showstopper – a take on a recipe from the River Café, in London, which was inspired by the myriad pear and almond tarts of Italy.

Place the flour and salt in a food processor, add the cold butter and pulse until the mixture resembles coarse breadcrumbs. Add the icing sugar and pulse until combined, then add the egg yolks and pulse again. At this point the dough should combine and start to come away from the side. If the dough is too dry, add the water, bit by bit, until it comes together.

Tip the dough onto a floured surface and bring together quickly into a disc. Wrap in plastic wrap and place in the fridge for 1 hour to chill.

Preheat the oven to 180°C. Butter and flour a loose-bottomed, 28 cm tart tin.

Roll out the dough quickly (so the dough doesn't become overworked) until it is about 4 mm thick. Lift the pastry quickly (so that the pastry doesn't stretch and become uneven) over the tin and press down into the sides. Trim the edge, cover with foil, and blind bake (see page 222) for about 20 minutes until light brown. Remove from the oven.

Reduce the oven temperature to 160°C.

FILLING Place the almonds in a food processor and chop until they are like coarse sand, not too fine. In a separate bowl, cream the butter and sugar until the mixture is pale and light. Add the almonds and blend. Beat in the eggs one at a time. At this point you should have a thick almond cream that can be scooped out with a spoon.

Peel, core, and halve the pears. Place one in the centre of the cooked tart case, and the rest around it facing inwards. Pour the almond cream roughly around the pears, leaving space between the rim and the pears, so the filling has room to spread. Bake the tart for 40 minutes, or until the top is golden brown.

This tart is best made in advance, and is even better on day two. Serve with some good double cream.

SERVES 10-12

250 g plain flour
¼ teaspoon salt
120 g unsalted butter, cold
75 g icing sugar
2 egg yolks
1 tablespoon iced water

FILLING
225 g flaked almonds
225 g unsalted butter,
  at room temperature
225 g caster sugar
2 eggs
4 ripe Packham pears,
  or similar

ONE BIG WHOPPER TRIFLE - ENOUGH TO FEED A SMALL ARMY

2 × 85 g packets raspberry jelly
  crystals, made as per packet
  instructions
2 large jam rolls from the
  supermarket
375 ml (1½ cups) sherry
750 ml (3 cups) thick custard
  from the supermarket
150 g frozen raspberries
1 × 400 g can peach slices, drained
200 ml thickened cream, whipped
80 g (¾ cup) flaked almonds,
  toasted

TIP: You can use Cointreau in place of
sherry and if you'd rather not use any
alcohol, use another packet of jelly and
dip the cake in the liquid jelly instead
of sherry.

Trifles are a hassle but using stuff you can find in any supermarket anywhere reduces the hassle and the fact it is so childishly delicious makes the patience-trying assembly well worth it.

Pour a little warm, unset jelly in the bottom of a large bowl and allow it to set a little but not fully.

Cut one of the jam rolls into 12 slices and dip one side of each slice into the sherry and layer the bottom and lower sides of the bowl with the cake.

Pour some custard over the cake, scatter on the raspberries then pour in some liquid jelly, covering any exposed cake. Place the trifle in the fridge at this stage to allow the jelly to set properly.

When it is set, slice the other jam roll in 12 and then each slice in half. Dip each slice in the sherry and line the sides of the bowl with the cake and place the rest in the middle. If there is any liquid jelly left splash it on the cake to moisten. Place a layer of peaches however you like, or arrange in a layer around the side of the bowl as pictured, saving a few to decorate the top. Pour in more custard if you have space, then finish with whipped cream to serve. Decorate the top with a few thinly sliced peaches and toasted almonds.

Refrigerate to allow the flavours to meld. Trifle is often better the next day. If you want to make it a day ahead, leave the cream off and add when you are ready to serve.

SERVES 10-12, PLUS LEFTOVERS

A CHEAT'S PLUM TART

1 tablespoon jasmine tea leaves

125 ml (½ cup) cold water

1 sheet of good, frozen
    shortcrust pastry

10 firm ripe plums

2 tablespoons caster sugar (or
    vanilla sugar if you have it)

375 ml (1½ cups) port, shiraz,
    cabernet or muscat

500 g mascarpone

3 tablespoons runny honey

1 teaspoon vanilla extract

juice of ½ lemon, strained

2 tablespoons caster sugar

Whipped cream, to serve

TIP: Decorate with white jasmine flowers if you want to be very on trend. Just make sure you use *Jasminum officinale* identified by its oval shiny leaves and white tubular flowers and NOT poisonous false jasmine aka woodbine or yellow jasmine!

TIP: This tart works wonderfully well with pretty much any stone fruit such as peaches, nectarines or apricots. If you are lazy, just use fresh figs and a pre-baked pie case with the mascarpone cream. Instead of using jasmine tea feel free to use Earl Grey instead, which I think works better with other stone fruit.

I have a little bit of a thing for stone fruit – from the soft fuzz and fragrance of apricots at the farm gate to plums piled high in supermarket aisles, their dusty bloom hiding shiny, dark skins and hearts that range from palest golden to dark, angry burgundy and every shade in between. This simple tart lets the plums really shine – even if they aren't at their ripest.

Butter a crinkly-edge metal tart tin, ideally one with a loose bottom – 24 cm in diameter is about right.

Preheat the oven to 180°C.

Place the jasmine tea in a large glass with the cold water. This means that the tea will delicately and slowly infuse the water with the minimum of tannins. Use hot water and it will be too astringent. The wonderful partnership of jasmine tea and plums is one that *MasterChef* contestant Kylie alerted me to.

While the pastry is still very cold, carefully roll out the sheet until it's thinner and about 20 per cent wider so it covers the tart tin. (If you are more generous than me just use a second sheet of pastry!)

Flop the pastry into the tart tin and press into the crinkle edges of the tin. Leave any excess overhanging.

Now blind bake the pie crust. Cover the inside base with baking paper and fill with rice or baking beans. Cook the pie crust for 10–15 minutes, or until the edges are turning golden. Remove the baking paper and your chosen weights. Now return the pie crust to the oven until the base goes golden too – about another 5–10 minutes. When fully cooked and golden all over, remove from the oven and leave to cool in a safe place. Trim off any excess pastry.

Reduce the oven to 160°C.

Cut the plums in half from top to bottom along their crease. Remove the stones.

Place the plums in a roasting pan cut-face up. Sprinkle the caster or vanilla sugar on the plums. Carefully pour the wine into the pan. Pop in the oven and cook until the plums have started to soften but aren't soft. Check them after 20 minutes. You want the fruit to still have its shape on top of the tart. Remember the plum halves will continue to soften and cook once out of the oven. Remove the plums while they are still a little firm. Place in a cool place on a plate. Strain and save any juices in the roasting pan.

CONTINUED OVERLEAF →

CHEAT'S PLUM TART (CONT.)

While the plums and the pastry are cooking, make your mascarpone cream. Whip up the mascarpone with the honey and vanilla. Pop in the fridge to firm up.

While everything is cooling down, make your syrup. Pour the strained plum and wine syrup from the roasting pan into a small saucepan. Add the strained lemon juice and 1 tablespoon of caster sugar. Heat gently until reduced to a syrup. Cut the syrup with 2 tablespoons of the strained jasmine tea. Taste, and assuming the tannins aren't too prominent, you can add another tablespoon of the tea if you like this mercurial combination of plums and jasmine.

Now that everything is cooled down, assemble your tart. Carefully lift your tart case out of the tart tin and place on a flat serving plate or board. Fill with the mascarpone cream and smooth evenly all the way to the edges. Now top with the halved plums. Choose the best, prettiest halves. Tumble these on top or organise in an overlapping wave. Keep in the fridge until needed.

Just before serving, brush with a little of the plum juice that will have leached from the plums while resting on the plate so that your plums glisten. If there is not enough use some of the jasmine plum syrup.

Serve with a jug of the syrup and some whipped cream.

SERVES 8

FRESH PINEAPPLE WITH LIME AND BLACK PEPPER SYRUP

'Eat fresh, eat light' has become one of our catchphrases on *MasterChef*. Yes, obviously our tongues are firmly in our cheeks when we say it. Sadly, we do have a well-documented obsession with animal fats that gets in the way but this dessert does fit the healthy bill. It's fresh and light but still supercharged with tastebud-busting flavour.

Put the lime juice and sugar in a small saucepan over low heat and stir to dissolve sugar. Add half the pepper, increase the heat to medium and simmer, without stirring, until you have a thick, viscous syrup. This will take about 15 minutes but keep an eye on it. If it gets too thick, without stirring, add a touch more lime juice or water.

Remove from the heat and add the remaining pepper.

Plate the pineapple, drizzle over the lime syrup and scatter over the mint leaves.

SERVES 4

250 ml (1 cup) lime juice (6–7 limes), strained through a fine sieve to remove pulp
300 g (1⅓ cups) caster sugar
½–1 teaspoon black peppercorns, freshly crushed
1 pineapple, peeled and cored, cut into wedges and chilled
¼ bunch mint leaves

GOLDEN SAFFRON PEARS WITH STOLEN LAVENDER CUSTARD

PEARS

200 g caster sugar
600 ml water
750 ml (3 cups) dessert wine
4 Beurre Bosc pears, peeled,
    with stalks left on
generous pinch of saffron threads

CUSTARD

450 ml full-cream milk
8–10 sprigs lavender flowers,
    stolen from a neighbour's garden
4 egg yolks
80 g caster sugar

TIP: Any leftover syrup can be refrigerated or frozen for next time you poach fruit, or use as a decadent topping for ice cream.

This is a heavenly combination that seems to have special appeal to the women in my life. In fact, I suspect the only reason the woman I love agreed to marry me was because I was deemed an 'OK' catch after I cooked this for her Sydney best friend and her girlfriends. If you can't find lavender, just serve the pears with vanilla ice cream but spritz it with a little rosewater. Rosewater and saffron is a match made where heaven touches earth in Istanbul. (Steal the lavender and call it 'foraging'.)

PEARS Combine the caster sugar, water and desert wine in a large saucepan. Bring to the boil and simmer for 3–4 minutes. Turn the heat to low and add the peeled pears with stalks left on.

Press some scrunched baking paper lightly over the pears and simmer for about 30 minutes to 1 hour, depending on the ripeness and size of your pears, turning them occasionally to ensure even cooking. After 20 minutes, add the saffron to the pan. When the pears are ready, remove with a slotted spoon and transfer to a container along with the poaching liquid and allow to cool.

CUSTARD Pour the milk into a saucepan, add the lavender flowers, place over medium heat and bring to almost boiling, then remove from the heat. Leave to infuse for about 10 minutes. Strain through a sieve to remove the lavender.

While the lavender is infusing the milk, whisk together the egg yolks and sugar until light and creamy. Carefully pour the hot milk slowly into the egg mixture, whisking constantly as you go. Pour the egg–milk mixture back into the saucepan and place over medium heat, stirring constantly with a whisk, until the mixture thickens and lightly coats the back of the spoon.

Serve the pears, removed from the poaching liquid, at room temperature with the hot lavender custard.

SERVES 4

CHOC CHIP ICE CREAM SANDWICH

600 g chocolate of your choice
(dark, milk, white or any
combination)
300 g (2 cups) plain flour
1 teaspoon salt
1 teaspoon baking powder
250 g unsalted butter, well softened
200 g light brown sugar
55 g (¼ cup) firmly packed
dark brown sugar
110 g (½ cup) sugar
1 teaspoon vanilla extract
2 tablespoons water
1 egg
120 g (¾ cup) whole almonds
150 g (¾ cup) whole macadamias
150 g (¾ cup) whole hazelnuts,
skins removed
vanilla ice cream in a cylindrical
cardboard tube (so you can
slice your ice cream into
evenly sized discs)
an extra 105 g (⅔ cup) hazelnuts,
skins removed (or nut of choice),
chopped

How do you make one chocolate chip cookie better? Have two. And then sandwich them together with ice cream. Rolling the edge in crushed nuts doesn't hurt either. But one side only, you want to be moderate!

Preheat the oven to 180°C.

Break the chocolate into 2 cm squares. You want the milk or dark chocolate hunks to be bigger than the white ones, because they'll melt more when cooked and if too small they will disappear. Reserve.

Sift the flour, salt, and baking powder into a bowl.

In an electric mixer, cream the butter and beat in the three types of sugar until light and fluffy. Add the vanilla, water and egg. Beat together. Beat in the flour mixture. Stir in the chocolate hunks and whole nuts. The mixture should come away from the side of the bowl and form a ball. If the mixture is sticky, add a little more flour.

Drop balls of the mixture, well spaced, onto baking paper on a baking tray. Use a dessertspoonful of dough for big bikkies. Bake for about 10 minutes, or until almost golden. Eat some immediately and allow the rest to cool before assembling the sandwich.

For the ice cream discs, snip the cardboard container to release the ice cream from the tub. Peel off the cardboard and slice the ice cream into 2–3 cm slices, place on a tray and return to the freezer.

When ready to assemble, place the ice cream slice between two cookies. Encrust one side of the wheel in the chopped nuts and eat immediately or return to the freezer until you have done as many as you need.

MAKES 8 SANDWICHES

RASPBERRIES AND CREAM ANOTHER WAY

What a great idea. Delicious tangy fruit topped with a thick seam of set cream that is reminiscent of a white chocolate mousse. Even better it's dead easy to make.

The recipe has a glorious set of antecedents. Setting cream with acidic liquids like lemon, cider, wine or even ale is something that dates backs to the Middle Ages with recipes for syllabubs and possets. However, the first time I tried this version was down on my friend Jen's remote farm last winter. Jen had taken a recipe for lemon set cream from the grand dame of the New Zealand country kitchen, Annabel Langbein, and then set it on a thick seam of her own stewed fruit.

The result was a delicious seasonal winter dessert but one with a creaminess and rosy redness that instantly conjured up the warmth of summer. No little feat when the rain is rattling the windowpanes and the winter wind howls round the house as it tries to whistle its way in under the doors.

Needless to say, I've tweaked this recipe, by adding rosewater to the raspberries which adds a lovely fragrance that seems to mellow the sweetness of the cream and softens the bright acidity of the raspberries a little. I've also added a topping of sugared almonds for crunch. You gotta have crunch!

Slowly heat the raspberries and caster sugar in a small saucepan over low heat until they are soft, warm and have released loads of juice. Season them with a few drops of rosewater. Taste after every drop and stop when you can just taste the rosewater under the sweetness of the raspberries. Leave to cool.

Take four ramekins, teacups or wide glasses and pack in a heaped tablespoon of raspberries at the bottom of each glass. Don't add too much syrup to the pots but reserve it for serving. Place in the fridge to chill.

LEMON CREAM Find your smallest saucepan and in it gently heat your honey, cream and caster sugar along with the cinnamon and nutmeg. Bring to the boil, stirring all the time and then reduce to a simmer for 3 minutes. Add the zest during this time.

Take the pan from the heat. Stir in 2 tablespoons of lemon juice. Take the raspberry-filled cups from the fridge. Strain the cream into the four cups. Place back in the fridge until set. This can take up to 6 hours.

SUGARED ALMONDS Heat the oven to 180°C. Pour your flaked almonds on a lined baking tray and spread them into one close-packed layer. Sprinkle with the icing sugar. Place the almonds in the oven for 6 minutes, or until just golden. Let them cool down before using.

Serve the cups topped with a little pile of sugar-roasted almonds. Add extra lemon zest on the top if you like and the remaining raspberry syrup on the side.

SERVES 4

300 g raspberries (frozen are fine when fresh raspberries are too expensive and not in season)
2 tablespoons caster sugar
couple of drops of rosewater, to taste

LEMON CREAM
1 tablespoon honey
300 ml cream
2 tablespoons caster sugar
pinch of cinnamon
fresh nutmeg, grated to taste
zest of 1 lemon plus 2 tablespoons strained lemon juice (about 1–2 lemons)

SUGARED ALMONDS
80 g (¾ cup) flaked almonds
2 teaspoons icing sugar

TIP: Basically you can put pretty much any stewed fruit in the bottom of your cups – rhubarb, apricots, plums, nectarines. Just pack in the fruit, not the juice so the cream will still sit better on top.

TIP: Alternatively, fill the bottom of your cups with roasted, peppery strawberries. Hull and halve your strawberries. Toss them in a little sieved ground black pepper, a squeeze of lemon and a very light dusting of caster sugar. Spread out on a baking tray and roast in a 150°C oven until the strawberries soften and collapse a little. This can take as long as 30 minutes. Instead of the raspberries, pack in the strawberries with a little of their syrup, if any has wept out. Do taste the strawbs just before using and grind on a little more black pepper if you fancy they need it.

QUINCE CLAFOUTIS

juice of 2 lemons
1 kg quinces
220 g (1 cup) sugar

BATTER
3 eggs
2 egg yolks
110 g (½ cup) caster sugar
375 ml (1½ cups) milk
½ teaspoon vanilla extract
1 tablespoon muscat (young,
  if possible, or sweet sherry)
finely grated zest of ½ lemon
50 g (⅓ cup) plain flour, sifted
30 g unsalted butter, melted

So here is the thing – this isn't really one recipe it's half a dozen of the best French recipes you could ever have. Master the clafoutis batter and it will become your best friend though the year. It's sort of like having a socket and wrench set that will sort any-sized nut. My apologies, that sounds awfully like a very clumsy euphemism but what I mean is you can pour this batter over pretty much any fruit.

Quinces are in season from about March through to July but for the rest of the year think about using other fruit for your clafoutis. Cherries are a French clafoutis classic. Use them in summer, from November onwards. Traditionally the first cherries of the season are used and left unpitted so the stones add an almondy fragrance to the dish. I pit mine because I am scared of dentist's bills and substitute a little of the flour with almond meal (or sprinkle over some flaked almonds) if I want that hint of almondy-ness. Feel free to freeze the fresh cherries if you want their texture to hold up better in the cooking process.

After cherries wane, think of stone fruit like halved and stoned apricots, peaches and nectarines that cascade into season through summer. These don't need any poaching and can just be added to the baking dish fresh. After Christmas you also have the option of a fig clafoutis but make sure you adjust the sweetness of your batter and perhaps make individual clafoutis, as these cook more quickly, allowing the figs to hold their shape better. Just cut the fresh figs in half and pop them in the little dishes.

For the poached quinces, put the juice of 1 lemon in a large, non-metallic bowl with 500 ml (2 cups) of cold water. Peel and core the quinces. Cut each one into eighths. Put the pieces in the lemon mix to stop them browning.

Heat 2 litres (8 cups) of water in a large pan then put the juice of the second lemon and the sugar and cook until the sugar dissolves. Add the quince pieces and cover with a circle of baking paper touching the surface of the fruit (posh people, snotty chefs and the French call this a *cartouche*). This helps keep the fruit submerged and cook evenly. Simmer until a knife slips in easily, then drain.

BATTER Whisk the eggs and yolks. Slowly whisk in the sugar. When the eggs go pale and creamy, add the milk, vanilla, muscat and grated lemon zest.

Place the flour in a separate bowl. Pour in some of the egg mix and whisk to a lump-free batter. Fold this back into the main bowl mixture. Cover with plastic wrap and set aside for 30 minutes so the batter thickens.

Preheat the oven to 180°C. Fold the melted butter through the batter. Butter a baking dish large enough to hold the quinces in a single layer. Arrange the quinces, pour on the batter and bake for 50 minutes, or until the batter is set and golden.

SERVES 8

CITRUS-MARINATED PEACHES

200 ml orange juice (2–3 oranges)
600 ml lemon juice (11–13 lemons)
6 large ripe peaches, white or
 yellow (not clingstone)
450 g caster sugar
ice cream or double cream, to serve

TIP: Look for fresh, ripe peaches. They should feel heavy for their size and smell like peaches. If the skin doesn't come away easily, blanch the peaches to make them easy to peel. Simply plunge the peaches in boiling water for 30–40 seconds, then transfer to ice-cold water to stop them from cooking. Dry them off and gently peel the skin from the flesh using a paring knife or fingers.

I love it when favourite recipes are given to me to share with you. It's a wonderful act of generosity. This recipe comes from my good friend Marnie who's helped me with both my books, being everything from a drudge to a scold but above all a soaring inspiration. I should note that the first two were my fault. This is a brilliant simple recipe and this is the note that came with it – I just love its directness, its economy and, above all, its humour.

'Matt, this is a recipe adapted from a regular on the menu of my mother-in-law. I don't know where she got it from, probably the Invergrowrie homecraft hostel guide to being a good housewife. I do hope it is not that of some well-known chef. I guess if it is he or she would be dead now, like my mother-in-law. Marnie.'

It's cheapest to make this recipe when both peaches and lemons are in season. So diarise it now for February and March!

Combine both citrus juices in a large, wide-based glass or ceramic bowl. Add the sugar and set aside, to allow the sugar to dissolve, stir occasionally.

Peel the skin from the peaches, gently taking care not to mark the flesh. Sit the peaches in the juice and marinate overnight. Turn occasionally.

Serve with the marinating juice and ice cream or double cream on the side.

SERVES 6

CHOCOLATE CAKE
WITH PRUNES

Scene: somewhere in the pantry. A phone rings.
'Prunes? Is that you? It's me Chocolate? I need to see you,'
'... but Chocolate, I thought we just agreed ... we'd just be friends.'
'I know that but without you I am nothing ... Your sweetness frees a dark fruitiness in me and I know you find my dark bitterness captivating.'
'Well ... OK, see you in the mixing bowl in 15 minutes when we can become one. By the way do you mind if I bring Vinnie?'
'Who? Not Vin Santo?'
to be continued ...
... and devoured in chocolate cake that looks like it's been designed by Austrian sculptor Erwin Wurm or just collapsed in a vacuum. Respect to David Lebovitz for the original recipe, from which this one has sprung.

PRUNES Simmer the prunes with the Vin Santo and sugar in a small saucepan until most of the liquid is reduced to a syrup. Remove from the heat, cover, and let stand until cool.

CAKE Preheat the oven to 170°C. Butter a 20 cm springform cake tin, dust the inside with the cocoa powder.

Melt the chocolate and butter together in a heatproof bowl placed over a saucepan of simmering water, ensuring that the bowl does not touch the water beneath. Stir until smooth, add half the sugar, remove from the heat and allow to cool slightly.

Separate 200 g of the prunes from the liquid, roughly chop them and stir into the chocolate. Add the egg yolks and stir until combined.

Using your electric mixer, whisk the egg whites with the salt until they begin to hold soft peaks. Continue whisking while adding the remaining sugar until the whites hold their shape but are not stiff. Fold one-third of the egg whites thoroughly into the chocolate mixture to aid sucessful incorporation, then fold in the remaining egg whites gently until completely incorporated.

Pour the cake mixture into the prepared tin and bake the cake for about 25 minutes. The centre should remain a little moist. Allow to cool completely before removing from the pan. Serve with the remaining whole prunes, their syrup and a dollop of cream.

SERVES 12

PRUNES
400 g pitted prunes
200 ml Vin Santo
30 g sugar

CAKE
cocoa powder, to dust cake tin
340 g good-quality dark chocolate, coarsely chopped
170 g unsalted butter
80 g sugar
200 g soaked prunes
6 large eggs, separated
¼ teaspoon salt
double cream, to serve

TIP: If you object to Vin Santo to soak your prunes, then try using muscat, madeira or pedro ximenez instead. If you object to alcohol altogether, then any flavoured tea can be substituted. Try Earl Grey or smoky oolong for starters but infuse the tea in 200 ml of cold water for an hour or so rather than in boiling water, which can free up too many tannins.

SO SIMPLE SO SOUFFLÉ

DEF. N, *SOUFFLÉ*: A VERY CLEVER WAY TO SELL HOT AIR

Soufflés are both ridiculously easy and amazingly cheap to make at home yet a prolonged campaign has us running scared of them. It's time for us home cooks to reclaim the soufflé from restaurant menus.

The best soufflé I've ever made at home was modelled on the best fruit soufflé I've ever eaten in Australia. Invaluable advice came from chef-owner Andy Davies, of Press Wine + Food in Adelaide, who claimed that his soufflé successes were all about the right oven temperature and correctly lining your moulds or ramekins with butter and then with an even coating of sugar, 'Your soufflés need the heat to kick start them and good lube to rise evenly,' he says.

Soufflés are a very simple science. It's the combination of these three scientific facts: egg proteins solidify as they cook; heat turns liquids to gases; and heated gases, like air, expand and rise. Think of when you boil a liquid and how bubbles burst from its surface, so it is with a soufflé. The hot steamy air has to force its way upwards as it can't escape from the sides of the ramekin. As it pushes upwards trying to escape, it takes the soufflé with it. If the soufflé has a good crust on top this gives the air something else to push against in its quest to free itself – just the way a boiling pan of water rattles the lid of the saucepan as the steam forces its way out. Then the egg whites trap the air as they set, giving us these high, handsome beauties. Simple! Now let's cook 'em.

12 TIPS TO KEEP YOUR SOUFFLÉS HIGH AND HANDSOME

1. Use eggs at room temperature to maximise your rise. Avoid super-fresh eggs.

2. Preheat your oven to 200°C. A hot oven is crucial to soufflé success as it cooks the outside making it hard for the hot air to escape the soufflé. This is what propels the soufflé skywards.

3. Use long, straight upward strokes to butter your ramekins. It helps the soufflé to rise if the strokes all run up the sides.

4. Evenly coat the inside of the ramekin with sugar (or breadcrumbs or cheese if you are doing a savoury soufflé).

5. Adding a little salt or sugar to your whites halfway through beating will keep them stable.

6. Beat your whites in a metal or china bowl rather than plastic as these surfaces repel fat. Fat (and egg yolk, which has fat in it) are the enemy when trying to achieve fluffy egg whites.

7. Fold in the egg whites gently to maximise the air incorporated in the soufflé. The expansion of this air will help the soufflé rise.

8. A flavour base that is cold – whether sweet or savoury – is harder to incorporate into your egg whites than a warm one, and you'll knock the air out of the whisked whites, which will affect the rise of the soufflé. So only incorporate warm flavour bases.

9. Score around the top edge of the soufflé with a thumbnail or blade of a knife to help keep the top loose and able to move upwards.

10. An old chef's trick to help the rise of the soufflé is to turn the grill on, to slightly gratinate the top of the soufflé first. This helps form a crust, which the steam created by cooking can push upwards against, taking the rest of the soufflé with it, as it tries to escape.

11. The cooking rate of the soufflé depends on the temperature of the soufflé mix. A cold mix results in cooked top and sides but a middle that's soggy and undercooked

12. Only cook the soufflés when the guests are ready to eat. Like love, soufflés can be fleeting; wonderful and voluminous one moment, flat and deflated the next.

1. TINNED PEACH SOUFFLÉ

This soufflé started out as Andrew Davies' apricot soufflé but has been steadily evolving into something a little less sweet and using tinned peaches so it's cheap to make at any time of the year. It still rises magnificently and is surprisingly delicious and delicate, given the provenance of the fruit.

First make the tinned peach base. Place **100 g caster sugar** in a pan and add **40 ml water** and place on high heat. Ensure the sugar is cooking evenly. Once you have reached a blond caramel (don't go too dark or you'll overpower the peaches), carefully add **250 g chopped, drained canned peaches**. Turn the heat to medium and cook them for approximately 5 minutes. Then sprinkle in a mixture of **2 heaped teaspoons cornflour** turned into a slurry with **35 ml water**. Stir for about 1 minute. Remove from the heat and purée in a blender. Add **25 ml Grand Marnier**. Set aside to cool.

Set your oven to 200°C at least 20 minutes before you want to bake your soufflés. Generously butter 4 soufflé ramekins using upward brush strokes, repeat and then evenly dust with caster sugar. Pop in the fridge until needed.

In a medium-sized, stainless steel bowl, whisk **4 egg whites** until soft peaks form, then sprinkle in about **40 g sugar**. Keep whisking until the whites reach semi-stiff peaks. Spoon in 6 tablespoons of the peach soufflé base and gently incorporate using a folding motion. Spoon the flavoured egg white mixture into each ramekin and smooth across the top. Run a knife or your clean thumbnail around the edge of the ramekin.

Bake for about 8 minutes until the soufflés are plump and tall. If you have filled the ramekins to the top you should get a good 4 cm rise. If you haven't gone that high after 8 minutes, give the soufflés about another 3 minutes to see if you can get more lift.

First time you make these soufflés, I'd suggest making an extra one that you can use as a tester. Taste it after 8 minutes and if the soufflés are ready, serve them. If they are still a little unset in the middle, give them a couple of minutes more. Serve with vanilla ice cream.

TIP: Using tinned peaches means you can have a soufflé through the year but do try this recipe with other stone fruit when in season. Andy Davies' original, from which this recipe has developed, used 250 g fresh and stoned apricots. I've found that half a dozen cardamom seeds add an exotic twist. Also try fresh plums or nectarines.

2. PHILIPPA SIBLEY'S CHEESE SOUFFLÉ

One of my most memorable moments of five years as the creative director of the Melbourne Food and Wine Festival was watching a hands-on MasterClass where ace pastry chef Philippa Sibley was teaching soufflé-making to a ragtag bag of soufflé novices. The look on their faces as they pulled out a succession of high and handsome soufflés first time was priceless! This savoury soufflé of hers should have you grinning proudly too.

Preheat the oven to 200°C. Butter 4 moulds or individual ramekins and dust with **20 g finely grated parmesan**. Boil a kettle and lay a clean tea towel in the base of a high-sided baking dish that will hold all 4 moulds with space around them.

Make a blond roux. To do this, cook out **40 g butter** with **2 tablespoons plain flour** until a paste forms. Whisk in **120 ml warmed milk** and bubble on the heat for a few minutes. Remove from the heat and whisk in **100 g finely grated gruyère**. Then add **2 egg yolks** with the mix still off the heat. Season with **salt and pepper** but remember that you will be adding whites so be generous to ensure the seasoning is right.

Whisk **200 g egg whites*** (about 7 egg whites) in a super-clean large bowl until they are airy. Then sprinkle in **1 teaspoon sugar**. This helps stabilise the whites. Whisk the whites some more until they get to good soft peaks – but take care not to over-whisk or the whites will become grainy or snowy and will not rise properly. Fold a third of the whites into the cheese mixture, then add all the rest. Doing this in two stages should aid amalgamation.

Divide the soufflé mixture between the 4 moulds. Place the moulds on the tea towel in the baking dish. This stops any wobbling of the moulds during cooking. Next pour hot water into the baking dish so that it comes halfway up the side of the moulds. Bake for about 12 minutes. Make sure everyone is sitting down at the table. Then sprinkle **extra gruyère** on top (25 g finely grated should do it) and continue cooking for another 8 minutes or so. Serve immediately.

TIP: Add cubes of cheese to your soufflé just prior to popping in the oven to give little melty pockets of goo in your cheese soufflé. Serve with a nice little chardonnay.

3. CLASSIC
CHOCOLATE SOUFFLÉ

This is a very elegant dinner party dessert based on an old Michel Roux recipe. The best soufflés I've ever tasted I have eaten at Roux's wonderful riverside restaurant, The Waterside Inn, just outside London. I sweetened it up to balance the chocolate's bitterness. As with the other soufflés, the process here is as simple as mixing a chocolate pastry cream with whipped egg whites for the soufflé base. Butter four 10 cm soufflé moulds with about **10 g softened butter per mould**. Use upward strokes of the brush to help the soufflés lift. Then coat the insides with a layer of **caster sugar** by rolling the sugar around in the moulds. Preheat the oven to 200°C and put a baking tray in the oven to heat.

Now we need to make the pastry cream. Slowly bring **350 ml milk** and **65 g caster sugar** to the boil in a small pan. In a small bowl, whisk **4 medium egg yolks** and **35 g caster sugar** until it forms a ribbon when you lift the beaters. Next, whisk in **30 g plain flour**. Then gently pour the hot milk over the egg yolks in a steady stream, whisking all the time. Return the pastry cream to the pan and whisk over low heat for a minute. Pour into a bowl, cover with plastic wrap and cool the pastry cream a little. Now take 280 g of the pastry cream and delicately mix in **25 g sifted cocoa powder** and **200 g finely chopped or grated dark chocolate** – 70% dark cocoa solids is best – using a whisk.

Beat **10 medium egg whites** to a thick foam, then add **40 g caster sugar** and continue beating until soft peaks form. Fold a third of the pastry cream into the egg whites with a whisk. Then fold in the rest with a large spoon. The mixture will be fairly loose. Divide the mixture between the prepared soufflé moulds, filling them ¾ full. Stand them on the hot baking tray and bake for 10 minutes. When the soufflés have risen, dust with **icing sugar** and serve with a good **vanilla bean ice cream** on the side.

TIP: This recipe will leave you with about 150 g of extra pastry cream. You could layer it with fresh raspberries between two sheets of puff pastry dusted with sugar as a simple mille-feuille or line a small tart shell.

RICH CHOCOLATE MOUSSE

170 g good-quality dark chocolate
  (70% cocoa solids)
80 ml (⅓ cup) full cream milk
2 large egg yolks
4 large egg whites
2 tablespoons caster sugar
2 peppermint chocolate bars (such
  as Peppermint Crisp), chopped,
  to serve

This is the Forrest Gump of chocolate mousses – it is so simple but so very, very nice. You also don't mind seeing it pop up again and again.

Melt the chocolate in a heatproof bowl over simmering water, making sure the bowl does not touch the water. Remove from the heat and allow to cool slightly.

Bring the milk to the boil, then pour over the chocolate. Using a small whisk, gently blend the milk into the chocolate until just combined. Cool for a few minutes, add the egg yolks and again whisk gently until combined.

Beat the egg whites in your electric mixer on medium until they hold soft peaks. Increase the speed and slowly add the sugar. Continue beating until the eggs are firm and glossy. Scoop a third of the egg whites into the chocolate and mix in completely to lighten the mixture. Now fold the rest of the whites in gently but thoroughly.

Pour the mousse into your serving bowls and refrigerate for at least 1 hour before serving.

Top with glistening shards of peppermint chocolate.

SERVES 4

CHOCOLATE SELF-SAUCING PUDDING

150 g (1 cup) self-raising flour
110 g (½ cup) caster sugar
30 g (¼ cup) cocoa, powder
60 g butter, melted and cooled
125 ml (½ cup) milk
½ teaspoon vanilla extract
1 egg
cocoa powder or icing sugar,
   to dust the top
cream, custard and/or ice cream,
   to serve

TOPPING
110 g (½ cup) sugar
3 tablespoons cocoa powder
500 ml (2 cups) boiling water

For as long as there have been records, people have been searching for the fountain of youth, whether literally, or with what they rub into their faces or what pills they pop. It's all a bit of a waste of money really. All they need to do is bake this old-fashioned country dessert and after one mouthful they'll feel like a kid again immediately!

Preheat the oven to 160°C.

Sift the flour, sugar and cocoa into a mixing bowl and combine. Make a well in the centre.

In a separate bowl, whisk the butter, milk, vanilla and egg and gradually pour into the well. Combine with a spoon, don't overmix.

Pour into a greased 6–8 cup ovenproof dish and flatten the top with the back of a spoon.

TOPPING Sprinkle the sugar and cocoa over the batter, then gently pour the boiling water over the top.

Bake for 30–35 minutes, remove from the oven and stand for at least 10 minutes before serving.

Dust with the cocoa or icing sugar and serve with cream, custard and/or ice cream.

SERVES 6

GOLDEN SYRUP DUMPLINGS

Few moments in my life have matched sitting at the wooden kitchen table where Margaret Fulton wrote all her recipes as she fed me lunch and told me stories of her rather amazing life. I wanted to include one of her recipes that we cook at home and as it is impossible to improve on something that is as perfect as her recipe for Golden Syrup Dumplings, I plumped for that. It is one of the many recipes I make regularly from the most used cookbook in my mighty arsenal of some 1000 tomes, an original and much dogged-eared edition of her *Encyclopedia of Food and Cookery*. Thanks for the recipe, Margaret!

Sift the flour and salt together and rub in the butter. Add the eggs and stir in with a knife, adding enough milk to make a soft dough. Divide the dough into 12 pieces and roll into balls.

SYRUP In a large saucepan, heat the water with the sugar and golden syrup, stirring until the sugar dissolves. Add the butter and bring to the boil. Place dumplings in syrup, cover and simmer for 20 minutes without lifting the lid. Serve the dumplings at once with the syrup spooned over them.

Serve with custard or cream.

SERVES 6

300 g (2 cups) self-raising flour
pinch of salt
45 g butter
2 eggs, beaten
a little milk (about ¼ cup)
custard, or cream to serve

SYRUP
500 ml (2 cups) water
110 g (½ cup) sugar
3 tablespoons golden syrup
30 g butter

80-SECOND SPONGE CAKE WITH 40-SECOND COMPOTE AND 20-SECOND CREAM

100 g caster sugar, and extra for
  dusting the inside of the ramekins
2 eggs
pulp of 2 passionfruit
100 g butter, melted
100 g self-raising flour
cream, to serve

COMPOTE
175 g berries (raspberries
  and blueberries)
50 g caster sugar

Nothing more needs to be said about this scrumptious pudding – by the time you finish reading one of my introductions, you could have made three of them!

Whip the caster sugar with the eggs and passionfruit. Throw in the melted butter and whisk. Add the flour to the mixture and combine.

Grease and lightly sugar the insides of six ramekins. Half fill with the sponge mix. Wrap loosely in plastic wrap so that it is covered but hot air can escape.

Microwave each ramekin for 40 seconds on high.

Use the first ramekin as a tester and increase or decrease the cooking time according to the power and efficiency of your microwave.

COMPOTE Cook the berries in a small saucepan over high heat with the sugar. Stir until bubbly and syrupy – about 40 seconds.

Turn out your sponges, pour a quarter of the fruit over each and dollop on whipped cream (or double cream, if that extra 20 seconds of whipping matters to you).

SERVES 4

TIRAMISU STOLEN FROM A KITCHEN IN BRIGHT

If it wasn't for Patrizia Simone I would never have got the job on *MasterChef*. It was a late night photo of me looking suitably dishevelled and like 'trouble' taken at her restaurant, Simone's of Bright, that got me the job. They didn't even consider my award-splattered CV.

As well as being a beautiful cook and the warmest of hosts, Patrizia is an inspirational woman. Years before foraging became fashionable, she would take me down lanes in the hills of her beloved North East Victoria looking for wild spinach and nettles to cook for dinner. And on a trip we made to her native Umbria, her family adopted me and the woman I love so comprehensively that we spent a week doing nothing but being guided by them through Medieval alleys, deep in the bush hunting for truffles, or eating feasts cooked in the most ingenious manner over no more than open fires in fine dining rooms and converted byres.

In my last book, her aunt's Tuscan chocolate tart was one of the hit desserts and this time it's only right that Patrizia takes her rightful place with this ridiculously light and simple tiramisu. I've tweaked it a little by adding the cream topping, which cuts against its custardy richness and adds a wonderful angelic white layer for the chocolate to smear against. I've also made it as one large tiramisu, unlike the single ones that we devoured on that fateful night six years ago that looked like this (on the right):

Place a large mixing bowl in the fridge to chill.

Beat the eggs and caster sugar together for 15 minutes. It is best to use an electric mixer for this. Now fold in *just* 500 g of the mascarpone until smooth. Do this by mixing some of the egg mixture into the mascarpone to loosen it up, and then little by little folding the mascarpone back into the egg. Place in the prepared cold bowl and place in the fridge.

Pour some of the coffee into a wide cereal bowl. Splash in 50 ml of cold water if the espresso is very strong. Roll the biscuits quickly in the coffee and then lay in a 24 cm square × 10 cm deep dish dish close together. When the base layer is done, pour over one-third of the mascarpone mixture. Repeat twice, until you have three layers of biscuits and mascarpone.

Lightly whip the remaining 250 g of mascarpone with the cream until it is thick and spoonable. Spread over the top of the tiramisu like a white blanket. Cover with plastic wrap and refrigerate for a couple of hours or overnight.

Place the block of dark chocolate in the freezer.

To finish, dust the top of the tiramisu with cocoa and finely grate over some dark chocolate.

SERVES 16-20

6 eggs
110 g (½ cup) caster sugar
750 g mascarpone
625 ml (2½ cups) cold strong (black) or espresso coffee (10 espressos from your favourite, Ned Kelly lookalike, bearded hipster barista)
250 g (1½ packets) savoiardi biscuits (1½ packs will do 2 layers but you need 2 packs for 3 layers)
200 g dark chocolate
the best possible cocoa powder
300 ml thickened cream

TIP: Hold the chocolate using the cardboard wrapping to stop it melting.

CHRISTMAS

WHAT I'VE LEARNED ABOUT FINGER FOOD
FROM HANGING OUT AT COCKTAIL PARTIES, CHRISTMAS SHINDIGS AND OTHER EVENTS AND HOW TO MAKE IT WORK FOR YOU AT HOME.

It may come as a little bit of a surprise to discover that a shy and shrinking violet like me just *loves* a party. Sorry, just saying the word, *party*, overexcites me and makes me WANT TO SHOUT and elongate the last syllable of the word 'party' in that most annoying *waaaay*!

There are few better reasons to party than the annual jamboree that we face at the end of each year. A time that incorporates for us on this side of the globe, the start of the summer holidays, the start of the new year, the birth of baby Jesus, the summer solstice, Yule, Hanukkah, Kwanzaa, Saturnalia and Pancha Ganapati.

It doesn't matter whether you are entertaining at home, opening Tupperware tubs from the back of your ute in a dusty bush paddock or catering for celebs, footballers and the divine Dannii Minogue in a million-dollar, cliff-top mansion, the basic rules are the same when planning your party:

* plan ahead
* don't forget to book the glasses
* if you want dancing, book some flashing lights and a smoke machine
* look for cohesion and variety in your menu
* keep the food dainty, tasty and remarkable
* pick a menu built around stuff that can be made in advance to lessen the stress on the day itself
* start with lighter bites, deliver something more substantial later to balance any alcohol consumption
* always have party pies and sausage rolls (even if you don't like them) because they are part of being an Aussie
* finish with something sweet to let everyone know that it's hometime!

You might even decide to start by passing around food and then move on to buffet-style dishes that can be prepped in advance like potato salad or whole poached fish. If so, remember disposable plates and cutlery will save on washing up but also think about how the people will 'be' at the party. Will they spread out and be sitting down, or will they be standing around holding a glass, a handbag and a bunch of mistletoe, in which case trying to cut up food with a plastic knife on a bendy paper plate is a recipe for disaster. That's why a lovely, delicately flaking fish or easily jabbable, bite-sized potatoes are ideal and sausages are not.

Also avoid party food with drippy dipping sauces that will ruin your guests' expensive party frocks (I've stopped eating spring rolls at cocktail parties for this very reason). Also avoid anything that will fall apart, topple over or that is difficult to pick-up, and anything that requires too much assembly. Remember, each two-second step taken to pull together a canapé will suck up valuable primping time when you have to repeat five steps 50 times! That's why a little bowl of risotto is good and a mini burger with the lot is a nightmare. Just make sure you don't make the mistake I did last Christmas of buying 5 kg of prawns that had to be peeled. It took a long time and I smelt of a trawler for most of the party, which is only good for attracting seagulls rather than pretty gulls.

OK, so let's rattle off some ideas to get you started with your party planning.

A large part of coming up with a good menu is about looking at those plates that you know you can do well and without taking too much of your party time. Think about things that can be prepared or finished in the oven while you are welcoming (and enjoying) your guests, such as crispy, retro vol au vent cases filled with something in a rich white sauce like mushrooms or chicken, or small blintzes. These are basically nanna's pikelets but topped with a little smoked salmon and dab of sour cream into which you push a weeny sliver of lemon and a tiny pluche or frond of dill.

If you have many little hands to help you, then skewers of prawns or chicken or meatballs are all great but are very time consuming if it's only you assembling them. So avoid them. Far easier is to do toast – just call it crostini or bruschetta! Split a ciabatta lengthways and grill the crust sides. Now flip it back over and toast the other side until just crisping but not brown. Now brush with olive oil (ideally infused with a little minced garlic) and top with your favourite but simple combos that deliver that number one rule of the kitchen – complement and contrast. So, lay sliced tomatoes on the toast, sprinkle on salt and top with slices of mozzarella. Pop back under the grill so the mozzarella starts collapsing loosely and then top each piece with a basil leaf or shard of prosciutto. Artichoke hearts, green olives and parmesan are a similarly ace bruschetta combination, as are pan-braised mushroom and goat's curd sprinkled with thyme or a few drops of balsamic.

Otherwise think about going for fritters, which also have the booze-friendly property of being fried, carry their own flavours really well and adeptly carry toppings. Think of corn fritters with salmon or bacon (perhaps dolloped with a herb mayo) or making round, green fritters with loads of crushed green peas, parsley, spring onions and mint. You'll find recipes for these fritters on page 104 and page 6.

Lamb cutlets are great, but expensive, and could come with everything from Moroccan to Indian flavours. Seasonally I like pairing them with dipping sauces; one of redcurrant jelly warmed with a little cranberry juice, the other of Greek yoghurt mixed with loads of chopped mint. This works especially well if you've doused the cutlets with a spice rub of 1 part ground cumin, 1 part ground coriander seed and 1 part salt before BBQing. Cook them a little underdone and keep them warm in the oven until needed. Garnish the plate with redcurrants. Chicken drumettes are the more Jerry Springer option.

You could just put out a bowl of peanuts and be done with it but there are lots of great ways to put a twist on your nuts – so to speak – whether it's roasting them with soy and sugar or mixing them with French onion soup mix and Nutrigrain to make 'nuts and bolts', which is a classic seventies combo from the era in which cocktail parties (as well as keys-in-the-bowl parties) hit their zenith. I'm far classier, so I make these **spiced nuts** from a recipe from Melbourne's posh Emirates Lounge! It's as easy as whisking **2 egg whites**. Then separately mix together **200 g sugar** with **2 tablespoons curry powder**, **1 tablespoon ground cumin**, **2½ teaspoons garlic salt**, **1 teaspoon cayenne pepper**, **1 teaspoon ground cardamom** and **½ teaspoon ground cinnamon**. Now stir in **1.5 kg mixed nuts**. Slowly add the sugar nut mix to the whisked egg whites. Spread them out on a well-greased baking tray and bake at 120°C for 45 minutes. Cool, break up and save in an airtight container until the party. Delicious!

While we are thinking of using the oven we might have a long hard think about whether we should make the effort to make our own sausage rolls. These are stupidly easy after all. It's just a matter of cutting sheets of puff pastry lengthways, using a piping bag to pipe in a long, fat finger of sausage on the pastry and then rolling it up, sealing and washing with a little egg glaze made from just beating an egg lightly. If you want to step this up, how about placing a long skinny line of prosciutto sheets along the spot on the pastry where you are going to pipe the filling and flavouring the filling with a Christmassy splash of muscat or two?

Here are the ratios. For every **3 sheets puff pastry**, you'll need about **900 g filling** made up from working together **400 g sausage mince**, **300 g chicken mince**, **a finely diced onion**, **1 grated carrot**, **2 cloves minced garlic** and **a loosely mixed egg**. Now work in **1 cup breadcrumbs**, **a handful finely chopped parsley** and about a **¼ cup muscat**. Work the mix between your fingers until it is sticky and then make the rolls. I use a piping bag with a big nozzle to apply the filling to the pastry, as it is neater and easier. Seal the rolls and then chill. Cut into 4 cm lengths and lay on a baking tray lined with baking paper. Keep in the fridge until needed, then bake in a 180°C oven for 35 minutes, or until golden and cooked through. Serve with tomato sauce, fat rounds of pickled cucumbers (aka gherkins) or sweet chilli sauce marbled with good dollop of whole egg mayonnaise. Red and white is soooo Christmassy!

Of course you'll be wondering what to do with all the leftover pickle juice and I have just the solution for this vexing problem – make Picklebacks. The Pickleback is a two-shot drink, thought to have originated in hipster bars in Brooklyn or as a favourite tipple of the NYPD. It is simply one shot of Jameson Irish whiskey and a second shot of pickle juice; first you take the whiskey, followed by the pickle juice ideally poured straight from a jar of sweet-and-sour gherkins. This drink is both surprising and tasty. It also goes very well with both sausage rolls and the desire to be talking authentic gibberish by the end of the night!

A little more blah-blah but still using easy frozen pastry, is knocking up some Moroccan filo parcels – basically just filled with a juicy but dry lamb mince cooked with toasted pine nuts, cumin, coriander seeds, ground cinnamon and a little sumac (if you have it). Serve with tzatziki.

A proper tzatziki is also always another winner. For the best tzatziki you'll need to do three things – deseed your cucumber, drain your yoghurt and blanch your garlic. To blanch your garlic, drop the garlic in boiling water for a minute to take away the harsh heat that raw garlic can give to this cooling mint and cucumber dip. To drain the yoghurt, spoon Greek yoghurt into a double sheet of muslin laid in a sieve. Gather the edges and tie them up so you have a sort of muslin ball of yoghurt. Hang this overnight in the fridge (over a bowl to catch the drips) to drain – or at least dry it out a little. You want it thick but not crumbly. If you over-dry your yoghurt, blitz it with the cucumber seeds to rehydrate it. The ratio to look for in a good tzatziki is **1 finely diced continental cucumber** to **2 cups yoghurt (drained)** to **3 blanched garlic cloves** mashed **with salt**. Finish with a **little lemon juice, salt and mint**. I always serve my tzatziki with warm triangles of Arab bread and some radishes that have been topped and tailed and then kept crunchy in a bowl of cold water in the fridge. Delicious.

While you've got the oven going, you might as well use it for some more sure-fire party winners. You might as well also make a **cannellini bean dip**. The main flavour of this is roast garlic, so using a serrated knife, slice the top off a **head garlic** – this will make it easier to squeeze out the flesh when it's all soft, sweet and roasted – then replace it and pop the garlic in a 180°C oven. When the garlic is soft and sweet smelling, around 45–60 minutes, blend it with a **large can cannellini beans** (well-drained and rinsed), a **little olive oil, lemon juice** and **salt** to taste. Serve drizzled with more oil and a light sprinkle of rosemary leaves. Serve with warm, supermarket flatbread or fingers of carrot and cucumber.

We are now stepping into the murky area of dips and while hummus, babaghanoush and tarama are all ace, none has the class of the **smoked trout dip** that the woman I love makes.

Making this is a breeze and it's a show stopper. Remove the skin from **1 whole, smoked trout** and gently flake the flesh. Check carefully for any bones and remove. Zest **a lemon**. Save the zest. Now blend **220 g cream cheese** with the **juice of lemon** and **75 ml sour cream** until it is smooth. Mix in **1 tablespoon chives** and **2 teaspoons thyme leaves or lemon thyme** if you can get it. Taste and season with **salt and a very good grind black pepper**. Mix. Finally carefully fold in the flaked trout and serve with thin slices of buttered toast or thin crunchy crackers.

For another change, how about forgetting the pedestrian cheese board this year and replacing it with a baked cheese like a slab of ricotta or a round of a melted washed rind or white wine cheese, if you are feeling more expansive. Put **400 g ricotta** on a lightly oiled metal skillet in a preheated 180°C oven and bake. When it has firmed up and is golden at the edges and warmed through, serve it in a skillet surrounded by **rocket** and dressed with **lots of extra-virgin olive oil**, **freshly chopped herbs like parsley**, **mint**, **oregano and basil** plus **a good sprinkle of lemon zest** or with **salt, oil** and **a generous tumble of seedless grapes**, plumped by warming in a pan with a generous splash of **wine vinegar** and **a little sugar**.

You can take a similar 'hot cheese' approach with the rinded round cheeses like **camembert**. Just bake them whole until them are oozy, warm and melted in the middle. While the heat is working its magic, take a leaf from *MasterChef* winner Andy's book, and warm **seedless grapes** and **dates** in a tablespoon or so of **warm honey** and the **tiniest splash of vinegar**. Tumble this over the finished cheese along with some **toasted almond pieces**. Serve with crackers.

And to mark the end of the night you can never go past serving your usual fudgy brownies with a dollop of thick cream or crème fraîche and a raspberry anchored in the centre of it. It's a far subtler way to mark the end of the party than just ordering cabs and starting to vacuum! If you want to get rid of your guests more quickly – and Christmas drinks parties can turn into 3 am epics rather than 9.30 pm finishes and heck you've still got the presents to wrap and the turkey to stuff – buy some red noodle boxes, line them with red, food-safe, tissue paper and fill them with a couple of brownies. Send your guests off with this little gift.

One final tip, don't forget the ice and to make sure the BBQ gas cylinder is full if you want to BBQ skewers, burgers or cutlets.

4 WAYS WITH CHRISTMAS GIFTS

Christmas has always been about sweetmeats and these four sweet treats are perfect to hand round to drop-ins or box up to give as gifts – assuming you don't eat them all yourself!

1. HEDGEHOG'S ROCKY ROAD

This is the first time a hedgehog meeting a rocky road has had a happy ending.

200 g dark chocolate
200 g milk chocolate
160 g (⅔ cup) glacé cherries
130 g (1½ cups) white marshmallows
about 125 g chocolate finger biscuits
  (look out for the mini finger ones)
130 g (¾ cup) raw peanuts

Line a 17 cm × 26 cm (or thereabouts) baking tray with baking paper.

Melt the dark and milk chocolate together in a glass bowl over a saucepan of simmering water, taking care not to let the water touch the bowl.

Place 60 g of the glacé cherries and 30 g of the white marshmallows to one side. Halve the cherries and cut the white marshmallows in half with a knife or scissors.

Toss all the other ingredients together in a bowl. If using the long chocolate finger biscuits, break them in half.

Once the chocolate has melted, leave it to cool off a bit before stirring the other ingredients through the chocolate. Spread and flatten evenly in the tray.

Press the remaining glacé cherries and half marshmallows cut-side down into the rubble-y chocolate for a Christmassy finish.

Place the tray in the fridge to set. Cut into squares as needed.

MAKES ABOUT 30

TIP: If you don't like hedgehog in your rocky road then make **RockStar Rider Rocky Road**. Replace the biscuits, peanuts and cherries with 200 g of only red and green M&Ms (peanut if you want) and 110 g of Turkish delight chopped into chunks. Stir this combo in with the marshmallows when the chocolate has cooled a little.

2. NUTTY RUMBALLS

Sure everyone loves a rum ball but how about stepping things up with the nutty flavour of Frangelico?

250 g plain sweet biscuits (such as Marie)
180 g (2 cups) fine desiccated coconut
3 tablespoons hazelnut spread, such as Nutella
1 × 395 g can sweetened condensed milk
3 heaped tablespoons cocoa powder
2–3 tablespoons dark rum or Frangelico

Blitz the biscuits in a processor or bash them in a strong bag with a rolling pin.

Add biscuit crumbs to a large mixing bowl along with 90 g (1 cup) of coconut and all the other ingredients. Stir to combine with a fork or clean hands.

Shape into balls and roll in the remaining coconut.

Place on a lined baking tray and refrigerate for a little while to firm up.

Store in an airtight container but these can also be frozen for later.

The coconut makes these rumballs look a little like snowballs (albeit dirty, London snowballs) but if using the Frangelico, you can also tweak the crust by rolling the balls in a cup of crushed, toasted hazelnuts so they look like London mud balls.

MAKES ABOUT 30

3. TOBLERONE TRUFFLES

Chocolates? Nuts? What could result other than deliciousness?

100 g Toblerone bar
240 g sweetened condensed milk
  (⅔ 395 g can, full fat or skim)
pinch of salt
125 g hazelnut spread, such as Nutella
30 g (¼ cup) good-quality cocoa powder,
  for rolling
50 g white chocolate, cut into very
  small pieces
dried cranberries, to decorate

Melt the Toblerone and condensed milk in the microwave or in a heatproof bowl over a saucepan of simmering water. Remove from the heat and add a pinch of salt and the Nutella. Put the mixture in the freezer for 20–30 minutes to firm up.

When it is about the consistency of firm ice cream, scoop out about a tablespoon at a time and roll it into balls. Place the balls on a tray lined with baking paper and freeze for at least 1 hour, or until hard. Roll the balls in the cocoa powder.

Melt the white chocolate in a bowl over a pot of simmering water. Be careful not to overheat or it may clump. Use a teaspoon to dribble a small amount of chocolate over each ball to resemble icing on a xmas pudding. Place a dried cranberry on each while the chocolate is still soft.

They can then be kept in the fridge in an airtight container.

MAKES 12–15

4. ANOOSKA'S WHITE CHOC AND PEANUT TRUFFLES

These are seriously rich. And seriously wrong. And seriously addictive.

450 g white chocolate
240 g sweetened condensed milk
  (⅔ can, full fat or skim, doesn't matter)
good pinch of salt
125 g (½ cup) Sanitarium Natural crunchy peanut
  butter (peanut butter with no added salt or sugar
  works best – normal peanut butter can make this
  recipe too sweet)

Melt 200 g white chocolate and all the condensed milk in a heavy bowl in the microwave on medium heat for 30 seconds. Stir well with a metal spoon and if not all melted, nuke again in 30-second bursts until smooth and runny when stirred. Add salt and peanut butter. (Feel free to add more peanut butter if it's not peanut buttery enough for you.)

Put the mixture in the freezer for 20–30 minutes to firm up. When it is about the consistency of firm ice cream, scoop out about a tablespoon at a time and roll it into balls. Place the balls on a tray lined with baking paper and freeze for at least 1 hour or until hard.

Melt the remaining white chocolate and, working quickly, roll frozen peanut butter balls in the melted chocolate, then put them back on the tray and into the fridge for 30 minutes, or until chocolate sets (or if you're in a hurry, whack them back in the freezer until set). They can then be kept in the fridge in an airtight container.

I must stress, these measurements really are approximate, so make sure you taste the mixture to see if it's salty enough and peanut buttery enough. Just don't taste too much, as I often do, as there won't be enough left to make many balls.

MAKES 25–30, DEPENDING ON HOW BIG YOU ROLL THEM

PRAWN COCKTAIL
'SANG CHOI BAU'

This is a real Aussie summer beach dish with the most Christmassy of colours that takes an easy seventies classic and adds some crunch by serving it in iceberg lettuce cups. This recipe is worth reading just for the tip on separating the iceberg lettuce leaves, which takes a bit of planning but which gives you lovely *intact* leaves.

Separate the iceberg leaves. It is good to do this a couple of hours before you want to eat. First remove the core of the lettuce. Do this my holding the lettuce in one hand like a basketball with the cut core/root end facing the ground. Now smash the lettuce on the bench top so the first point of contact is the root end. This will drive the core up into the lettuce severing its connection with the leaves. It will also loosen the leaves. Lift out the core and soak the lettuce in a bowl of iced water for at least 1 hour. This will help the leaves lift away from each other so you don't have the usual problem of tearing when you try to prise them apart. Dry the leaves and trim them neatly with scissors if you are that sort of a person. Store them stacked together in a plastic bag in the fridge until needed. This will help crisp them up too. Do remember to dry each leaf before serving – they need it.

Now make a mayo by whisking the egg yolk along with the mustard, a good squeeze of lemon and a good pinch of salt. Slowly, little by little, drizzle in some of the grapeseed oil while still whisking. When the oil is incorporated, drizzle in a little more oil. Keep going like this until the whisk starts leaving trails in the thickening mayonnaise.

Now flavour the mayo by whisking in 10 drops of Worcestershire sauce and 1 tablespoon of ketchup. You need to use tomato *ketchup* as it is sweeter and thicker than the more acidic and thinner good old Aussie tomato sauce.

Taste and address the balance of flavours by adding more lemon juice and tomato ketchup for tang and Worcestershire sauce to add savouriness. The tomatoey flavour should be there but never taste 'ketchupy'! This will loosen the mayo and I like it thick enough so it sits like a light doona on top of the prawns.

Thickening the mayo is just a matter of whisking in more oil. This seems counter-intuitive but honestly, it ain't. It's all about the science of emulsification. One egg yolk can actually emulsify a surprising amount of oil but it needs liquid to do this. According to Harold McGee's must-read book on kitchen science, *On Food and Cookery*, more mayos fail because of lack of liquid rather than lack of yolk. He says the liquid like lemon juice or Worcestershire sauce forms an important barrier between the oil molecules in the emulsification process. This stops the mayo collapsing. Now you have your Marie Rose sauce.

To serve, dollop a little sauce at the bottom of each lettuce cup. Top with avocado, a little tumble of tomato dice and prawns. Just before serving nape over a thick blanket of the sauce.

SERVES 8-10

1 head iceberg lettuce
4 ripe avocados, flesh cut
   into cubes
250 g smallest cherry tomatoes
   you can find, cut into quarters
1 kg shelled, cooked prawns

MARIE ROSE SAUCE
1 egg yolk
1 scant teaspoon Dijon mustard
1 lemon
salt flakes
250 ml (1 cup) grapeseed oil
10 drops Worcestershire sauce
2 tablespoons tomato ketchup
(keep these 3 bottles handy as you
   may need more)

INGREDIENT TIP: In winter, instead of the tomatoes, use a bulb of fennel and garnish with the snipped fennel fronds, then you might like to spike the mayonnaise with a little Pernod or ouzo as well as the tomato ketchup.

FLAVOUR TIP: Feel free to customise this dish by adding finely diced red chilli for pep, small cubes of cucumber flesh for extra crunch or just lime juice instead of lemon, garnish with coriander and throw a handful of pan-browned corn kernels into the mix. You can also tweak the Marie Rose sauce further by using sour cream instead of mayo and adding a little sweet chilli sauce along with the fresh, diced chilli.

ROLLED TURKEY WITH ORANGE, PISTACHIO AND HERB STUFFING

2 onions, finely chopped

2 tablespoons olive oil

2 garlic cloves, finely chopped

3 rashers bacon, cut into
   2 cm squares

40 g butter

zest and juice of 1 orange

100 g (⅔ cup) dried cranberries

1½ cups chopped mixed fresh
   herbs, such as flat-leaf parsley,
   sage and thyme

320 g (4 cups) fresh breadcrumbs

140 g (1 cup) shelled, salted
   pistachios

1 egg, lightly beaten

TURKEY

1 × turkey (5–6 kg) boned,
   wings removed

olive oil, to rub into the turkey

salt flakes and freshly ground
   black pepper

2–3 small sprigs rosemary and
   thyme or sage

2 tablespoons maple syrup

TIP: Take your stuffing to your butcher and ask them to stuff the turkey and tie it in a roll.

Most families have one. Someone who has appointed themselves the keeper of the Christmas flame; the person who makes sure Christmas keeps with tradition and reminds you what must happen when. They are like those pagan priests from the days before Christmas existed always consulting some hidden book of Christmas law to decide whether this year we can have a star on top of the tree instead of a fairy. I have two of them in my life. They have been called Christmas Nazis, which is unfair because they neither wear a uniform nor jackboots.

Nowhere is their obsession with keeping up tradition and the status quo as rabid as with the Christmas dinner. Let me see if I can sum up their differing credos. There must be a lolly tree, bonbons, tomato savoury, ham and turkey, restraint in the table decorations plus brandy custard and never, ever brandy butter or there must be bread sauce, Brussels sprouts, two stuffings (one of which must be sausage meat with sage and onions), crackers, far too much tinsel on the table, Neil Sedaka's and Johnny Mathis' Christmas albums on constant rotation, and brandy butter. BTW, what in Odin's name is brandy custard?

Apparently if all these things don't happen the gods will be angry and either the harvest will fail or we'll be tormented by a plague of frogs, weevils or chanting Swedish backpackers at the tennis.

STUFFING Sauté the onion in the oil over medium heat until the onion is lightly golden in colour and starting to caramelise. Add the garlic and cook for another few minutes. Add the bacon and toss occasionally for another 4–5 minutes until the bacon is cooked through. Take off the heat and add the butter to melt. Throw all the hot and cold ingredients into a large bowl and mix together. Season with lots of black pepper and taste for salt. If not using immediately, wrap the mix in plastic wrap and refrigerate until ready to use. It will be fine for a couple of days. Once your turkey is stuffed, ready to cook and at room temperature, preheat the oven to 190°C.

TURKEY Place the turkey on a roasting rack over a large baking tray. Massage some oil and salt and pepper into the skin. Tuck the pieces of thyme and rosemary under the string. Cook for about 2 hours until the meat thermometer reads 60°C. Take the turkey out of the oven, glaze with the maple syrup and return to the oven for about another 20 minutes or until the internal temperature of the meat reaches 74°C.

Remove the turkey from the oven and rest for 20 minutes.

Serve as part of the Christmas extravaganza!

SERVES 10

3 WAYS WITH CHRISTMAS VEGETABLES

Here are three perfect Christmas vegetable side dishes to keep both sides of my family happy. Oh, and the cabbage in the middle makes the table look very pretty and colourful without the need for a blizzard of red and gold lametta/tinsel shreds.

1. BRUSSELS SPROUTS

500 g Brussels sprouts
4 slices thick streaky bacon or pancetta
salt flakes and freshly ground black pepper
1 tablespoon lemon juice

Trim the bottoms and remove the outer leaves of the Brussels sprouts and cut in half. Boil a large pot of salted water and blanch the sprouts for 3 minutes. Refresh in cold water.

Chop the bacon into 5 mm strips and fry in a non-stick frying pan until they are crispy. If your bacon is not very fatty, you can add a little goose fat or butter to the pan. Remove and drain on paper towel.

Leave the pan on the heat and add the sprouts, and sauté in the leftover bacon fat until they begin to brown. Season with salt and pepper, return the bacon to the pan, add the lemon juice and serve immediately.

SERVES 8–10

2. RED CABBAGE

1 medium red cabbage
2 Golden Delicious apples
1 large brown onion
2 tablespoons brown sugar
1 teaspoon ground allspice
1 bouquet garni
4 tablespoons white wine or cider vinegar

Preheat the oven to 150°C.

Remove the outer leaves of the cabbage and reserve. Cut the cabbage into quarters and discard the hard centre. Using a mandoline or a food processor, slice the cabbage finely.

Peel, core and slice the apples and onion.

In a large enamelled or cast-iron casserole, layer the cabbage, apple and onion, sprinkling the sugar and seasoning between the layers as you go. Place the bouquet garni in the centre layer. Pour over the vinegar and top with the reserved cabbage leaves. Cover this with baking paper and a lid. Cook in the oven for 3 hours.

SERVES 10–12

3. TOMATO AND ONION SAVOURY
(BUT SOME MIGHT INSIST ON IT BEING CALLED A PIE)

8 ripe tomatoes
2 onions
salt flakes and freshly groud
**   black pepper**
fresh breadcrumbs
50 g butter, cubed

Preheat the oven to 170°C.

Slice the tomatoes and onions about 5 mm thick. Butter a casserole dish, and layer the tomatoes and onions, alternating as you go. Sprinkle some salt and pepper between each layer. When you have finished layering, cover the top with the fresh breadcrumbs. Dot the top with the butter and bake in the oven for about 40–60 minutes. The breadcrumbs should be golden brown and crispy.

SERVES 8

GLAZING THE HAM

4–5 kg leg ham on the bone
1½ cups marmalade of choice –
   orange, cumquat, lime,
   blood orange
60 g (¼ cup) Dijon mustard
60 ml (¼ cup) orange juice
40–50 cloves

TIP: Choose a ham with a layer
of fat at least 1–1.5 cm thick.

Contrary to what I might have said in the past, glazing a ham is worth the effort. Well, it is when it's got nice burny burnished spots where the pig fat has started to blister along with the sugar of this tart, orangey glaze. It should be a Christmas tradition like stirring the Christmas pudding or photographing your bum on the office photocopier at the office party.

Preheat the oven to 190°C.

Remove the skin from the ham, leaving the fat intact.

In a small saucepan over low heat, dissolve the marmalade, Dijon mustard and orange juice. (If you are using lime marmalade use verjuice or a tart white wine like South Australian riesling, instead of the orange juice.)

Score the fat in a diamond pattern, cutting about 1 cm deep. To do this, run a sharp knife down the leg with equidistant lines about 4 cm apart, and then across the leg with more lines at the same distance apart. Voila! Diamonds. Avoid cutting into the flesh of the ham.

Stud each diamond with a clove or arrange them in whatever pattern you like.

Sit the ham on a rack over a large baking pan. Pour 2–3 cm of water into the bottom of the pan, this will help stop the glaze from burning as it drips into the pan.

Brush the ham with the glaze, keeping enough to be able to brush the ham at least 3–4 times during its 40 minutes in the oven.

Remove from the oven and allow at least 15 minutes to rest before carving.

SERVES 20 PLUS A LOT OF HAM SANDWICHES

GINGER YULE LOG

16 (250 g) ginger snap biscuits
250 ml (1 cup) cream
dried and fresh fruit, or white
    chocolate leaves,
    for decorating
icing sugar, to serve

TIP: To make the white chocolate leaves, melt 100 g white chocolate (or more if you fancy a forest-worth of leaves) in a double-boiler. Take washed and dried holly leaves and, using a paintbrush, paint the white chocolate on the back of the leaves. Chill and do another layer. When the second layer has set completely, carefully peel off the real leaf and you should be left with a perfect white chocolate duplicate.

TIP: You can flavour the cream with a little sherry, some ginger wine or even instant coffee granules or cocoa and a little icing sugar if you want to be really retro like my mum – and not cool and stripped-back like me, who is modernising a classic and giving it a new meaning as we are here. Got that mother?!

When we were kids Christmas was all about the Christmas Yule log. It was also all about warm spices like ginger. When I arrived in Australia I discovered that the chocolate ripple cake was one of the country's finest inventions, to match the fridge, the ultrasound and the black-box flight recorder. Culinary cross-pollination now brings you the Ginger Yule log, inspired by a chocolate ripple cake. I was quite proud of this and felt it might rival other smaller Aussie inventions like the Super Sopper and biodegradable marine degreaser until my mother pointed out that she used to make this in the seventies. 'Stop stealing my air mother!' I cried.

Pick a presentation plate that is long enough to hold the ginger snaps in a horizontal stack.

Whip the cream in your electric mixer or by hand until thick but be careful not to overwhip.

Place a large blob of cream on one of the biscuits and sandwich it with another. Stand the biscuits up on their ends and continue until all the biscuits are joined together in a log. They should be evenly spaced about 1 cm apart. Carefully begin to cover the log with the rest of the cream, beginning with the top and the sides. When one side is completely covered, gently roll the log onto that covered side, and continue to coat the rest of the log.

Now place a large container or casserole dish upside down over the log to cover it, and place it in the fridge overnight.

When you are ready to decorate your Yule log, run a fork or something pointy along the side of the log to create the lines, smooth out the ends and draw concentric circles. To decorate, you can cover with white chocolate leaves and a dusting of icing sugar until your log looks suitably festive.

When you are ready to serve, slice or spoon the log in long diagonal lines. The biscuits should be soft and spongy.

SERVES 6

INDIVIDUAL STRAWBERRY PAVLOVAS

OK, no beating about the bush. There's an elephant standing over there by the bookcase. All the current evidence points to the fact that pavlova was first a New Zealand dish but just like Russell Crowe, Derryn Hinch, the Finn brothers, Rebecca Gibney and Keith Urban, it felt far happier moving here and, in true ANZAC spirit, we adopted it as one of our own. This was good news for the pavlova, which was ill-suited to a New Zealand life where career options seem to consist of playing rugby, playing guitar in The Datsuns, or playing hobbits in movies. With no fingers, no toes (hairy or otherwise) and a soft and giving personality, the pavlova is ill-suited to any of these pursuits.

Preheat your oven to 110°C. Line three baking trays with baking paper.

Place the egg whites into the bowl of an electric mixer. Using the whisk attachment, begin to beat on low speed, gradually increasing the speed until the egg whites are stiff. With your mixer on high speed, start to add the sugar bit by bit until all the sugar has been added. Continue beating until the egg whites are stiff and glossy.

To make individual pavlovas, spoon large dollops of meringue onto the baking trays, using a dessert or serving spoon. Spread them out slightly by tapping the top with a spatula and forming into circle shapes, creating a small well in the centre of each as you go. You should fit about 5 on each tray. Remember that they will expand as they cook.

Place the trays in the oven and bake for about 1 hour, if you like your meringue a little drier, leave them in for longer. I don't!

Loosely whip the cream and fold in the yoghurt. Refrigerate.

BERRY DRIZZLE

Blitz the ingredients in a food processor for about a minute until it reaches a smooth consistency.

Serve each meringue with a dollop of cream mixture and decorate with the strawberries. Dust with a little icing sugar, pour over the berry drizzle, garnish with the mint leaves and serve immediately.

MAKES 12–14

9 egg whites
500 g caster sugar
200 ml pure or double cream
200 ml Greek-style yoghurt
75 g demerara sugar
2 punnets strawberries, washed, to serve
icing sugar and mint leaves, to serve

BERRY DRIZZLE

1 punnet strawberries, washed hulled and halved
1 punnet raspberries, washed
juice of 1 lime
2 tablespoons icing sugar, or to taste

JUDE'S CHRISTMAS
ICE CREAM PUD

100 g (½ cup) proper glacé cherries (not those nasty fakes made of jelly)

110 g (¾ cup) blanched almonds, toasted

60 g (⅓ cup) candied peel

75 g (½ cup) of dried cranberries

85 g (½ cup) raisins

80 g (½ cup) sultanas

2 level teaspoons mixed spice

1 teaspoon ground cinnamon

1 teaspoon ground nutmeg

2 teaspoons brandy (you can use rum, Frangelico or vanilla extract)

1 litre your favourite vanilla ice cream

holly, for decoration

fresh redcurrants and cranberries, to serve (optional)

When I first arrived in Australia twenty years ago I could never get the whole obsession with having some sort of Northern European Christmas with heavy pudding and vast amounts of roast meats when it was 35 degrees and the cicadas were humming like chainsaws. Now I'd militate against the traditional Christmas pudding if it wasn't for the brandy butter. This mix of butter and caster sugar spiked with brandy is the shiny-winged golden angel on the Christmas tree of my lunch and it is as unmissable as crackers and a stocking. Then I had my first Christmas with my one-day-to-be mother-in-law and she brought out this. All the joys of a Christmas pudding but in a refreshing ice cream and – as it is officially pudd – then brandy butter can be served with it. Brilliant!

Take 40 g of the glacé cherries and 50 g of toasted almonds. Reserve them for decoration.

Roughly chop all the remaining fruit and mix with the spices. Pour the brandy over the fruit and allow it to stand overnight.

Roughly chop the almonds into large pieces.

Let the ice cream soften a little, but not melt, then fold in the chopped fruit and almonds.

Line a pudding bowl with enough plastic wrap so it spills over the sides of the bowl. We want to totally encase the ice cream when we finish, so be generous! Scoop the ice cream into the pudding bowl, cover by pulling the edges of the wrap back over the pudding and return it to the freezer to firm up. When it's time to serve up, hold your serving plate over the bowl and turn out your pudd. Remove the plastic. Decorate your serving plate with holly and the pudding with the reserved glacé cherries and almonds or fresh redcurrants and cranberries and serve.

SERVES 10-12

XMAS PANNA COTTA WITH REDCURRANT JELLY

JELLY

125 g (1 punnet) fresh or
  frozen redcurrants
100 ml water
30 g caster sugar
1½ gold-strength gelatine
  leaves, or ¾ teaspoon
  powdered gelatine

PANNA COTTA

500 ml (2 cups) pure cream
350 ml full-cream milk
100 g caster sugar
1 vanilla pod, halved lengthways
  and seeds scraped
5 gold-strength gelatine leaves,
  or 2½ teaspoons powdered
  gelatine
fresh seasonal berries, to serve

TIP: Most fruit can be substituted for the cranberries.

Just like Santa, normal Christmas desserts tend to be fat and jolly but if this panna cotta was a Santa it would be the sexiest, coolest Santa ever. Lean, buff and very well defined, with milky-white flesh that moves with a taut hydraulic will all of its own, covered by the merest slip of see-through red that is more a tease than a covering. This is not the sort of Santa who'd slip down your chimney with a sack but I suspect you'd still be very glad to see them! I'll leave it up to you to decide if this Santa is male or female!

JELLY Measure your jelly mould. If the mould is more or less than 1 litre you can scale the ingredients up or down to suit. You will have to start this recipe a day ahead as the jelly will need time to set.

To make 150 ml of jelly, place the fruit, water and sugar in a heatproof bowl and cover with plastic wrap. Place the bowl over a pot of simmering water and leave it for about 30 minutes, to allow the juices to release. When the fruit is ready, strain it through a fine sieve and measure out 150 ml of liquid.

Soak the gelatine in cold water for 5 minutes. (If you are using powdered gelatine, sprinkle it over 2 teaspoons of cold water and mix to soften.) Squeeze out the gelatine leaves and add it to the hot redcurrant syrup. Give it a stir to make sure the gelatine has dissolved completely, and then pour the liquid into the jelly mould. Leave in the refrigerator to set completely.

PANNA COTTA When the jelly has set, heat the cream, milk, sugar and the scraped vanilla pod and seeds in a saucepan until just before boiling point. Remove from the heat and take out the vanilla pod. Soak the gelatine in cold water for 5 minutes. When the cream is ready, squeeze out the gelatine and add it to the hot cream, and stir well to dissolve. Leave the cream in the refrigerator to chill until it is very cold and starting to thicken. When it is ready pour it over the set jelly to fill the rest of the mould. Leave in the refrigerator to set.

When ready to serve, fill a container or the sink with very hot water. Immerse the mould for about 2 seconds. If you have a ceramic mould this might take a little bit longer in the hot water. Invert the mould onto your serving plate and gently shake out the panna cotta. Serve with fresh seasonal berries.

SERVES 8–10 (MAKES 1 LITRE JELLY MOULD)

XMAS PANNA COTTA - PART 2

If the ice cream Christmas pudd is a bit too naff for you 'cos you are a classy sort, then you'll love this alternative, which is about the sexiest thing in this book. The fruit here also has all those bell-ringing Christmas flavours and combined with the softest and ever-so-saucy wobble of the panna cotta, which is about as intoxicating as that first barrage of kisses from your one true love, you'll be in heaven. The little jelly made from the syrup adds some extra textural relief from the creamy assault of the panna cotta. It's also dead-set elegant.

And as it is Christmas, treat yourself to a new jelly mould. Something geometric and square with a good recessed pattern on the bottom would be ideal for this dessert.

POACHED DRIED FRUIT Soak the fruit in hot water for several hours, then drain. Make the poaching syrup by bringing the remaining ingredients to the boil in a large saucepan. Reduce to a simmer and add the drained fruit. Poach gently for 1½ hours until the fruit is swollen and soft, and the liquid has reduced slightly.

JELLY First measure your jelly mould by filling it with water and then pouring the water back into a measuring jug. If your mould is larger than 600 ml. You can scale up the recipe to suit. Soak the gelatine in cold water for about 5 minutes to soften. (If you are using powdered gelatin, sprinkle it over 2 teaspoons of cold water and mix to soften.)

While the fruit is poaching remove 100 ml of liquid into a bowl, squeeze out the gelatine and mix with the hot liquid until dissolved. Pour into your jelly mould, using just enough to fill the relief in the mould. If there is no relief, use as much or as little of the liquid as you want. Place in the refrigerator until set.

PANNA COTTA Heat the cream, milk, sugar and the scraped vanilla pod and seeds in a saucepan until just before boiling point. Remove from the heat and take out the vanilla pod. Soak the gelatine in cold water for 5 minutes. When the cream is ready, squeeze out the gelatine and add it to the hot cream and stir well to dissolve. Leave the cream in the refrigerator to chill for 30 minutes or so. When it is cold, give it a stir and then pour it over the set jelly to fill the rest of the mould. Leave in the refrigerator to set.

When ready to serve, fill a container or the sink with very hot water. Immerse the mould for about 2–3 seconds. If you have a ceramic mould this might take a little bit longer in the hot water. Invert the mould onto your serving plate and gently shake out the panna cotta. Serve with the poached fruit.

SERVES 2 (MAKES 1 X 600 ML JELLY MOULD)

400 ml cream
200 ml full-cream milk
80 g caster sugar
1 vanilla pod, halved lengthways
   and seeds scraped
3½ gold-strength gelatine leaves, or
   1¾ teaspoons powdered gelatine

JELLY

1 gold-strength gelatine leaf,
   or ½ teaspoon powdered gelatine
100 ml poaching liquid (retained
   from poaching the dried fruit)

POACHED DRIED FRUIT

200 g prunes
200 g dried apricots
100 g sultanas
100 g dried baby figs
100 g dried cranberries
300 g caster sugar
375 ml (1½ cups) dessert wine
1 litre (4 cups) water
1 cinnamon stick
1 vanilla pod, halved lengthways,
   seeds scraped

TIP: The dried fruit can be poached a few days ahead of time and kept in the refrigerator until needed. Just bring to room temperature before serving.

630 g (7 cups) rolled oats

165 g (1 cup) linseeds

170 g (1 cup) sultanas

80 g (1 cup) slivered almonds

160 g (1 cup) pepitas

160 g (1 cup) sunflower seeds

150 g (1 cup) chopped unsalted pistachios or rather hip and apparently miraculous chia seeds

pinch of salt

TIP: You can grind half of the linseeds, sunflower seeds and almonds together if you are concerned about drawing as much nutritional goodness out of this muesli as possible but it's better to just buy some ready-ground LSA from the supermarket and add 2 cups of this powdered LSA to the mix along with another 2 cups of rolled oats and a handful of sultanas. This way you still get all the textures of crunchy almonds, almost chewy sunflower seeds and popping little brown linseeds.

My life is a roller coaster, a switchback that soars with good intentions and swoops back down to earth with a screaming rush of indulgence. So it was with this book. After the excess of the last hundred pages or so, culminating in Christmas, it's time to pull things back into line; to start the New Year with the best of intentions and an achievable suite of resolutions.

First, eat breakfast, every morning. A good breakfast is the foundation of a day of virtuous eating. Second, eat oats. Oats keep you full for longer, which helps your self-control when the plate of biscuits comes round at elevenses, or the chips at lunchtime. It's that whole low GI thing. Oats are a solid foundation on which you can build your day.

This is not loaded with sugars or bad, sweet fatty stuff such as coconut but it's still loaded with trendy ingredients that are currently cited as wonder foods.

At the centre of my muesli are the components of 'so-hot-right-now' LSA (it sounds rather space-age and sexy but it is little more than linseeds, aka flaxseeds, sunflower seeds and almonds) in a crunchy form. Linseeds are reportedly a good source of omega-3 and amino acids while the combo is also believed to help detox the liver so the organ can keep pumping out that 'good' HDL cholesterol. It should be noted that you'll get more goodness out of your linseeds, sunflower seeds and almonds if you grind some of them – or at least chew them thoroughly if you want to enjoy their texture in your muesli. I am especially enthralled with the smooth satiny curves of linseeds.

To be truly virtuous, you can leave out the sultanas but I think that makes the muesli a little bird-seedy and the occasional chewy burst of intense sweetness they provide is vital to me in making this muesli something I want to eat again tomorrow.

Tumble all these ingredients together and store in a large, clear airtight container in a cool dark place.

Serve 1 cup of this power-packed muesli per person each morning. Add slices of fresh banana or a handful of blueberries on top if you are entertaining.

Oh, and remember to chew every mouthful 20 times like your mother told you to. This encourages 'mindful eating', and will give you time to contemplate how you will approach the challenges of the day. So much better than bolting and running!

MAKES 10-15 SERVES

ACKNOWLEDGEMENTS

What started as a modest follow-up cookbook has turned into a far bigger and far sexier beast than I could ever have imagined. This is solely thanks to the enthusiasm of all the people who have worked on the book, starting with the team at Plum and Pan Macmillan. Publisher Mary Small once again willingly threw herself into the eye of the storm, providing invaluable insights, wise counsel and a quirk-embracing enthusiasm for this book. Ellie Smith who helmed the project has a rare eye for beauty, an exquisite sense of humour and enough grit to de-ice all the roads of Scotland. She worked crazy hours to make this book what it is and I love that. I owe them both a great debt of gratitude as I do to Tracey Cheetham and all in the publicity, marketing and sales departments at Pan Macmillan.

Allison Colpoys is the woman behind the beautiful, vibrant design of this book – she even designed a unique typeface to capture the tone. I LOVE what she has done. Editor Margaret Barca tried to rein in the words and beat my ramblings into some sort of sense. It was a thankless and massive task but she was more than up to it. Megan Johnson proofed and Pauline Haas did the rather fine typesetting – two roles too often criminally undervalued. But not here; not now!

Huge thanks also have to go to my old friend and wunderkind photographer Mark Roper, who once again has managed to shoot some truly stunning images that make my pedestrian food look shockingly (to me) good! His commitment to the project was such that he allowed us to shoot everything at his house, taking over his lounge, kitchen and the kids' playroom for weeks at a time –a mark of the generosity of the man and the long-suffering nature of his beautiful wife Deb and their children Jack and Ella. Thank you!

Mark would be the first to give über food stylist Caroline Velik much of the credit for how beautiful she made the food look with her styling and propping of each shot. Like Mark, she really is the best at what she does and it was an honour to work with her again. Caroline was backed in the kitchen by some truly talented cooks – Marnie Rowe, Karina Duncan, Emma Christian, Kate Quincerot, Deborah Kaloper and Jamie Humby – who all contributed to fine-tuning these recipes as well as ensuring that the food looks page-lickingly good. I owe these guys a huge debt of gratitude too.

Great food is far easier with great produce and throughout the whole process, Gary the butcher at the Prahran Market acted like my own personal meat consultant and kept me supplied with the best meat – he's one of my culinary heroes BTW. The boys at Pino's helped with the veg. Thanks!

When it comes to what actually made it onto these pages from my end, there is a dizzyingly long list of people who I need to thank. As you flick through the preceding pages you'll see copious mentions of my personal brain trust; inspirational home cooks who have shared ideas, brainstormed improvements and generally just inspired me. You'll find cooks like Jen Clarke, Jennifer Preston,

Jude Bennison, Peter Mitchell and Caroline Roessler. Closest of all on this project have been the wonderfully exact Ms Kate Quincerot who is something of a pastry whisperer, and the divine, insightful and very funny Ms Marnie Rowe who cooks and pirouettes flavours like a T1000 version of me. They have become my food team and their fingerprints shine like burnished silver over this book. I value their wisdom, honesty, dedication and creativity in equal quantities. They have made this book a joy to write.

And of course I need to thank the army of food lovers who share their ideas, recipes, food experiences and images of what they've cooked with me on both Facebook and Twitter (@mattscravat).

Inspiration and wisdom doesn't just come from those I work with, so I'd also like to acknowledge the dizzying number of light-bulb moments and knowledge shared by so many chefs and cooks both here and overseas. Some are represented in the book – the likes of Margaret Fulton, Lylah Hatfield, Tina Li, Marco Pierre White, Heston Blumenthal, Mario Batali, Andrew Davies, the late Rose Gray, Pascal Barbot and Philippa Sibley. Then there are Gary and George. Having food's Mr Technique and Mr Creativity on permanent speed dial is just one of the joys of working with them, but they also keep me on an even keel through the working week! *MasterChef*'s in-house chef Monty Koludrovic, along with new *MasterChef MasterClass* producer Sandy Paterson, have helped me immeasurably with my first faltering steps along the rocky path of cooking on TV. (Props and thanks also to Georgia, Sam, Olivia, Tiffany, Brendan and the always-inspiring food nerd D-Mac for helping in this area too.)

Working for Danielle Opperman, Fiona Nilsson and Nicole Sheffield at NewsLifeMedia and at *delicious.* magazine, and with the team at News Ltd's *Taste* section including John McGourty, visual wizard Steve Moorhouse and editor Jana Frawley, continues to inspire and push me. Guys, you are also part of the reason this is a better book! Thank you to them and to my other great photographic collaborator Catherine Sutherland.

This book would never have been possible without the support of Hamish, Beverley, Karen and Anthony at Network Ten, who do as much as anyone in this country to promote good food through their work. Thank you.

A huge thank you to my *other* family, my beautiful and extremely smart manager Henrie Stride, wily business manager David Vodicka, legal eagle Yasmin Naghavi, moneyman Aaron Hurle, and Charlotte James and Aleesha De Mel-Tucker who keep me social!

Too often I leave my family until last and yet again I appear to have done this! My children Jono, Will and Sadie have been both willing and unwilling critics of the recipes here, while my beautiful wife Emma is the reason that I am happy. I love you all very much! Thank you for letting me do this!

INDEX

There are some dishes that are just too disgraceful to risk impressionable eyes stumbling across. These are they. None are recommended as part of a low-calorie diet!

SEALED SECTION

ROAST FIVE-SPICE PORK BELLY

FIVE-SPICE POWDER

1 tablespoon Sichuan peppercorns
8 star anise
½ teaspoon ground cloves
1 tablespoon ground cinnamon
1 tablespoon ground fennel seeds

PORK BELLY

1.3 kg pork belly
1 teaspoon salt
1 tablespoon peanut oil
1 red onion, halved

＊Please treat any implied or direct claims of working-class credentials here with the sort of wariness and suspicion usually reserved for a saltwater crocodile with a room to rent.

No sealed section could be complete without a certain amount of juicy, porky goodness and 'a certain amount' in this case translates as 'rather a lot'. Here this is pig at its best with bubbly, crunchy crackle, fat that weeps the sweet sticky tears of the damned and a price tag that says 'I'm still a man of the people even if I am eating like a king'.

And oooooo look, we are making are own five-spice spice mix in this recipe just like a real chef. So eat your heart out Mr $50 Main Course, I'm not so sure I need your white damask-draped world anymore.

FIVE-SPICE POWDER

In a dry pan, roast the Sichuan peppercorns by shaking the pan over low–medium heat until the aroma of the peppercorns is released (about 3 minutes). Grind the roasted peppercorns and star anise in a coffee grinder or mortar. Add the cloves, cinnamon and fennel and grind again.

Now, wash and pat dry the skin of the pork. Using a Stanley knife or very sharp paring knife, score the skin of the pork diagonally at 1 cm intervals, essentially creating a diamond pattern on the skin.

Mix 1 tablespoon of the five-spice powder with the salt and oil. Massage this all over the pork, including the skin and leave in the fridge for at least 2 hours, or overnight if you can.

Preheat the oven to 250°C.

PORK BELLY

Put the seasoned pork belly on top of a rack inside a roasting pan, or slice up a large onion to create a platform to sit the pork on. Place in your very hot oven for 25 minutes, or until the skin of the belly starts to bubble and is golden brown. Turn the oven temperature down to 160°C and roast for another 2–2½ hours.

Serve in a buttered roll or with fried rice and roast carrots.

SERVES 6

AVOCADO AND GORGONZOLA GRILL

This Italianate take on an open toastie breaks loads of rules, most notably cooking avocado and being so guiltily rich. So eat it sparingly, seldom and definitely serve it with the suggested guilt-free salad of crisp leaves, apple and celery. Beware – the friend who loved this most had his cholesterol checked and dialled in an impressive 12. I deny this dish was implicated in any way.

Preheat the grill to high.

Split the loaf in half lengthways. Grill one side of both pieces.

Remove from the heat and top the untoasted sides with the avocado and gorgonzola. Toast under the grill for 4 minutes until the cheese melts and runs over the avocado.

To make the salad, toss the witlof, cucumber, celery, apple, walnuts and parsley together in a bowl. Season well with salt and pepper, then dress with the lemon juice and olive oil.

Cut the Turkish bread into wedges and serve immediately with the salad.

SERVES 6

1 large Turkish loaf
4 ripe avocados, sliced 1 cm thick
500 g gorgonzola dolce, crumbled

SIDE SALAD

2 witlof, leaves separated
½ continental cucumber, thinly
  sliced on an angle
1 celery stalk, thinly sliced
  on an angle
1 crisp green apple, halved,
  thinly sliced
50 g (½ cup) walnuts, toasted,
  roughly chopped
½ cup flat-leaf parsley leaves
salt flakes and and freshly ground
  black pepper
juice of 1 lemon
1 tablespoon extra-virgin olive oil

TIP:
Gorgonzola
dolce or dolcelatte
is a creamy blue
Italian cheese
from delis.

NICE BUNS
OR CRACKLING PORK
AND PRAWN BAGUETTES

1 sheet of pork skin (ask your
    butcher for a piece about
    30 cm × 20 cm, and to score
    it too)
olive oil
2 teaspoons salt flakes
4 small baguette rolls
2 teaspoons English mustard
4 teaspoons whole egg
    mayonnaise
    (S&P, Hellman's, Best's)
50 g prawn crackers
12 green prawns, peeled and
    deveined with tails intact
¼ white cabbage, thick seams
    removed, finely shredded
juice of ½ lemon
¼ iceberg lettuce, finely shredded
lemon wedges, to serve

I am a fan of anything that can be eaten one-handed. It means that it is ideal when the other hand is nursing a drink on the deck, in the backyard or down the beach. Or nursing anything else for that matter.

This recipe breaks the rules and is far more fun when shared with a large mob of people. Make lots because these will have your guests baying for more, like a pack of hungry wolves after a long, hard winter sensing that the first scout troop of spring is about to get lost in the woods.

Preheat the oven to 180°C.

Score the crackling skin (if your butcher hasn't done it for you) and rub with the olive oil and then the salt. Place the crackling between two metal baking trays and pop in the oven for 45 minutes. This will help the fat render.

Cut a wedge out of the top of your baguettes.

Mix your English mustard with the mayo. Add a squeeze of lemon.

Drop the prawn crackers into a pan of hot oil (160°C or when a cube of bread turns golden brown in 30–35 seconds) so they puff up. Drain on paper towel.

As soon as the crackling's fat is soft and melty, check the surface. It is likely that the skin side is still a little leathery. Remove from the oven and turn the grill to high.

Fry the prawns in a tiny bit of the drippings from the pork crackling until cooked and pinkish in colour.

Toss the cabbage and lettuce in the juice of ½ a lemon.

Place the crackle skin-side up under the grill, if necessary, to puff it up and make it crisp. Watch it as it will burn easily. Cut the crackle into thumb-length pieces.

Line the bottom side of each baguette with lettuce and cabbage. Drop in the prawns – 3 per roll – and splotch on some mustard mayo. Top with a few pieces of crackling and a few prawn crackers. Serve with lemon wedges.

MAKES 4 ROLLS

150 g (1 cup) potato flour (rice
flour would be about the only
alternative)
2 firm, shiny and fat eggplants
rice bran oil, for frying
spring onion, finely sliced,
to serve (optional)

THE 'FISH SAUCE'

1 teaspoon grated fresh ginger
2 teaspoons grated garlic
1 dessertspoon broad bean
paste
3 dessertspoons Chinese
pickled chillies
2 dessertspoons neutral oil
(like groundnut or grapeseed)
2 teaspoons potato starch flour
(or you could use cornflour)
2 tablespoons water
125 ml (½ cup) Chinkiang black
vinegar
165 g (¾ cup) caster sugar, plus
more for balancing the sauce
good pinch of salt

TIP: If making the eggplant chips by
themselves, try using rice flour, which
is more readily available – you'll get
a thinner crust but less oil
absorption.

Few dishes inspire the sort of 'rats clawing at your brain' cravings then
this simple eggplant dish from Melbourne's Dainty Sichuan restaurant.
Such is the demand that they get through 15 kilos of eggplant every day.
After resisting all sorts of bribes and inducements to part with it, chef and
co-owner Tina Li agreed to teach me how to make it for my newspaper
column. It is based on a traditional Sichuan dish made with slippery
eggplant, but Tina has stepped it up by making eggplant chips that stay
chewy and a little crispy even under the rich, sweet and sour 'fish sauce' so
called because it was once used on fish.

The ingredients in the sauce will require an expedition to a decent
Chinese grocery but the crunchy eggplant is brilliant by itself with anything
from spiked mayo to pulled lamb shoulder roasted with a dry rub of
cumin and Sichuan pepper. One other note – Li uses a Chinese spoon for
measurements, which most closely resembles a dessertspoon in volume,
which is why all the measurements in the recipe are dessertspoons rather
than tablespoons.

The success of this dish is about having all the elements on the dish prepped
and ready to go before you start, which is very Chinese.

First, prepare your base sauces. You need three small bowls. In the first bowl,
mix the ginger and garlic together. In the second bowl, mix the broad bean
paste with the pickled chillies and oil. In the third bowl, mix the potato starch
flour with water to make a slurry for thickening the mixture.

At the heart of this sauce is the combination of sugar and fruity black rice
vinegar. Much depends on the acidity of your vinegar. In a medium-sized
bowl, mix the vinegar, sugar and salt together. Taste. If vinegar is the primary
taste, increase the sugar by stirring in another tablespoon. Stir until it
dissolves. Taste again. Do this until the sauce is a little more sweet than it is
vinegary but still has a little vinegar bite.

Fill a metal mixing bowl with the potato flour and keep handy. Line up three
bowls: one two-thirds filled with cold water, another empty and the final one
being the large bowl full of the potato flour.

Now prep the eggplant. Cut the cheeks of skin off two opposing sides of
one eggplant, and cut off the stalk end and discard. Rest the eggplant on
one of the cut sides and slice into 1 cm thick slices lengthways. Hold the
eggplant together and rotate it. Cut the rounded end off at a slight angle and
discard. Then cut the bunched-together slices into batons by cutting down
and crossways on a diagonal at the same angle. You want 1 cm batons of
eggplant that are about 6 cm long with a little skin at each end. Repeat with
the other eggplant.

CONTINUED OVERLEAF →

Now your *mis en place* is done and you are ready to cook.

Place a large pan of the oil on the heat and watch it. A large wok is good for this. We want the oil to be very hot, and this means it will froth up when the eggplant is added, so make sure the pan is stable, has high sides and that the oil doesn't come more than halfway up those sides – less in a wok. The oil needs to be about 200°C+ when you start frying.

Now you need to work fast and multi-task, as this dish is best pulled together quickly. You can even work in a team with one of you making the eggplant chips and the other the sauce.

Douse your eggplant chips in the bowl of cold water. Leave for a second and then push your hand down on the chips in the water and release. Now using two hands, lift up the eggplant chips, hold them above the water for a few seconds to let some of the water drain off and drop them into the empty bowl.

TIP: Sprinkle on fresh spring onions to garnish if you want an oniony kick.

Tilt the eggplant bowl to drain any water and then toss the damp eggplant chips into the bowl with the potato flour. Immediately, and very carefully, drop the chips into the hot oil. Be careful – and maybe use a slotted spoon or wok ladle, as the oil will foam and froth up quite madly. Keep the eggplant chips moving while you fry them for about 5 minutes, or until the flour turns into a hard, almost glassy, just golden crust. Do this in batches. Now carefully scoop the crunchy, crusted eggplant into a sieve and tap the sieve a couple of times to encourage any oil on the eggplant to drip off.

As the chips are cooking, in a hot wok assemble the following: 3 dessertspoons of the chilli and broad bean oil, 2 teaspoons of your ginger–garlic paste and 150 ml of the vinegar mixture. It should taste sweet with some vinegary bite afterward. The chilli and the salty broad bean paste should be a murmur not a shout. Add a good splash of the potato starch slurry (about 1 tablespoon) to your chilli vinegar sauce to help it thicken, then give it a good toss. Taste and add another 1 dessertspoon of the chilli oil if it needs more pep.

At the restaurant they immediately toss the crunchy eggplant in the sauce and then throw in the spring onion, toss a couple of times and serve. I reckon you have more control if you serve the eggplant on a platter with a couple of spoonfuls of the sauce splashed over and the rest of the sauce on the side.

SERVES 4

NORMANDY CHICKEN

'The calm before the storm' we called it as children; the three weeks we
were taken out of school to holiday in Normandy before our youngest sister
was born. I was nine and some things I can remember vividly: camembert,
nuns, nun-shaped pastries filled with coffee cream, the D-Day beaches,
the rushing tide at Mont Saint-Michel, my first taste of tripe (which was
far better than my father's advert for it – 'it's just cow's stomach') and my
frugal grandmother boiling water for hot chocolate with a boilette in a bidet
to avoid paying for room service.

All of these memories I realise now revolve around food in some
manner, including the D-Day beaches. There was a restaurant there
that served 'Chicken in the Normandy style', a dish that is all about the
cream and apples that the area does so very well. Here was a dish worth
liberating France for – and one worth returning for.

Each time I taste it again that first memory is reignited. Whether on a
particularly funny weekend, with an actor friend and our squeezes, where
that chicken was followed by about the best idea in the world ever – an all-
you-can-eat cheeseboard in Normandy – or a dinner where returning chef
Philippe Mouchel talked about (and cooked) this childhood dish from his
birthplace. The version of the recipe here has evolved from scribbled notes
and wonky Calvados-sodden reminiscences of all those meals, through a
sort of pot-roast version from Diana Henry (although Diana uses thyme,
leeks, no mustard, more cider, less apple and flour in her version) and, I am
a little ashamed to admit, an English supermarket website recipe.

This dish is decadent, delicious and, I fear, deadly if you eat enough of
it. And you may well do. It is that sort of dish.

Oh, and I do sometimes use crème fraîche rather than double cream,
as I am sure that I read somewhere that it was healthier … or maybe …
come to think of it … actually I think that was jogging.

CONTINUED OVERLEAF ➔

30 g butter

1.8 kg chicken, cut into 8 pieces
(ask the butcher to leave all the
pieces on the bone)

100 g streaky bacon, cut into
1 cm strips

2 brown onions, finely diced

300 ml dry cider

salt flakes and freshly ground
black pepper

3 Granny Smith apples, peeled
and cut into wedges

2 teaspoons sugar

300 ml double cream

3 teaspoons Dijon mustard

Preheat the oven to 170°C.

Melt half the butter in a large flameproof casserole dish over a medium heat. Season the chicken on all sides and place in the dish to brown. Remove the chicken and set aside.

Cook the bacon the same way until it is golden brown, then add the onion and cook for a few more minutes.

Place the chicken back in the dish, pour in the cider and bring to the boil. Season with salt and pepper and cover the pot. Cook in the oven for 1½ hours.

While the chicken is cooking, sauté the apple in the remaining butter. Sprinkle with a little sugar to help them colour.

When the chicken is cooked, remove from the dish and keep warm. Bring the juices in the dish to the boil. Add the cream and mustard. Simmer for 10 minutes until the liquid has reduced, and you have a sauce the consistency of thickened cream that will coat the back of a spoon.

Check the seasoning, return the chicken to the dish and add the apples. Serve immediately with mash and peas.

SERVES 6-8

CAULIFLOWER CHEESE WITH HAM HOCK

1 smoked ham hock
4 whole cloves
3 dried bay leaves
¼ teaspoon black peppercorns
1 large cauliflower
60 g butter
1 small brown onion, chopped
60 g (just over ⅓ cup) flour
300 ml cream
2 dried bay leaves
1½ tablespoons Dijon mustard
200 g (2 cups) tasty cheese,
    coarsely grated
50 g (½ cup) finely grated
    parmesan
salt flakes and freshly ground
    black pepper

The best assassins are the best because you'd never suspect what they are up to. They look so familiar, so normal. A bit like this cauliflower cheese, which looks like hundreds you've seen – and eaten – before, yet a dark porky secret lurks close to its heart.

Place the ham, cloves, bay leaves and peppercorns in a large saucepan. Cover with cold water and bring to the boil over medium heat. Reduce the heat to low and simmer, adding extra water to keep the ham covered, for about 3 hours, or until very tender and the meat starts to fall from the bone. Allow the ham to cool before shredding the meat. Place the shredded meat evenly along the bottom of a buttered casserole dish.

Preheat the oven to 180°C. Cut your cauliflower into florets and place in a steamer, and cook for 4–5 minutes. Then place the cauliflower over the ham in the casserole.

Melt the butter in a saucepan, add the onion and cook until soft. Stir in the flour and allow to cook for a few minutes before adding the cream and bay leaves. Stir continuously while the sauce thickens.

When the sauce is ready, turn off the heat, remove the bay leaves, stir in the mustard and tasty cheese. Season to taste, and pour over the cauliflower. Sprinkle with the parmesan and bake for 30 minutes, or until golden brown on top. Serve hot.

SERVES 4–6

A PLUM BOOK
First published in 2013 by
Pan Macmillan Australia Pty Limited
Level 25, 1 Market Street, Sydney,
NSW 2000, Australia

Level 1, 15–19 Claremont Street,
South Yarra, Victoria 3141, Australia

A CIP catalogue record for this book is available from
the National Library of Australia.

Design by Allison Colpoys
Typeset by Pauline Haas
Edited by Margaret Barca
Index by Fay Donlevy
Photography by Mark Roper
Prop and Food styling by Caroline Velik and Ellie Smith
Food preparation by Emma Christian, Karina Duncan, Jamie Humby,
Deborah Kaloper, Kate Quincerot and Marnie Rowe

Colour reproduction by Splitting Image, Clayton, Victoria
Printed and bound in China by 1010 Printing International Limited

Some of the material in this book has been adapted from articles previously published in the Taste section of News Ltd
metro newspapers. At the time of writing, recipes on the following pages have appeared in Taste: 8, 12, 19, 24, 30, 40,
67, 69, 73, 81, 88, 91, 92, 98, 101, 102, 107, 117, 129, 136, 140, 148, 152, 191, 211, 216, 224, 234, 242, 263, 280 and 296;
in delicious. magazine: 28, 96, 155, 157, 171 and 295; and the Age 187 and 188.

10 9 8 7 6 5 4 3 2